The factory model of education most of us remember so well—the scripted lesson plan, assembly-line-style regurgitation of factoids by successive cogs in the teacher's seating chart—won't cut it anymore. *Teach Our Children Well* is a compendium of success stories emerging from hands-on classroom trials in settings ranging from bucolic suburban campuses to graffiti'ed inner-city bastions. It is a reasoned argument that no school reform can succeed unless it can be plugged in directly at the level of the atomic unit of public education: the classroom. And it is a step-by-step "how-to" manual for teachers, parents, grandparents, who can draw on the book's numerous concrete examples of graphic organizers and instructional strategies to help their young learners prepare for an information-intensive 21st century that will require the expert use of language *in all its forms* for thinking, problem solving, and communication.

Teach Your Children Well:

Bringing K–12 Education into the 21st Century

by Robert C. Calfee

and

Cynthia L. Patrick

In memoriam

Miriam Miller

Portable Stanford Book Series
Editor and Manager 1983–89

Editor: Bruce Goldman
Book Design: Amy Pilkington
Cover Design: Paul Carstensen

THE PORTABLE STANFORD is a book series
sponsored by the Stanford Alumni Association.
The series is designed to bring the widest possible
sampling of Stanford's intellectual resources into the
homes of alumni. It includes books based on current
research as well as books that deal with philosophical
issues, which by their nature reflect to a greater degree
the personal views of their authors.

THE PORTABLE STANFORD BOOK SERIES
Stanford Alumni Association
Bowman Alumni House
Stanford, California 94305-4005

ISBN: 0-916318-55-9

Acknowledgments

This book recounts the story of an unusual collaboration between a private university and public schools. A complete listing of all the individuals who have played a major role in this endeavor would fill pages. We will mention, in chronological order, a sampling of those people who typify the collaboration.

The story began with Jean Funderburg, principal of Graystone School in San Jose, California, and with teachers like Doris Dillon, who saw the promise of extending their dreams of a genuinely integrated and engaging literacy program through the curriculum structures and instructional strategies that we created in the summer of 1980. It was supported by doctoral students in the Stanford School of Education—Andrea Whittaker, Robin Munson, Marcia Henry—who blended practical knowledge about teaching with what they were learning in our program. And the early work was made possible by a small but vital grant from an anonymous donor who believed in public schools.

The proof of the pudding was established early on by testing the ideas in other places and with other leadership. Rita Bean at the University of Pittsburgh, Roger Bruning at Nebraska and Barbara Schweiger in the Omaha Public Schools, Ruth Mach and Harriet Spilker at Meramec School in St. Louis, Clay Wadleigh in the Whisman District south of Stanford, Myrna Cooper and Vinnie Danzer of the New York City Teacher Centers Consortium, Alice Furry of the Sacramento County Department of Education, Pat Masonheimer of the Elk Grove, California, District—researchers and practitioners from a broad spectrum of backgrounds saw in the concept of critical literacy the potential for a more challenging curriculum in the early grades.

The North Shoreview experience was of fundamental importance in moving from the level of classroom practice to school change. Evelyn Taylor is a believer, and her teachers showed what can happen when the commitment and intelligence of classroom teachers is harnessed. Ed Boell and Morris Houck are two who were especially memorable. The "second stage" of the project built on the contributions of a new group of Stanford students: Shelby Wolf, John Shefelbein, Carrol Moran, and Robin Avelar La Salle stand out in this group. The project continued to focus on urban districts serving the needs of students from at-risk backgrounds: Ginger House Shattuck in the Norwalk–La Mirada District in Southern California, Mary and John Cooke in the Oakland Unified Schools, Associate Superintendent Bob Martin in South Central Los Angeles, along with principals and faculty at the 59th and 102nd Street schools in Martin's region, stand out in memory. The Weingart Foundation provided support for the Los Angeles project.

Most of these early project activities are still alive in one way or another. The current work centers around three activities: (a) Developing the phonics program into a balanced format that is equally accessible to practitioners at both ends of the "great debate." Gillian Johnson and her primary team at Mack School, along with Rita Kimball at Walnut Grove School in Pleasanton, Calif., are centrally involved in continuing development of the program. (b) School change based on curriculum reform, which seems within reach; work in Chicago schools with Gail Ward and a network of collaborators is still alive, despite the turmoil in the system. (c) A focus on collegiate teacher education. The ideas in this book could revolutionize the way that schools of education prepare practitioners, but changing traditions is difficult. In Los Angeles, Mary Lewis and her colleagues have developed an intern program that builds on this book's ideas—the District now graduates hundreds of teachers every year through a process that connects candidates with the realities of urban education and the possibilities of cognitive-social schooling. The collaboration that began with Graystone Elementary remains the hallmark of this project.

Finally, turning these years of experience into a book would not have been possible without the assistance of Bruce Goldman and Amy Pilkington. They turned ideas and experiences into words and pictures.

Table of Contents

Teach Our Children Well 1

The year is 1985. From the outside, North Shoreview Elementary School in San Mateo, California, looks like many other schools constructed during the suburban buildups of the 1950s. The long, low, brick structure was built when San Mateo was an ethnically homogeneous middle-class community south of San Francisco. Passing decades brought urbanization and economic disparities. In 1985, Principal Evelyn Taylor can describe Shoreview as "the school across the tracks, a place for throw-away kids." Its student body encompasses virtually every social and educational ailment one can imagine. The 357 students speak 31 different home languages. Neighborhood children are mostly poor and often hungry. Many live in nearby residence motels, dwellings for the borderline homeless. Immigrant children frequently appear in the principal's office for their first day in any school.

Now let us fast-forward to the year 1992. Within the walls of North Shoreview, things have changed. At first glance, the cacophony suggests educational disaster. Yet upon closer inspection of the goings-on in any classroom (the school welcomes visitors), you see that the students are working enthusiastically at high-level tasks, noisily exploring academic matters in various languages. You can see that they are learning to like learning.

For the adult visitor accustomed to orderly classrooms, North Shoreview classrooms in the year 1992 are chaotic on first encounter (Figure 1.1). Walls are crowded with pictures and diagrams messily scribbled on large sheets of paper—fourth- and fifth-graders read Hesse's *Siddhartha*, comparing it with Moses' life. Student compositions drop from clotheslines strung around the room. The children are noisy. Even while the teacher is lecturing, students may interrupt, sometimes several at the same time. As you enter, the teacher stops to find out who you are and what you want. She introduces you to the class, and the students return to their work while she chats with you.

You begin to realize that, despite the apparent disorder, the children are genuinely involved in schoolwork. They talk about books as sources of enjoyment, information, and understanding. Some work in groups, others on individual tasks. But all are working, and none seem bored. From one perspective, this picture is not really news. Kids are learning to read and write, and that's the goal in the early years of schooling. But these children live in troubled conditions, and we might expect them to be troubled in school. Even students from more-advantaged backgrounds often find schoolwork not all that interesting. They may do fine on tests, but they often lack the motivation or interest to pursue learning for its own rewards.

Critical Literacy: Reading and Writing for an Information Age

The Shoreview students are immersed in a curriculum of *critical literacy: learning to use all forms of language for thinking, for problem solving, and for communication.* A crucial shift—from the basic-skills curriculum found in most U.S. classrooms toward one that embodies the principles of critical literacy—can lead all our children to achieve high academic standards.

Most Americans have experienced basic-skills instruction as children and as parents. The teacher presents a specific skill ("The vowel *a* makes the long sound when the word ends with a silent *e*."), students recite the pattern and practice on worksheets. Then they take a test. Rote practice is the method; individual mastery is the goal. Yet a half-century of cognitive research[1] indicates that learning is faster, more long-lasting, and more far-reaching when it is active, social, and reflective—when (a) students work on problems that mean something to them, (b) they work in cooperative groups, and (c) they learn to reflect on how current learning applies to new tasks.

The curriculum of critical literacy described in this book builds on these three principles. Instruction starts with problem solving rather than skills. Kindergartners deal with simple tasks: "What should we do for our Thanksgiving play?" For sixth-graders, the problems are more sophisticated: "You have read two books, *James and the Giant Peach* and *Where the Red Fern Grows,* that both deal with persistence and striving. As sixth-graders, what can you learn from these themes to help you with next year's move to middle school?"

To support students as they wrestle with these problems, instructional strategies can guide students in collecting information from a variety of sources (textbooks, computers, the library), while graphic structures can help to portray a topic visually. These graphic organizers encourage cooperation in framing and solving problems. They help make thought public. Ask a group of young children to "web" or "cluster"[2] about the concept of Thanksgiving, and you will discover that they possess a wealth of creative ideas. You can see examples in Figure 1.1. Business calls these techniques "brainstorming," and is willing to invest substantially to teach them to managers. Children can learn to web as early as kindergarten.

Finally, critical-literacy methods teach kids a technical language for talking about problem solving and learning, the essence of reflection. The technical language includes words like "web" for brainstorm, "character" and "plot" for story analysis, and "report" for informational writing.

Thinking about thinking is hard work. If you focus on your thoughts while reading this sentence, it distracts and slows your reading. Mental processes usually run on autopilot, so you can focus on the content.

Pausing to reflect is important in two circumstances: (a) when learning something new, and (b) in emergencies. New learning, for both adults and children, works better if the learner has a big picture of the situation and if he or she can talk it out, preferably with someone a little more expert. Trial and error is essential, but we often need help if we are to learn from errors.

Performance in an emergency also profits from reflection. Learning a computer program by rote works fine until you meet the unexpected. Then a capacity for reflection pays off, because you know how to step back from the problem and look beneath the surface. Here is where technical language comes in handy. You can ask yourself questions like "Is it the operating system or the software? Should I restart the machine or try to save the files?" In school, tests are often emergencies:

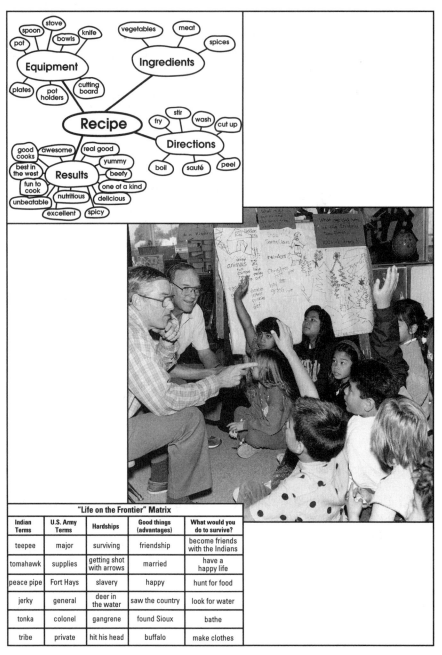

"Life on the Frontier" Matrix

Indian Terms	U.S. Army Terms	Hardships	Good things (advantages)	What would you do to survive?
teepee	major	surviving	friendship	become friends with the Indians
tomahawk	supplies	getting shot with arrows	married	have a happy life
peace pipe	Fort Hays	slavery	happy	hunt for food
jerky	general	deer in the water	saw the country	look for water
tonka	colonel	gangrene	found Sioux	bathe
tribe	private	hit his head	buffalo	make clothes

Figure 1.1, Panel A
Bob Calfee in Ed Boell's third-grade classroom at North Shoreview Elementary School. Above is a web on the recipe for dragon stew; below is a weave, or matrix, on frontier life.

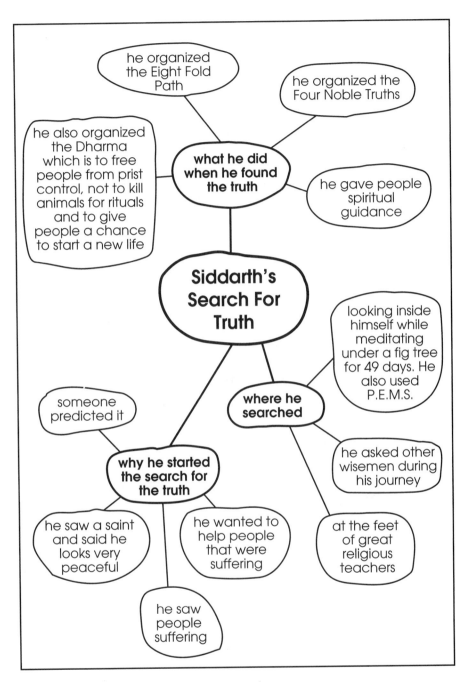

Figure 1.1, Panel B
A web on Siddhartha constructed by a team of
upper-elementary students.

"Compare and contrast the Revolutionary and Civil Wars"; or "List the advantages and disadvantages of environmental controls." Students handle such challenges more effectively when they have the tools to analyze the problem, to create a structure for organizing what they know, and to talk it out.

Tests that require analysis and writing are reappearing in schools across the nation, replacing the multiple-choice, fill-in-the-blank exams that reinforce rote skills and memorization. The shift toward higher standards on more-demanding tests is a worthwhile endeavor, but we need a parallel shift in curriculum and instruction.

As you walk through the classrooms during your virtual tour of circa-1992 North Shoreview Elementary, you see critical literacy in action. The students appear connected with their tasks. The noise is productive; students are not goofing off but arguing about real issues. They are reflective; they can answer questions like "What are you doing; why are you doing it?" Lest you take this feat for granted, visit a few other schools and talk with students.

Something unusual happened at North Shoreview. In 1985, North Shoreview students' scores on the California Assessment Program (CAP) test placed them at the 10th percentile, meaning that 90 percent of the schools in California had higher scores. This wasn't surprising; for this type of population, scores would be expected to be in the low percentiles. Children from poor families do poorly in school. Yet by 1989, Shoreview scores had risen to the 55th percentile; the school was above the state average. San Mateo schools serve mostly middle-class families, and the district was impressed by North Shoreview's improvement. The school attracted visitors—partly because of the changed test scores, but even more because of the evident enthusiasm of teachers and students, backed up by the quality of classroom work and student writing.

How did the change at North Shoreview come about? How did it persist for almost a decade? What lessons does the story offer other schools? These questions are important for all Americans. They are obviously important to those who care about the children of the poor. But they also concern middle-class parents who want the best education for their children. Children from financially stable households, whose parents are well educated, whose native language is English, and whose family is intact—these students have historically outperformed their less-advantaged peers on standardized tests. But our world is changing. Schools need to teach *all* our children to handle unknown tasks in unconventional situations. A classical education is no longer a guarantee of a comfortable position in society. And children's profiles are changing. Students from impoverished backgrounds are entering schools in disproportionate numbers. Yet we know enough to ensure that all students, whatever their background, secure the best education that we can imagine for the most promising of our children.

A Little History

Everyone knows that schools are in trouble. Educators, businesses, citizens, and parents have advanced several factors to explain America's educational failure:

The trouble with today's schools is:

(a) Students are unprepared and lazy
(b) Teachers are incompetent and unmotivated
(c) Administrators are overpaid and underworked
(d) The public is unwilling to provide adequate money
(e) All of the above

Based on newspapers and newscasts, you might pick *e* as the correct answer. Or you might add alternatives of your own: money wasted for special programs; schools distracted by non-school tasks. In any event, the starting point is that schools are failing. Americans expect a lot from their schools, and rightly so. Since Jefferson first proposed public education as the foundation for democracy, Americans have invested substantially in public education. Two centuries after Jefferson, we demand both quality and equality. In a diverse nation such as ours, these competing aspirations pose a conflict.

Popular interest in education rises and falls like the tide (or a roller-coaster). Sputnik went into orbit in 1957, and so did the public. Citizens complained—not about the space program, but about the schools. The federal government responded with programs to fund research on new instructional approaches, especially in science and math. Research on cognitive learning produced major insights, the foundation for much of the work described in this book.

In 1964 the Office of Education commissioned the first nationwide survey of America's schools. The Coleman report, *Equality of Educational Opportunity*,[3] confirmed that students from poor and minority families attended schools with fewer academic resources and performed less well on standardized tests. The government responded with special funding for schools serving the children of the poor. Federal support for education was a small fraction of school budgets during the 1960s and 1970s, however, and the dollars were spread broadly but thinly.

The Vietnam War overtook the war on poverty, and schools were mostly ignored until midway through the Reagan presidency, when *A Nation at Risk*,[4] a report released in 1983 by the new Department of Education, proclaimed:

> If an unfriendly power had attempted to impose on America the mediocre educational performance that exists today, we might well have viewed it as an act of war. . . . We have squandered the gains in student achievement made in the wake of the Sputnik challenge. . . . We have, in effect, been committing an act of unthinking, unilateral educational disarmament.

The evidence actually did not support these charges. There were no "post-Sputnik achievement gains"; student achievement has remained quite stable from the 1950s to the present. The fact that the proportion of high-school graduates and college-bound youth has increased dramatically had little or nothing to do with Sputnik, which mainly spurred accelerated-education programs for kids who surely would have graduated in any case.

There *were* changes in students, however, with more children coming from backgrounds of poverty and broken homes (Figure 1.2). These changing family circumstances reflect broad and deep movements in U.S. society. Today's student is more likely to live in a single-parent household, to live in a distressed community, and to be poorer than used to be the case. These trends all lead to the expectation of declining academic achievement.

The classroom realities are poignant. In a Bronx classroom we visited, only two of the 32 students lived in traditional families with biological parents. The demographics of North Shoreview's student body—children from poor and splintered families, children of ethnic and linguistic minorities—have always posed problems for U.S. schools, which are better suited to mainstream and middle-class families. But besides these obvious cases, students from single-parent families have become commonplace in classrooms across the social spectrum. In more and more two-parent families, both adults take on jobs for economic and social reasons, leaving latchkey children to make their way to and from school. When Robert Calfee, one of the co-authors of this book, ran for the Palo Alto, California, Board of Education in 1987, he was amazed to find, even in that tony suburb, home-alone children answering the door as he canvassed neighborhoods in the late afternoon.

The federal response to *A Nation at Risk* was the bully pulpit. Education Secretary William Bennett prodded teachers, students,

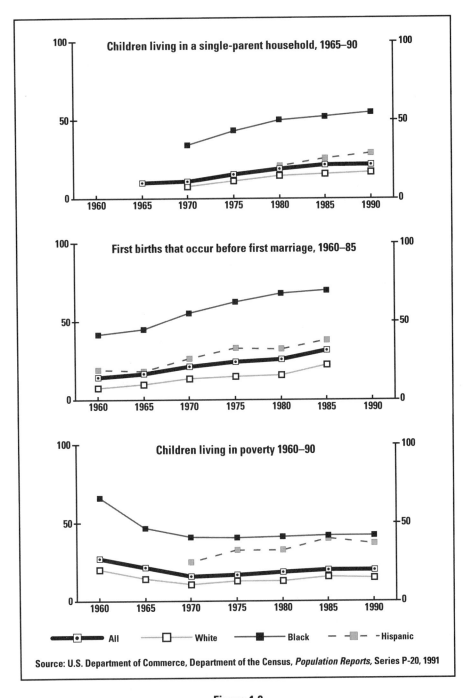

Figure 1.2
Trends in student and family demographics in the United States.

administrators, and families to higher achievements. Media and politicians announced that the schools were falling apart, victims of a conspiracy of incompetence and irresponsibility. After Bennett, Secretary Lauro Cavazos urged parents to provide their children quiet places to read and do homework. Little comfort in this advice for children who lacked homes and parents.

In 1988, George Bush was inaugurated as the "education president." Foreign events occupied much of his time, but one singular event focused on education. The 1989 Education Summit in Charlottesville, Virginia, chaired by then-Governor Bill Clinton of Arkansas, committed the U.S. to a set of desiderata called *Goals 2000:*[5]

- Children start school ready to learn.
- Ninety percent of students graduate from high school.
- Students demonstrate competency in challenging subject matters to prepare for citizenship, lifelong learning, and employment.
- U.S. students are first in the world in math and science.
- Adults possess the knowledge and skills to compete in a world economy.
- Schools are safe and drug-free, conducive to learning.

The federal role in *Goals 2000* was to exhort the nation's schools and families to attain higher, world-class educational standards of achievement. The tool for implementing these goals was a system of national tests. For President Bush, the remedies were choice, competition, and privatization of schooling. The reform flagship was a network of New American Schools, many aglitter with high-tech computers. Teachers were largely unrepresented at the summit, and none of the goals addressed their realities or their needs. The most immediate fallout was a marked decline in federal support for schools.

President Clinton, building on *Goals 2000,* hewed to familiar themes: codifying national goals, establishing a system of national tests, urging state and local agencies to reform themselves. "Opportunity to learn," a placemarker for equity issues, appeared briefly on the administration's program, but quickly fell by the way. Administrations had changed, but the messages remained the same.

Here is an alternative view of this history:

- Schools are actually doing a pretty good job under difficult conditions.

- Schools need to tackle a *new* agenda—not higher but *different* standards.
- Public schools will be the mainstay for educating our children.

In a nutshell, the correct answer to the multiple-choice question posed earlier is "None of the above." Today's schools still operate like the assembly lines of an earlier *factory* model (Figure 1.3). Speeding up the line will not help, nor will making a few refinements in the basic model. Changes are needed in several areas—in what is taught, in how it is taught and tested, in textbooks and materials, and in the social organization of the classroom. Tomorrow's graduates need not to read faster and write more, but to read more critically and write more effectively.

Views of Literacy

We focus in this book on the elementary and middle years of schooling, the nine years from kindergarten through eighth grade, years when reading is an essential outcome. Educated people often view literacy as a low-level skill, so simple that something must be wrong with anyone who does not easily master the task. In fact, reading is such an automatic process that you cannot appreciate its mysteries unless you try to analyze it while you are doing it—or try to teach a novice.

Reading is partly about print. A reader can translate scribbles on a printed page into meaningful messages. One view of teaching literacy emphasizes the spelling-sound code, or *phonics*. After acquiring this skill, students can get on with the "good stuff," like literature and history, science and technology, serious pieces and fun articles.

This view of reading, while partly true, is too limiting, and gives the wrong message to both students and teachers. Learning the code is important, but critical literacy goes beyond the *medium*, even beyond the *message*, to the *manner* of using language. The print medium (paper, computer screens, and so on) assists the literate person in thinking and communicating. As Figure 1.4 illustrates, today's messages combine words and graphics in complex ways. It is one thing to settle back to enjoy a paperback novel, where minimal phonics suffices. When you study the income tax manual, more is required than casual reading. Here is where the cognitive strategies of critical literacy become essential—unless you have a good accountant.

Critical literacy can also be illustrated by the contrast between a televised situation comedy and a public-broadcast documentary. This contrast in manner shows up when you chat informally with a friend

INDUSTRIAL SOCIETY/ FACTORY SCHOOLS	INFORMATION/ INQUIRING SCHOOLS

Curriculum

Basic skills, functional literacy	Transferrable skills, critical literacy
Separate subjects: reading, writing, arithmetic, science, history	Interdisciplinary relations in humanities, arts, and sciences
Specialized body of knowledge to be memorized, content emphasis	Processes and strategies for analyzing new information and emerging knowledge
Print-based textbooks and worksheets	Multiple technologies, electronic libraries, multimedia sources, information networks

Instruction

Teacher teaches, students recite	Students construct, teacher manages
Student receives information; teacher the source	Student builds meaning; teacher guides to resources
Individual work on assigned objectives	Cooperative learning, "real" tasks, flexible scheduling

Assessment

Standardized multiple-choice tests	Performance-based assessments and portfolios
Achievement reported by external authorities	Achievement assessments based on teacher judgment

Organization

Hierarchical structure, principal as manager	Collaborative decisions, principal as head teacher
Individual work by isolated teachers	Professional community of inquiry
Separate grade levels, pull-out programs for problem students	Multigraded program, schoolwide services

Figure 1.3
Comparisons between schools for an industrial society
and those for an information age.

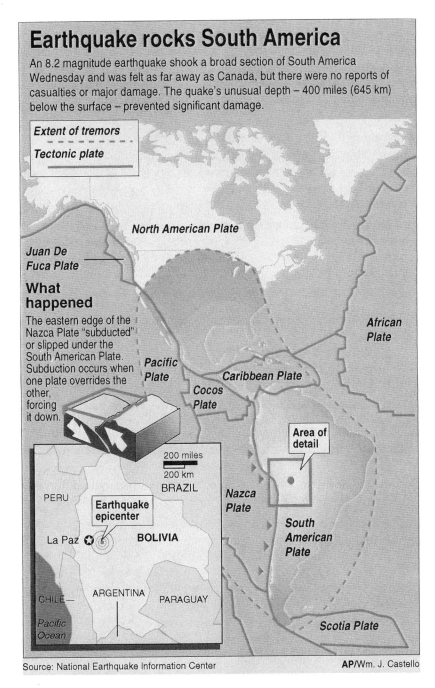

Earthquake rocks South America

An 8.2 magnitude earthquake shook a broad section of South America Wednesday and was felt as far away as Canada, but there were no reports of casualties or major damage. The quake's unusual depth – 400 miles (645 km) below the surface – prevented significant damage.

Extent of tremors
Tectonic plate

North American Plate

Juan De Fuca Plate

What happened

The eastern edge of the Nazca Plate "subducted" or slipped under the South American Plate. Subduction occurs when one plate overrides the other, forcing it down.

African Plate

Pacific Plate

Caribbean Plate

Cocos Plate

Area of detail

200 miles
200 km

BRAZIL

PERU

Earthquake epicenter

Nazca Plate

La Paz   BOLIVIA

South American Plate

CHILE

ARGENTINA   PARAGUAY

Pacific Ocean

Scotia Plate

Source: National Earthquake Information Center   AP/Wm. J. Castello

Figure 1.4
An example of the type of writing that graduates encounter in the daily newspaper.
The "meaning" of this article, which appeared in the *San Francisco Chronicle*
on June 10, 1994, is more than the sound of the words.

about a traffic ticket, and then prepare to plead your case before the judge. Both situations illustrate the difference between natural and formal styles of language use. Both styles (and many variations in between) have value in the right context. Talking with friends at a party is stultifying if you lecture; your case in traffic court will go badly if you address the judge like a buddy.

A curriculum of critical literacy builds foundations for formal language from the earliest years. Kindergartners can learn to handle problems, to work together, and to reflect, even before they have mastered the printed word. The single most important outcome of the early years of schooling is competence in the literate use of language, through the study of literature, social studies, science, mathematics, the arts, and even school culture. Taught consistently and well, virtually all of our children should be able to achieve this competence.

The following chapters describe in more detail how critical literacy can be taught, and then show the results for students in a variety of locations around the country. Two questions may puzzle you at this point: First, can today's schools and teachers handle this task? If they are doing such a terrible job with the basics, how can they possibly aspire to higher-level outcomes? Second, is it reasonable to hope that all children will attain high levels of literacy? Without supportive families, schools surely cannot press disadvantaged students to achieve high academic standards.

Chapter 2 presents evidence that today's schools are actually holding their own in teaching the basics. Equally important, schools provide children and families with a safe haven at a time when many other supports are faltering. Elementary teachers are, by and large, caring adults who dedicate their lives to the well-being of children. They are, by and large, intellectually capable of handling the curriculum described in this book. Chapter 3 tells how their talents are undercut by mindless textbook routines that bore them as well as their students. A rigid curriculum guarantees that many students will fail to learn—and learn to fail. The classroom teacher is the key to adaptive instruction.

For more than a century, American reading instruction has swung between two polar extremes. At one extreme, the teacher follows a recipe. Skills-based *phonics* programs teach reading in a series of stages, beginning with simple words and moving through short sentences to simple stories. Students who encounter problems along the way are recycled back to the beginning, ensuring that they fall further behind. At the other extreme, teachers are left on their own. *Look-say* or *whole-language* programs emphasize the naturalness of reading. Give children good books, give them a little help now and then, and they will learn to read "naturally." Some children may prosper with this approach, but many others will fall by the way. The curriculum described in Chapter 3 is not an amalgam of these two philosophies, but embodies innovative concepts to ensure high levels of literacy for all students.

Good News for "Throw-away" Kids

Can we expect all students to attain high levels of literacy? The answer is "yes." Cognitive research shows that virtually all children possess the cognitive potential to read and write. But children in our society differ markedly in the experiences they bring to kindergarten. Our schools amplify the differential; academically perhaps more than economically, the rich become richer and the poor become poorer.[6]

Schooling transmits a society's cultural traditions to succeeding generations. In contrast to some cultures, where these traditions are reserved for the elite, a democratic society aspires to give virtually every child the endowments for individual and collective well-being. The gifts include cultural literacy, an awareness of the facts and figures that "everyone knows."[7] Even more important are strategies for learning, interaction, and full participation in society.

To some extent, the goal of equal educational opportunity is at odds with the reality of individual differences. Schools are caught in the tension between grading or growing. A *grading philosophy* builds on the notion of selection, where bigger is better. Apples pass through a sorter, the small fruit falling through the narrow slots at the beginning and the largest fruit surviving to the end. The big apples are the most costly. School systems around the world rely on a similar principle. U.S. schools are also dedicated to the principle of equality, which is better served by a *growing philosophy*. U.S. farmers grade, but they also work at increasing the yield. They create growing conditions—soil, water, and fertilizer—that maximize the number of "big apples." Schools need to enhance growing conditions for students—and for teachers. *This book questions the immutability of the bell-shaped curve.* It calls for redirecting educational philosophy and practice toward growth rather than grades.[8]

One of the nation's official goals is that all children enter kindergarten "ready to learn." The members of the Goals Panel have had a hard time with this one, because they don't know what to measure. Kindergarten teachers expect children to know their ABCs and numbers, to behave and cooperate in the classroom, to understand how to play the school game. Not all of today's 5-year-olds are prepared for school in this sense, but if you enter virtually any kindergarten, you will be impressed by the eagerness of these children to learn.

In the project described in this book, we have repeatedly found that most students, including those identified as low-achieving, have sharper minds than they get credit for. They have experiences of enormous academic value and pedagogical potential, but they don't know what they know. They cannot recognize and use their background experience until someone—a teacher—offers the cognitive tools for expressing themselves and participating in group problem solving.

Witness this remedial ninth-grade social-studies classroom at San Jose High School in San Jose, California, where Hispanic and Vietnamese students struggle with limited English. The students have been placed with an art teacher in her studio-*cum*-classroom. Art courses are rare in the school, and the teacher, who has been assigned the castoffs, has asked Calfee (in the latter's capacity as visiting coach), "What can you possibly do with students like these?" His response: "Let's see what they know about the world."

Calfee begins the lesson by scrawling on the blackboard, in large letters, "Where do you live?" The students can read the words, but are understandably puzzled by the question. Calfee offers a frame of reference: "Pretend I'm from Mars, green face, buggy eyes. How would you tell me where you live?" The conversation during the next 20 minutes is alternately whimsical, practical, serious, humorous, ingenuous: "I live in San Jose." "I live at 1401 North First Street." "I live down the street from Taco Bell." "I live in the U.S." "I live in the world."

One student's response is especially memorable: "We all live in a galaxy—sort of like a Frisbee of stars, and we're on the westward spiral arm." "Where did you learn that?" "I read it in a book." In fact, the reference is Douglas Adams' *Hitchhiker's Guide to the Galaxy*. This college cult classic is loaded with cultural jokes, bizarre historical references, and science-fiction spoofing—scarcely the literary fare one expects from a remedial reader. The student has been identified as a failure, but in this case the system is failing the student.

Project READ: Critical Literacy in Action

In addition to the formal research on student potential, our experiences in varied classrooms show that virtually all children can acquire the skills and knowledge of critical literacy. The techniques and strategies described in this book, based largely on the development and implementation of a program called *Project READ*, offer one strategy for achieving this goal. Since 1981, Project READ has helped schools in troubled neighborhoods throughout the country—as well as quite a few average, middle-class communities—to promote reading and writing achievement appropriate for an information age. The project began in a Silicon Valley school, Graystone Elementary, as a collaboration between Calfee and the Graystone teachers. Chapter 3 gives more detail about this story, but the essence was the combining of teachers' beliefs that their students should be challenged with Calfee's conviction that a curriculum designed around cognitive principles would lead to just such a challenge.

Cognitive theory, as espoused in the project design, builds on the premise that while students vary in their experiences, interests, and styles, they all possess the intellectual potential and the motivation needed to read and write, to think and communicate. Moreover, *this goal is attainable with the resources now available to schools, families, and communities.* The key is a shift from prevailing instructional extremes—rote practice or unstructured experience—toward a curriculum design that provides students with strategies and structures to handle high-level tasks.

Like several other innovative programs for improving instruction in the elementary and middle grades,[9] Project READ promotes academic learning that is *constructive, social,* and *metacognitive.* "Constructive" means that students are actively engaged in authentic tasks. "Social" emphasizes a balance between individual and group activities. "Metacognitive" means learning to reflect, to think about thinking. Project READ is unique in that, rather than package a program for students, it aims at professional development for teachers. The goal is the establishment of a *community of inquiry,* where teachers collaborate around a shared conception of critical literacy to adapt instruction to student experience and interests while remaining mindful of achievement standards.

Success for all students does entail change. First, it means a focus on "teaching a few things well."[10] Today's elementary and middle schools try to do too much. State and federal mandates have become prescriptive burdens, detailed but vague, fuzzy in concept and lacking in practicalities. *It's Elementary,*[11] a California Department of Education document that spells out what the state's elementary schools ought to be doing, lists more than 30 goals for elementary schools, ranging from "Invest shrewdly in technology to help promote the thinking curriculum" to "Support teacher professionalism with a classroom supply budget, secretarial help, and a well-equipped workplace." The framework says little about curriculum. Other state documents lay out mandates for reading and writing, science, social studies, mathematics, and the arts. Teachers spend little time reading these stacks of publications.

What should be taught in the elementary and middle grades? We repeat our earlier answer: "The single most important outcome of the early years of schooling is competence in the literate use of language, through the study of literature, social studies and science, mathematics, the arts, and the school culture." Success for all students requires a focused curriculum in place of today's scattershot efforts to cover everything. It means moving toward a developmental view of learning.

Kindergarten through eighth grade spans nine years, easily enough time to ensure that all students meet high standards on graduation from middle school. Experience with the various disciplines is important. Students should understand history and geography, the relation of time and space to the working of societies. They should be able to apply these understandings across a range of situations, from the neighborhood to the world community. They should be familiar with significant geographic features and historical events, and should understand the conceptual importance of these facts. But memorizing the specifics is less important than acquiring strategies for finding information and using it intelligently.

Finally, success for all students calls for better ways to assess achievement.[12] The federal call for national standards is leading to the construction of national tests. But while standardized tests provide one index of learning, they cannot tap the high-level competence that is the essence of critical literacy. The present reliance on multiple-choice tests is a relatively recent trend. Fifty years ago, classroom teachers handled assessment. The Friday tests covered material presented during that week. On Monday morning students learned how they did. Students had to show their work. The right answer based on wrong reasoning was less valued than the wrong answer reached by valid methods.

Today a few adventurous teachers are employing portfolios to judge student performance. Informed teacher judgment is the soundest basis for evaluating students, especially in the elementary and middle grades. It is essential that teachers possess the knowledge, skill, and time for this task, and they also have to have a clear idea of the curriculum—the course of study.

What Can We Learn from North Shoreview?

Newspapers and newscasts often feature schools that appear to be successful under tough conditions. Leadership is a key theme. North

Shoreview Principal Evelyn Taylor played a key role in turning her school around. How can the North Shoreview experience be reproduced in the tens of thousands of "ordinary" schools around the country? Taylor is hard to clone.

One thing to be learned is that students can attain a quality education under difficult circumstances. In 1992 North Shoreview still did not look much like a "New American School." Like most schools serving hard-hit communities, this one's funding was meager. The faculty would have liked to renovate the library, and wished for a computer in every classroom.

North Shoreview had not replaced the teaching staff. Promising students were not selected and bused in. No large grants were received. What did change—fundamentally—was the central core of schooling: what was taught, how it was taught, and how learning was assessed. North Shoreview teachers set their sights not on minimal competence but on excellence, not on proficiency in the basic skills but on the acquisition of critical literacy. Evelyn Taylor set the stage for change, but the key was the teachers' response to a new view of reading and writing.

These elements of the North Shoreview experience are reproducible. Later chapters describe how a strategy based on curriculum change transformed elementary schools around the nation. The techniques are not particularly sexy. Today's educational klieg lights spotlight "innovations"—science and math, high schools, multimedia and virtual reality, and lots of money for a few earthshaking projects. How do you get the public excited about elementary schools, teachers, reading and writing, and changes that don't cost a lot?

The program outlined in the following chapters relies on *people rather than paper*. Young children, especially those from troubled home and community situations, need nurturance and understanding to support their academic growth. Project READ assumes that, on the surface, *new schools will look a lot like old schools*. Neighborhood schools are a reality, and we can't wait another decade for new institutions to be created and built. Project READ focuses on *the early years of schooling and the learning of literacy* as the primary target for reform. Civics and deportment, drugs and health, assertive discipline and cooperative learning—these are all important, but today's eighth-grader who enters high school lacking critical literacy is in trouble.

To sum it all up: School reform calls for strategies that ensure a quality education for all children, within the existing realities of people (students, teachers, and families), institutions, resources and needs; strategies that support the well-being of our children and our society during the next few decades. How to attain this holy grail? Reform proposals and the bully pulpit emphasize money, technology, standards, parental choice, and restructuring, all couched in a simplistic "pull your socks up" approach.

But the key is what happens in the classroom. America's schools have actually been doing a pretty good job, as we will show in Chapter 2. But the job has changed. Project READ structures and strategies demonstrate the potential for moving beyond basic skills to cognitive learning in ways that are feasible with existing resources and knowledge. We describe the research, theory, and practice of Project READ in Chapter 3. The techniques have been applied in a wide variety of settings (not only in San Mateo, but also in New York City, Omaha, Pittsburgh, St. Louis, Sacramento, Oakland, and Los Angeles, to name a few), over many years, under unsettled conditions. We recount these experiences in Chapter 4. A unique feature of the READ strategy is that school restructuring begins with classroom instruction, the "engine" that drives schooling. Chapter 5 describes the linkage between school reform and professional renewal. Finally, in Chapter 6, we discuss ways in which you can help schools. You can make a difference by knowing what to look for, and by knowing when and how to put your shoulder to the wheel. It takes the entire village if we are to teach all of our children well.

Are American Schools As Bad As They Seem? 2

The scene was rushed, the players fast-talking and harried—just what you'd imagine in a Washington government office at the beginning of a busy workday. Education heavyweights came and went in the downtown office, while swarms of young lawyers buzzed through the Department of Education corridors. In the middle of the confusion, A tieless Undersecretary of Education Marshall S. Smith pored over charts showing the latest test scores from NAEP—the National Assessment of Education Progress, undeniably America's best audit of its education system. The scores were once more on the rise. He scowled at a local headline that bannered the same report as continuing evidence of the nation's educational decline. It was 1994. Midterm elections lay just ahead. "Look at these results! What do we have to do? What more can we say?" asked Smith in perplexity and frustration.

How well are America's schools doing? It depends on whom you believe. In a book called *The Learning Gap*,[1] two researchers asked American mothers to judge how effectively their neighborhood schools are educating their children. Nine out of ten rated their schools as doing an "excellent" or "good" job. Only 40 percent of the Japanese and Taipei mothers rated their schools so favorably.

If U.S. parents seem to like their own children's schools, that is only part of the story. In 1994, George Gallup conducted the 26th *Phi Delta Kappan* poll on American schools.[2] Of the 1,300-plus American adults who "graded" their neighborhood schools, 44 percent gave them an A or B, a decline of 3 percent from the year before (Figure 2.1). Only 7 percent flunked their local schools. When asked to grade the rest of the nation's schools, however, just 22 percent—about one in five—gave them an A or B. These trends have remained relatively stable for a decade. The low point occurred in 1983, just following the alarms of *Nation at Risk.*

Maybe parents just don't understand the problem? In *We Must Take Charge: Our Schools and Our Future,* former U.S. Assistant Secretary of Education Chester Finn points to several other surveys that confirm the Gallup results.[3] A 1989 Harris poll showed that 92 percent of American teachers thought education at their school to be either good or excellent. In a 1990 Allstate survey, 91 percent of school administrators reported public education as excellent, very good, or at least good. A 1989 study of school board presidents found that 79 percent gave their own schools either an A or B. Not exactly disinterested parties, to be sure. Finn is convinced that our schools have undergone major decline, and concludes that our educational leaders simply don't grasp the seriousness of the situation.

Finn is one of a large group of opinion-shapers who decry the public's complacency and self-satisfaction. But self-deception is not the only possibility. Perhaps America's schools are *not* as bad as politicians and others would have us believe. Perhaps the adverse press releases spring from government and media inclinations to promote perceptions of a national crisis. Might parents' high ratings of local schools reflect their observations that today's classrooms aren't much different from what they were in years past? We hear unrelenting horror stories of schools riddled by drugs and crime. What is actually happening to the character and quality of education on a daily basis in the school down the street a couple of blocks from your home?

How Bad Are Our Schools?

The state of our educational system depends on what you read. Consider this sample of articles gleaned from a few months of media-watching:

• "SAT Tests Show Gains Made in 1980s Eroding," *Los Angeles Times,* August 23, 1994. This article about the Scholastic Assessment Test for college entry concedes students' "plodding progress in math," but adds that they are "slipping back to historic lows in verbal skills." Girls are making gains, "but boys are slacking." It does not mention the swelling numbers of students taking the test. Nor does it note that national scores are holding steady— even rising slightly for math. Small 2- and 3-point yearly fluctuations on the 600-point scale are described as "grim."

• "Writing Tests Show Many Children Still Can't," *San Francisco Chronicle,* June 8, 1994. This squib cites an Education Department report that "many students at each grade level continue to have serious difficulty in producing effective informative, persuasive, or narrative writing." The study reviewed writing samples from 30,000 children in grades 4, 8, and 12. Funny, but the article did not quote another section of the same report showing that students, on the whole, have improved skills. The piece goes on to decry the hours that students spend watching television. Another item in the same section highlights another "education" story from Kansas City: "Students Find Body—Tell Only Friends." Good news is hard to come by.

• "SAT Increases the Average Score, by Fiat," *New York Times,* June 11, 1994. This article presents a balanced account of the decision by the College Board to renorm the SAT. The test was originally designed in the 1940s with 500 as the baseline. Most publishers renorm standardized tests every few years; the College Board waited for a half-century. Most national coverage of this event intimated that something suspicious was occurring—that the wool was being pulled over our eyes vis-a-vis our children's education. Even the *Times* couldn't resist a dig: "The SAT score of the average American high school student will soon be going up 100 points. However, that doesn't mean that anyone is getting smarter." Nor does it mean that our students are getting dumber.

Are today's children less able academically than previous generations? Most reports of school decline, including *Nation at Risk,* have relied on standardized-test results as evidence. A multiple-choice exam is a frail indicator of the quality of schooling, but it's a starting point. Chester Finn and then-Assistant Secretary of Education Diane Ravitch, in a much-publicized book *What Do Our 17-Year-Olds Know?*,[4] reviewed

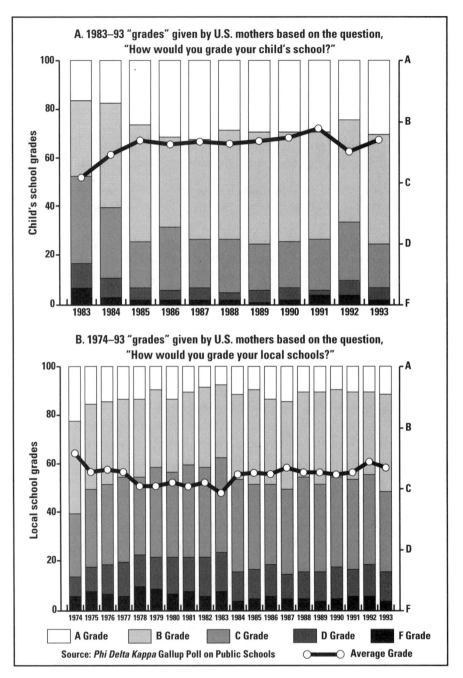

A. 1983–93 "grades" given by U.S. mothers based on the question, "How would you grade your child's school?"

Child's school grades

B. 1974–93 "grades" given by U.S. mothers based on the question, "How would you grade your local schools?"

Local school grades

☐ A Grade ▨ B Grade ▨ C Grade ▨ D Grade ■ F Grade

Source: *Phi Delta Kappa* Gallup Poll on Public Schools ○——○ Average Grade

Figure 2.1
Results from the Gallup polls of "grades" for public education
conducted for the *Phi Delta Kappan.*

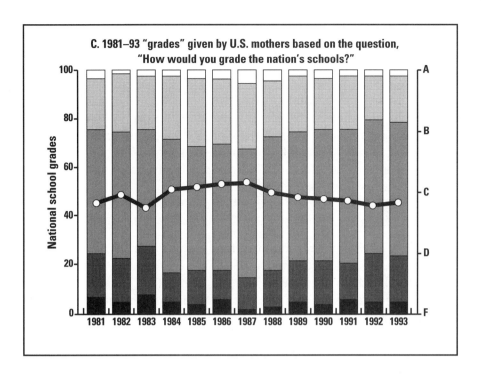

C. 1981–93 "grades" given by U.S. mothers based on the question, "How would you grade the nation's schools?"

data from a 141-item multiple-choice test and found evidence that today's teens know little or nothing about history. Parents, grandparents, and great-grandparents would surely have done better. But in 1991, in the prestigious *American Educational Research Journal,* researcher Dale Whittington attacked those conclusions. Examining tests going back to 1915, Whittington found 43 items from the Ravitch-Finn test that paralleled earlier test data. Her analysis showed that today's students scored about the same on a third of the items, worse on another third, and better on the final third compared with earlier times. Average performance was virtually identical, even though, as we shall see, a much higher proportion of today's 17-year-olds are still in school than was the case in 1915.

Whittington commented that students have always known less than their elders expect of them:

> The perception of decline in the "results" of American education is open to question. Indeed, given the reduced dropout rate and less elitist composition of the 17-year-old student body today, one could argue that students today know more American history than did their age peers of the past.[5]

The image of educational decline is rooted in American tradition. When the going gets tough, public schools are convenient scapegoats. For instance, schools were blamed for America's economic woes during the recession of the late 1980s. Stanford educator Larry Cuban wondered why the recent economic upturn did not result in praise for public education: "For the last decade, U.S. presidents, corporate leaders, and critics blasted public schools for a globally less competitive economy, sinking productivity, and jobs lost to other nations." Once the economic upturn occurred, he noted, "Not even a cheaply framed certificate of merit is in the offing for public schools."[6]

Blaming schools is part of the American Way. Witness these commentaries from past generations:

> • It is hard to imagine a more grossly stupid, a more genuinely asinine system tenaciously persisted in to the fearful detriment of over 17 million children . . . a system that not only is absolutely ineffective in its results, but also actually harmful in that it throws every year 93 of every 100 children into the world of action absolutely unfitted for even the simplest tasks of life? Can you wonder that we have so many inefficient men and women; that in so many families there are so many failures; that our boys and girls can make so little money. . . . (Ella Francis Lynch, *Ladies' Home Journal*, 1912)

> • Forty percent of high-school graduates haven't a command of simple arithmetic, cannot multiply, subtract and divide correctly in simple numbers and fractions. Over 40 percent of them cannot accurately express themselves in the English language or cannot write in their mother tongue. (Chairman of the National Association of Manufacturers education committee, 1927)

> • Frustrated university professors and angry business people [complained] that public-school students were woefully unprepared for college as well as for work. The typical high-school student could not write a clear English sentence, do simple mathematics, or find common geographical locations such as Boston or New York City. There were no basic standards. . . . As one critic put it: "We are offering them a slingshot education in a hydrogen-bomb age." (*The Scientific Monthly*, 1951)

While many seem to recall a golden age of American schooling, schools aren't what they used to be—but then, they never were. But what about trends in actual achievement data over the last few decades? "Everyone knows" about declining test scores, increased dropouts, lowered standards. "We all know" that schools have gone to hell in a handbasket since the 1960s.

The evidence suggests otherwise.

The Story You Haven't Heard

Since the 1989 Bush-Clinton Educational Summit, voices have emerged to challenge the conventional wisdom. In October 1991, Gerald W. Bracey wrote a cover article for the *Phi Delta Kappan*, "Why Can't They Be Like We Were?"[7] At the time, Bracey was a policy analyst for the National Education Association. After reading "Johnny's Miserable SATs" by *Washington Post* columnist Richard Cohen, he decided to look into just how miserable the scores really were. He examined "sources available to any interested person," and concluded: "I can only assume that people have heard the opposite [i.e., that schools are bad] so often and for so long that they have come to assume it to be true." But, he wrote, achievement data showed that "American schools have never achieved more than they currently achieve. And some indicators show them performing better than ever."

Bracey's findings were backed up by an engineering team at the federal government's Sandia National Laboratories in Albuquerque, New Mexico. The Lab had been commissioned a year earlier by the Energy Department to review the state of the nation's schools. The Sandia Report[8] did not conform to official federal policy, and it was years before it was officially released. Since Bracey's article and the Sandia report, however, several other scholars and researchers have uncovered evidence that undercuts current shibboleths of American education.

The November 13, 1991, issue of *Education Week* front-paged the problems of the Sandia report, Bracey's analysis, and the work of other researchers who concurred with their conclusions. While critics have picked at statistical fine points, these researchers' overall conclusions have proven robust. Subtly, the argument has shifted. The 1983 *Nation at Risk* gave the impression that student achievement had plummeted during the 1960s and '70s. By 1991, critics were charging that U.S. schools had been bad for a long time and that schools in competing countries were improving. Ravitch: "I don't remember anyone being happy with schools in 1970." Albert Shanker, president of the American Federation of Teachers: "Our economic competitors have improved their school systems. . . . If I buy a car, I don't give a damn whether it's better than the 1970 model. I care whether it's better than the Japanese model across the street." Columbia University's Linda Darling-Hammond makes the point more clearly: "America's schools are in bad shape relative to what they need to be. Even America's 'good' schools provide little preparation for kids to be independent thinkers. They do not prepare students for democratic life."

This is a serious indictment, but America's aspirations for its public schools have always exceeded its grasp. Joe Schneider of the Southwest Regional Labs:

> Students are not learning as much as they could. But then, folks have been saying that about students for about as long as there have been schools. After all, few things provide adults with more pleasure and a greater sense of accomplishment than ordering youngsters to exert themselves.[9]

But we now face a future where we need to shape the rhetoric into reality. This book is about that task. First, let's take stock of where we are. Let's examine the shibboleths.

Standardized-test scores are plummeting. The "bad news" about U.S. education has traditionally been heralded by dismal standardized-test scores. We begin with the headliner, the Scholastic Assessment Test. The SAT, as it is popularly known, was developed in 1941 by Princeton's Educational Testing Service for the College Board as a guide for universities in admitting freshmen. Originally labeled an *aptitude* test, it was renamed in 1993, an admission that it measured the influence of schooling as well as innate capacity. Until 1994, the test norms were based on the original sample of 10,000 highly selected applicants. Based on this sample, the average score was set at 500, with a range from 400 to 600 that covered two-thirds of the sample. The original norming remained the standard until 1994, when the test was finally renormed to reflect the changing, growing population of students applying for college— more than 1.2 million in 1994. The renorming in no way constitutes a "dumbing-down" of the test. During the past half-century, ETS has taken every precaution to sustain the SAT at a constant level of difficulty.

Many citizens look to SAT scores to grade the nation's schools, and the news does not appear good. Headlines seem to report declining SAT scores every year or so. SAT verbal scores are certainly lower today than they were in 1963, the starting point of the current hullabaloo (Figure 2.2). Scores tumbled 30 points between 1965 and 1975. Performance has remained fairly constant since then.

But there is more to the story. As Figure 2.2 also shows, the proportion of high-school graduates taking the test increased substantially over

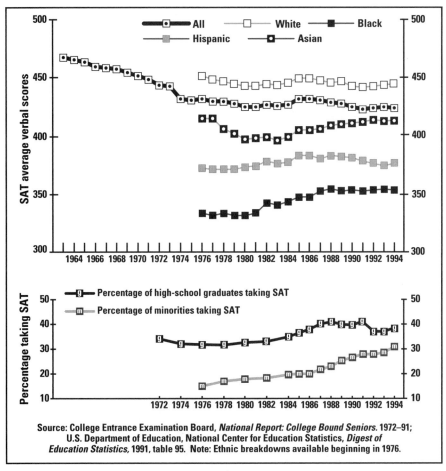

Figure 2.2
Trends in verbal performance on the Scholastic Assessment Test, and proportions of high-school graduates and minorities taking the test, 1963–94.

the decades, and more minority students entered the pool. If you test only the top two students in a classroom, the scores will be higher than if you test the top half of the class. A good deal of the decline in the SAT average reflects this pattern—on average, the top two students took the test in the 1960s; today, it's more than a third of the graduates. The 1960s marked a time of social change, with equity on the front burner. High schools encouraged students to graduate and to enter college. Before 1960, students were unlikely to think about college unless they were in the top 25 percent of their class; after 1960, students from a far broader range attempted the test.

During recent decades, SAT performance for all socioeconomic strata and all ethnic groups has remained relatively stable or risen (Figure 2.3). The overall decline since 1965 demonstrates "Simpson's paradox": An average can change in a direction opposite from all subgroups because of changes in the representation of different subgroups. That's what's been happening with the SAT. Today's test-takers are more likely to come from poorer communities and to attend schools with a thinner academic curriculum and fewer advanced offerings than the smaller, comparatively elite cadre of 1965. On average, they may do less well on standardized tests than more-advantaged students, but as Figure 2.3 shows, scores of every subpopulation (except whites) have improved.

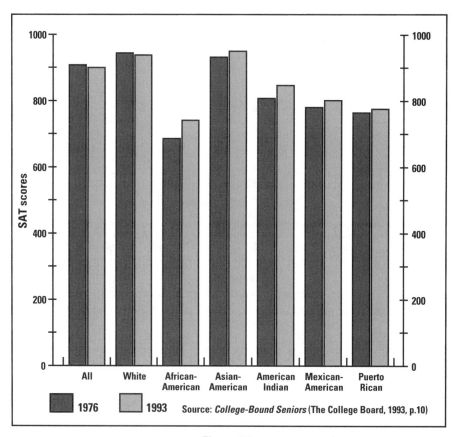

Figure 2.3
Illustration of "Simpson's paradox" for Scholastic Assessment Test verbal scores, 1976 and 1993. Virtually every group (whites were the exception) improved during these years, but changes in the representation of different groups meant that the overall average dropped.

What about performance at the top? Many worry that academic opportunities for middle-class children may be undercut by the focus on the needs of disadvantaged children. The percentage of students scoring above 600 (the 84th percentile) on the Verbal test dropped from 1965 until 1975, when it stabilized. Math scores fell until 1975 but recently returned to a level slightly above that of 1972. According to Bracey, "more people score above 600 on the math subtest than one would expect, given the characteristics of a normal curve—and substantially more than would be expected for scores above 700."

Another approach is to look at matched groups—for example, consider scores for test-takers in the top 10 percent of high-school graduates. The Sandia researchers sorted SAT test-takers from 1975 to 1990, matching 1990 students with 1975 students by several criteria including high-school rank. Over this 15-year period, the matched scores rose by about one-third of a standard deviation—in laymen's language, the current 50th percentile is where the 60th percentile was 15 years ago.

Another view of our top students comes from the Graduate Record Examination (GRE), ETS's standardized test for admission to graduate school. The trends follow those for the SAT (Figure 2.4). From 1965 to 1991, the percentage of college graduates taking the GRE increased substantially, especially during the 1960s. Math and verbal scores, after dropping during the 1960s and '70s, increased during the past decade. The gains in mathematics are especially impressive. By the way, these scores are for U.S. citizens only.

A final note on our top ranks. In 1954, the College Board developed the Advanced Placement (AP) tests to provide gifted high-school students with college credits. Prior to the 1970s admission to AP courses (and hence to AP tests) was highly restrictive. The College Board, responding to equity concerns, mounted an aggressive program to increase enrollment in AP courses. The Board could encourage, but the burden was on high-school teachers to develop demanding but attractive courses. The effort has been remarkably successful. In 1978, 90,000 high-school students took AP tests. By 1990, the number had increased 255 percent to 324,000. Did AP scores plummet as a consequence? No—the average score on a five-point scale was 3.16 in 1978 and 3.05 in 1990.

What do these results say about student achievement in our public schools? Both ETS and the College Board have issued warnings about relying on these tests to evaluate our schools. Participants in the SAT, GRE, AP, and other exams in this category are self-selected, and they vary over years and places. In states that spend the most money per student on public education, for example, the proportion of SAT-takers

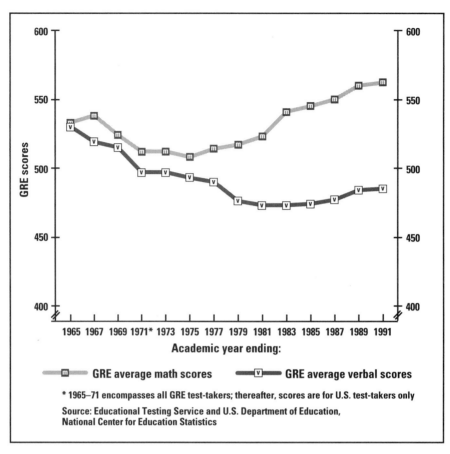

Figure 2.4
Trends in Graduate Record Examination scores, 1965–91.

is more than ten times greater than states with the smallest investments. Nonetheless, even with these caveats, it seems clear that these measures do *not* portray a system in decline and disarray—to the contrary.

Now a look at the local scene. Most school districts and many states currently administer their own standardized tests of reading and mathematics, usually multiple-choice format. Differences in tests and contexts make it hard to compare trends over time and situations. One trend made the headlines, however, when West Virginia physician John J. Cannell announced in 1987 that he had discovered the "Lake Wobegon" effect. He found that virtually every major school district in the country was scoring above average on standardized tests.[10] Something was surely rotten in Wobegon! In fact, Cannell had actually discovered long-term improvements in test performance. Six reading-math tests account for most business in the U.S. market. Publishers renorm and revise these tests about every seven years or so. The data show yearly increases for virtually every published reading test, averaging 1.1 percentile per year—a total gain over seven years of 7.7 percentile points. Average scores in 1993 are close to the 60th-percentile level in 1986. With each renorming, the publishers reset the average to the 50th-percentile level—schools are on a treadmill when it comes to standardized tests. This trend has been observed by publishers for more than twenty years. The developer of the Iowa Test of Basic Skills said of the 1984–85 norming (just after *Nation at Risk*) that "composite achievement in 1984–85 was at an all-time high in nearly all test areas." Achievement continued to increase during the 1990s.

Publishers' norms are not front-page news, and neither is the National Assessment of Educational Progress (NAEP). This test was developed in the 1960s as a "low-stakes" measure of student achievement in U.S. schools; the idea was to produce a national report card without direct consequences for students, teachers, districts, or states—i.e., to answer the question: "How well are we doing when students are assessed without duress?" Chester Finn has described it as "far and away our best barometer of student performance in the United States as a whole." Beginning in 1969, NAEP tests have been administered in several subject matter areas to national samples of 9-, 13-, and 17-year-olds. Until recently, NAEP findings seldom made the headlines. Snippets occasionally appeared in the back pages, but politicians and the media paid little attention to the results.

Statistics are seldom exciting, and even less so when they are not especially newsworthy. The Sandia report summarizes the findings from the NAEP reports: "The national data on student performance do not indicate a decline in *any* area." Figure 2.5 shows the results in several ways. The first thing to note is that trends in reading are flat over the past two decades. Reading scores for minority students have increased noticeably during this time, although they continue to lag behind white students. Students whose parents have completed some college courses outperform those whose parents are high-school grads, while children of dropouts are 20–30 points lower. College appears to be a good investment for children as well as grown-ups. Writing scores present a mixed pattern over the past ten years, with a downward trend for all groups in the 1990 assessment followed by upward trends in 1992.

But beyond the trends, what about absolute levels of performance, in both reading and writing? The scale labels in Figure 2.5 suggest that

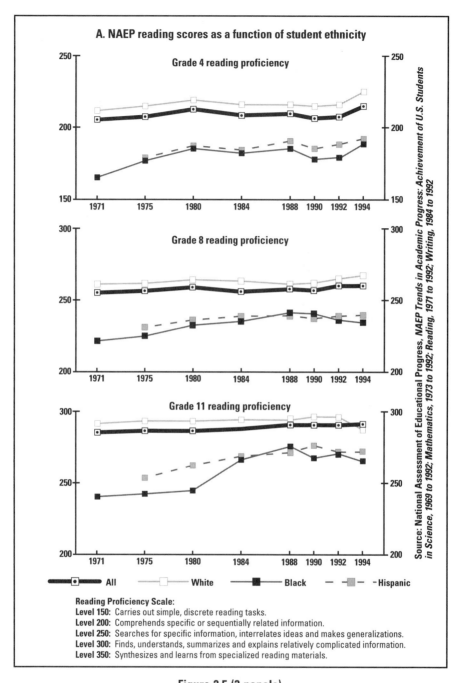

A. NAEP reading scores as a function of student ethnicity

Grade 4 reading proficiency

Grade 8 reading proficiency

Grade 11 reading proficiency

Source: National Assessment of Educational Progress, *NAEP Trends in Academic Progress: Achievement of U.S. Students in Science, 1969 to 1992; Mathematics, 1973 to 1992; Reading, 1971 to 1992; Writing, 1984 to 1992*

All — White — Black — Hispanic

Reading Proficiency Scale:
Level 150: Carries out simple, discrete reading tasks.
Level 200: Comprehends specific or sequentially related information.
Level 250: Searches for specific information, interrelates ideas and makes generalizations.
Level 300: Finds, understands, summarizes and explains relatively complicated information.
Level 350: Synthesizes and learns from specialized reading materials.

Figure 2.5 (3 panels)
Reading and writing scores on the National Assessment of
Educational Progress as a function of student ethnicity and parent education.

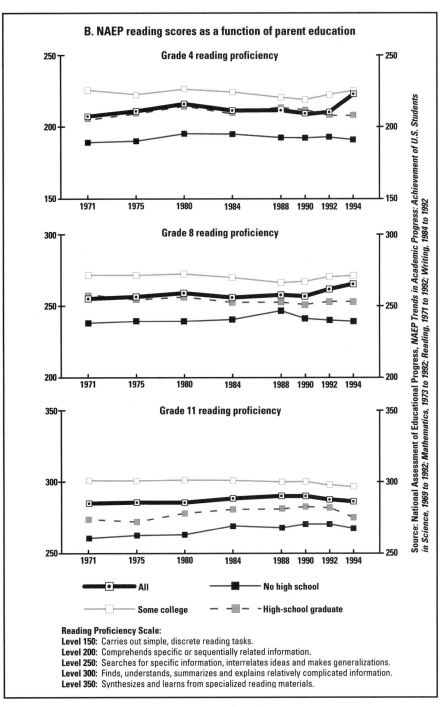

B. NAEP reading scores as a function of parent education

Grade 4 reading proficiency

Grade 8 reading proficiency

Grade 11 reading proficiency

All — No high school — Some college — High-school graduate

Reading Proficiency Scale:
Level 150: Carries out simple, discrete reading tasks.
Level 200: Comprehends specific or sequentially related information.
Level 250: Searches for specific information, interrelates ideas and makes generalizations.
Level 300: Finds, understands, summarizes and explains relatively complicated information.
Level 350: Synthesizes and learns from specialized reading materials.

Source: National Assessment of Educational Progress, *NAEP Trends in Academic Progress: Achievement of U.S. Students in Science, 1969 to 1992; Mathematics, 1973 to 1992; Reading, 1971 to 1992; Writing, 1984 to 1992*

Figure 2.5 (cont.)

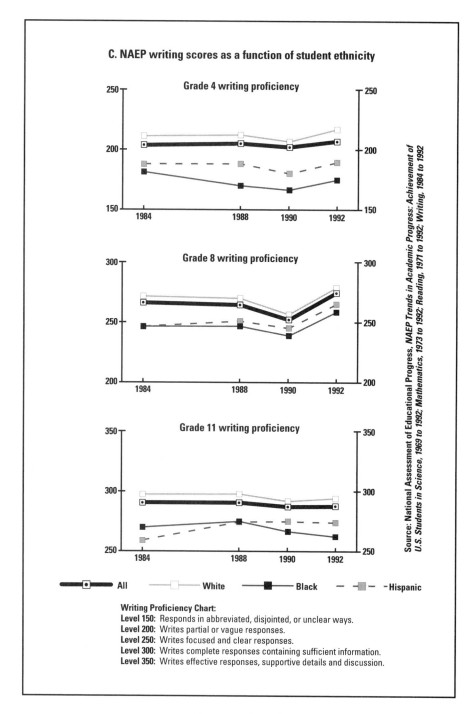

C. NAEP writing scores as a function of student ethnicity

Grade 4 writing proficiency

Grade 8 writing proficiency

Grade 11 writing proficiency

All — White — Black — Hispanic

Writing Proficiency Chart:
Level 150: Responds in abbreviated, disjointed, or unclear ways.
Level 200: Writes partial or vague responses.
Level 250: Writes focused and clear responses.
Level 300: Writes complete responses containing sufficient information.
Level 350: Writes effective responses, supportive details and discussion.

Source: National Assessment of Educational Progress, *NAEP Trends in Academic Progress: Achievement of U.S. Students in Science, 1969 to 1992; Mathematics, 1973 to 1992; Reading, 1971 to 1992; Writing, 1984 to 1992*

Figure 2.5 (cont.)

our students are, on average, barely adequate. That certainly appears to be bad news, but we need to take a closer look. In the early days of NAEP, the results were straightforward. Sample items were presented along with percent-correct scores. In 1988, after *Nation at Risk*, NAEP changed the game. The program developed "proficiency scales" for each subject area in an effort to judge absolute performance. The scales are subjective, reflecting the best guesses of the committees in each subject area. Except for writing exams, in which real writing samples are graded, the tests are all multiple-choice. Each committee decides how to convert the number of correct answers to a statistical "scale score" by setting the boundaries between *unsatisfactory and minimal, minimal* and *adequate,* and so on. The compositions are graded in a routine fashion, and then the grades are converted to the scale scores shown in Figure 2.5. Level 200 on the writing scale, for example, is designated as *minimal*—"recognized the elements needed to complete the [writing] task, but were not managed well enough to ensure the intended purpose." Both co-authors of this book have been guilty of this short-coming from time to time, but do not think of ourselves as "minimal."

The result of all these machinations is that the *San Francisco Chronicle* can decry the wretchedly "inadequate" writing of U.S. students, while reporting in the same article that writing has improved markedly from 1990 to 1992.[11] Parents and teachers have little basis for understanding these scales—nor do reporters. For that matter, neither does the Federal government. According to the Government Accounting Office: "NAGB's [National Assessment Governing Board] aim . . . was to make NAEP scores more interpretable. . . . As we have seen [earlier in this report], however, NAGB's interpretations have been misleading."[12] Our point is not that U.S. students are reading and writing as well as they should, but that the guideposts are virtually impossible to understand.

Japan is beating us. NAEP scales may be arbitrary, but what about cross-national standards? Americans' insecurity is world-famous. We wonder what other nations think about us, and look over our shoulders to compare ourselves, often unfavorably, with others. In recent years Japan has been the major point of comparison. The spirit is captured by a 1981 *Chicago Tribune* cartoon captioned, "News item: United States and Japan evaluate each other's educational systems."[13] In one panel, American educators look intently at a Japanese classroom, tape recorder and notepad in hand. In the other panel, Japanese observers double up in laughter as they view American students.

A counterpoint comes from a 1993 survey of more than 1,000 Japanese students who had spent part of their school years in the United

States. More than 35 percent of the respondents found American schools superior to Japanese schools in fostering logical and analytic thought; fewer than 30 percent thought the opposite. More than 60 percent thought U.S. high schools better at teaching teamwork; only 10 percent said that Japanese schools did a better job. An overwhelming 80 percent saw U.S. high schools as more conducive to the development of creative and independent thought.[14]

American critics might disagree with this assessment. In October 1985, returning from a study tour of Japanese schools, then-Assistant Secretary of Education Finn remarked: "[The Japanese] have demonstrated that you can have a coherent curriculum, high standards, good discipline, parental support, a professional teaching force and a well-run school. They have shown that the average student can learn a whole lot more."[15]

While Finn was clearly impressed by his personal experience in Japan, he did express some puzzlements and reservations:

> Exactly how [the educational miracle] has been accomplished in Japan, however, involves familial, social, and institutional arrangements that are alien to contemporary American assumptions. . . . Nor is every facet of Japanese education wholly appealing. . . . Even at the elementary-secondary level, the Japanese themselves are restive about the scanty attention their schools pay to individual differences, and about their lackluster results in nurturing independent thinking and creativity.[16]

Would you really prefer a Japanese-style education for your children? Education professor David Berliner of Arizona State University culled several thought-provoking items from the Japanese media:[17]

- Because they didn't like a lecture on how they might lead a better life, eight junior-high toughs demanded an apology from their teacher. He refused, so they hit him, kicked him, threw his papers all around, and fought with ten other teachers as well. Finally, the teacher knelt before the youths and apologized to avoid any further confusion.

- Ten percent of Japan's public middle schools request police guards for their graduation ceremonies.

- Parents pay teachers "thank you" money for giving good grades and letters of recommendation to their children.

- A teacher was taunted by his colleagues for being too soft on students, so when a student on a field trip used a hair dryer—an act forbidden by the school—that teacher beat and kicked the student to death. At the trial, the defense was that everyone at the school expected this teacher to use corporal punishment. This seemed perfectly reasonable to the judge, whose sentence was quite lenient.

Lest you think that Berliner's examples are extreme, the *Japan Times* summarized the current state of affairs as follows:

> Bullying, suicides among school children, dropping out from school, increasing delinquency, violence both at home and at school, heated entrance exam races, overemphasis on scholastic ratings, and torture of children by some teachers are the result of the pathological mechanisms that have become established in Japan's educational system.[18]

Or read this 1993 letter to the *Phi Delta Kappan* editor, written by educator Peter Boylan, who had taught for years in Japan. Applauding Bracey's analysis of American schools, he offered the following comments about the Japanese educational system:

> One important effect of Japan's education system is . . . the incredible stunting of the students' social and psychological development. My [Japanese high-school] students have all the emotional maturity of American elementary-school students. If I ask a girl a question, often she will sink to the floor in embarrassment at being asked to answer a question. These are 19-year-old high-school seniors I'm talking about. The boys aren't so dramatic; they just pretend that the teacher doesn't exist if they are unsure about things. Socially, these students are almost incapable of doing anything on their own. . . . I consider the Japanese schools to be a national, institutionalized system of child abuse.[19]

Berliner ponders the meaning of these stories for American schools, and expresses concern:

> Do we have the gumption and willpower to resist turning our schools into institutions where 26,000 junior high-school students and 4,000 elementary-school students refuse to go to school *at all* because they are tormented by teachers and bullied by students, and where 47,000 others miss at least fifty days of schooling per year because of the abuse they must face at school? Where the number of pleats allowed in a girl's skirt is specified? Where stu-

dents with curly hair are required to carry certificates attesting that their hair is not permed? Where some of the teachers at a middle school kicked and beat the students regularly, in full view of other teachers, finally killing one student by bashing in his skull, and were then supported by all the other teachers, who threatened the students to make them remain silent?[20]

While they may not be perfect, the Japanese certainly excel when it comes to academic achievement—right? Well, not always. Harold Stevenson, a psychologist at the University of Michigan and author of *The Learning Gap*, is renowned for his comparative research of students in the U.S., Japan, and Taiwan. In a series of studies spanning almost two decades, he and his colleagues have looked at motivation as well as achievement, at parents as well as students. His data on mathematics scores show that, across all grade levels, Japanese and Taiwanese students perform better than American students. He finds that American schools spend less time on mathematics than schools in the other two countries do. Reading and writing tend to receive more emphasis in our schools, and our sixth-grade readers outperform Japanese readers. But this finding has not made its way to the top of the charts.

A broader and more representative survey of educational achievement comes from the International Association for the Evaluation of Educational Achievement (IEA), which conducted a worldwide study of reading achievement during the 1990–91 school year.[21] Thirty-two nations participated in the study, which assessed performance of 9- and 14-year-olds. International comparisons are tricky, but IEA has been in the business since the late 1950s, and most experts consider its studies reasonably trustworthy. Figure 2.6 shows the results for eight of the 32 nations. Neither Japan nor Taiwan participated in the 1990–91 reading study; Singapore serves as a stand-in for the Asian sector. Six of the countries are highly industrialized, while Venezuela is a developing nation.

Figure 2.6 contains lots of information. The Composite Development Index combines several indicators: per capita gross national product, expenditure per student, life expectancy, percentage of babies with low birth weights, per capita newspapers, and adult literacy. As with the SAT, student scores were scaled at a mean of 500 and a standard deviation of 100 for each age level. We have grouped the countries in clusters: the United States, Canada, and New Zealand (English-speaking); the European nations; Singapore; and Venezuela.

The Index places the United States on a par with most other devel-

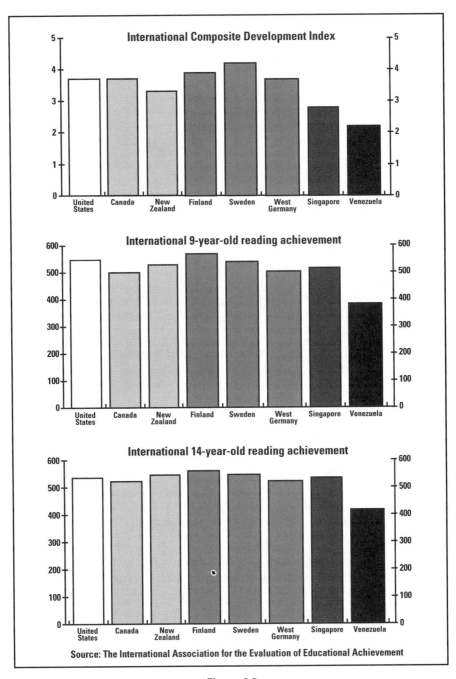

Figure 2.6
Results of the International Assessment of Education:
reading achievement of 9- and 14-year-olds in selected countries.

oped nations in this sample. As a nation, we are pretty well off. We knew that. But guess what? Our students read as well as any others in the world. Among 9-year-olds, only Finnish children score better; Finland, Sweden, and New Zealand have slightly higher measures among 14-year-olds. We're a tad higher than the former West Germany and Canada. Our country may be suffering from widespread illiteracy, but then so is the entire industrialized world.

The IEA researchers conducted several analyses of the factors responsible for cross-national differences in reading achievement. We cannot give all of the details here, but the findings are fascinating because they go against the grain of several prevailing beliefs. For instance, "crazy" English spelling is often the scapegoat for poor reading performance. The IEA survey reports an advantage for *less regular* orthographies like English. We hear that American students don't spend enough time in school. Countries with *shorter* school years tended to do better. Other, less counterintuitive findings speak to the quality of schooling. For instance, good school libraries helped, as did better-educated teachers.

The bottom line is that U.S. kids do reasonably well on international comparisons of reading, even though they don't get much credit. Moreover, our schools are supporting these achievements while attaining high rates of secondary and postsecondary enrollment. The Paris-based Organization for Economic Cooperation and Development (OECD) reports that the United States has the highest percentage (35 percent) of young people enrolled in postsecondary education of any nation—another success story that flies in the face of conventional beliefs.

Kids are dropping out; they can't make it to or in college. Over the past half-century, the percentage of U.S. students completing high school has increased from less than 40 percent in 1940 to almost 90 percent in 1990 (Figure 2.7). Completion rates count all enrolled students, including those who "stop out" but then obtain a diploma through the General Equivalency Degree or other nontraditional means. The completion rate for black students has risen over the past two decades from 78 to 85 percent. Hispanic students still have much higher noncompletion rates; only two out of three Hispanics acquire a high-school diploma. Bear in mind, however, that these reports count *all* 17-year-olds resident in the United States, including the immigration wave of the last decade.

In addition to completion rates are *on-time* graduation percentages, the proportion of students finishing high school when they are "supposed to." This indicator has also increased in recent years, and is currently about 75 percent. Japan, with a homogeneous society and strong

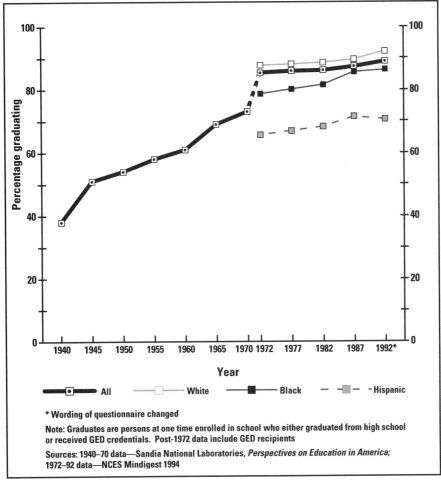

Figure 2.7
Trends in high-school completion rates.

emphasis on education, has an on-time graduation rate of about 85 percent. The authors of the Sandia report estimate that the overall on-time graduation rate would rise by as much as 3 percent if the impact of recent immigration were factored out. The current completion rate may be the best that can be expected for a large, heterogeneous population.

But what are students doing with their time in U.S. high schools? What about the dumbed-down curriculum and the proliferation of goof-off courses? The Department of Education surveys course-taking patterns, and a quick glance at the 1992 *Condition of Education* seems to support the prevailing pronouncements; "on average, a high-school graduate in 1987 earned a larger number of course units than in either 1969 or 1982 . . . [but] earned a smaller percentage in *academic* units."[22] Aha —the kids are goofing off!

In fact, the kids are not goofing off. A closer look at the data reveals that, while the *percentage* of academic units has declined slightly, the *number* of academic units actually *increased* from 15 to 15.6 between 1969 and 1987. Not a big change, but certainly not a decrease. A 1994 Educational Testing Service report shows that this trend is continuing:

> There is much good news. . . . Over the decade, there were steady improvements in the proportion of students taking a "minimum academic program" [four years of English and three years of social studies, science, and math; 13 percent in 1982, 47 percent in 1990] and a 'core curriculum' [the minimum plus foreign language and computer science; 2 percent in 1982, 23 percent in 1990].[23]

The report concludes, "There is much room for improvement." Hard to disagree, although one might also ask about the costs needed for such improvement, and the conditions confronting schools in the 1980s. Incidentally, these upward trends held for every ethnic group, for boys and girls, for public and private schools.

Similarly, in 1989 the prestigious Center for Policy Research in Education made an intensive study of state reforms in six states and found "modest, but significant" toughening of the curricula.[24] Schoolchildren were being asked to write more, they were taking more math and science courses and fewer electives, they were doing more homework than at the initiation of the reforms in the 1970s. "One legislator told me, 'I just want the little buggers to work harder,'" said Stanford's Michael Kirst, one of the report's authors. "Well, the little buggers are working harder."

Is all this schooling worth it? We have heard of Ph.D.'s working in MacDonalds. Education doesn't seem worth what it used to be. Well, that gloomy prospect turns out not to be true, either. The 1992 *Condition of Education* reports that the employment rate is strongly influenced by amount of schooling. Educational level makes an even greater difference in hard times. A high-school diploma used to be a critical breakpoint between high and low salaries; increasingly it is a college degree, especially for women and minorities. The good news, according to the *Condition of Education*, has been a steady increase since 1973 in the percentage of high-school graduates (recall that this group has been increasing proportionately) entering college, from the mid-40s in 1973 to over 60 percent today. The percentage of black high-school graduates entering college dropped in the 1980s (federal support for education dropped precipitously during these years), but moved sharply upward in the late 1980s. Enrollment rates for women have overtaken those for men in the last few years. And the college graduation rate puts the U.S. in the top ranks worldwide. A 1993 National Center for Educational Statistics report compared graduation rates in OECD countries with individual states in this country. Japan, Canada, and Norway led the ranks with a graduation rate of 25 percent, compared with a U.S. rate of 22 percent (for 25-year-olds). Thirty of 50 states in the U.S. equalled or exceeded this rate, with Ohio and Michigan at 25 percent, New York and Pennsylvania better than 30 percent, Iowa and Massachusetts over 40 percent. New Jersey and California were the only large states substantially below the top-ranked OECD nations, and they came in at 20 percent, slightly below the national rate.

In short, American students are completing high school, taking a demanding but balanced array of courses, and making it in college. While there's room for improvement, the federal government's own statistics offer good news about our students' achievements and our schools' accomplishments.[25]

We're spending more and getting less. Given the amount that we're spending on schools in this country, are we getting our money's worth? The word on the street is that we spend much more per pupil than any other nation on education. Before the 1989 education summit, then-White House chief of staff John Sununu stated: "We spend twice as much [on education] as the Japanese and almost 40 percent more than all the other major industrialized countries of the world." Critics complain that too much money is wasted on school administrators. Statisticians pronounce that money isn't what really matters anyway.[26]

Such comments may be politically popular, but they can also be misleading if not mischievous. What about the data? According to UNESCO, the U.S. ties with Canada and the Netherlands, all three behind Sweden, in the amount spent per student on education. This figure, however, includes expenditures for *higher education*. America's universities and colleges, beyond debate, are the best in the world. We have, comparatively at least, lavished our resources on this system, to good advantage if one counts Nobel laureates and the like. When higher education is factored out, America's educational spending is no longer at the top. An estimate from the OECD, adjusted for purchasing parity power, presents figures on spending for primary and secondary schools (in 1988 dollars).[27] This comparison of 18 Western nations placed the U.S. fourth after Luxembourg ($10,646), Sweden ($9,569), and Norway ($8,742). The U.S. investment was $7,936—a lot of money, but not consistent with the image that we are throwing money at our schools relative to comparable nations.

Besides, more is involved than the average. The United States commitment to educating all students also affects the finances. In the past few decades, the largest increases in educational expenditures have been for students with special educational needs. True, per-pupil outlays in U.S. public schools climbed by more than 50 percent (adjusted for inflation) between 1975 and 1990. But the proportion of students requiring special education has risen substantially, siphoning those spending increases away from mainstream students. According to the Sandia report, "The cost of educating a special-education student is 2.5 to 7 times as large as the cost of educating a regular student. The country's dramatic increase in educational spending over the past 30 years is due largely to the costs of special education." Federally mandated special-education programs today enroll more than 12 percent of all students. When these costs are factored out, expenditures per regular student during the last thirty years have remained virtually constant.

What about administrative and overhead costs? The Department of Education addresses this matter in the *Condition of Education:* "School district administrators as a percentage of full-time staff and the number per 100 students have remained fairly constant since 1950." How can this be? In 1950, according to the national statistics, there were 3.6 classroom teachers for every 100 students; today that number is 5.8. Much of that increase occurred in the 1960s and 1970s as part of special-education programs. Support and other instructional staff increased from 1.2 to 4.6 per 100 students—librarians, counselors and psychologists, teachers' aides, secretarial, transportation, food service, plant maintenance, health. Administrators rose from 0.3 to 0.5 per 100 students during these forty years—a noticeable increase, but still a small piece of the pie relative to increasing staff size, and incommensurate with the deluge of paperwork required by federal and state mandates.

We are not economists, and will not pursue this line of argument any further. Our main point is that money is not the only issue. The United States spends a great deal on its schools, but other countries invest an equal proportion of their resources on schools—and even more on children and families. Moreover, we have adopted policies intended to educate all children in normal settings rather than isolating those who are different. This is a noble policy, and an expensive one.

The people who care for our children in today's schools—teachers, secretaries, custodians, and administrators—are, almost without exception, exceptional. Young men and (more so) women continue to enter the education profession even though the demands on the individual have become increasingly draconian during recent decades. They are not there because of money or working conditions, but because they care about children.

Schools, kids, families—they're all going to hell! American society has undergone a fundamental transformation in the past several decades. Teachers have sensed for more than thirty years that something is happening. Surveys by several organizations have documented worries over parents motivating and disciplining children, ensuring that homework is done, and getting their students to school on time.[28] Teachers say that they are working relatively harder, especially in tough inner-city schools where a large proportion of tomorrow's students are being educated.

But relief is hard to find. We have a lot of children in our future, but they are increasingly likely to be troubled. The Department of Education estimates that K–12 enrollment will increase by more than 10 percent between 1994 and 2004. A large proportion of the parents will be poor and poorly educated. A UNICEF survey reported that one of five U.S. children lived below the poverty level in 1991, more than twice that of comparable nations like Canada and England. Even in the suburbs, divorce, single-parenthood, and families with two working parents are on the rise. The 1991 Census Report found only one in every two children living at that time in a nuclear family. As noted in Chapter 1, an increasing percentage of children live with a single parent, often an unmarried woman. These conditions are unlikely to improve during the next ten years.

Today's student population is incredibly diverse, a trend that is also likely to continue. In 1941, the Scott Foresman publishing company could produce the Dick and Jane readers for children whose father went to work every morning, whose mother stayed home to prepare dinner, and all of whom were middle-class whites. They had a dog, Spot. Today's highest birthrates are among nonwhite ethnic minorities. In California, New York, Florida, and Texas, the highest increases in enrollment in elementary schools are among immigrant children. Many of these families are struggling to establish themselves economically in their new land. Many speak a language other than English.

The institutions that taught children the values of respect and responsibility have lost much of their influence. Families were crucial—but so were churches, clubs, libraries, parks, and even swimming pools. Especially in the inner cities, these sources of support for children have virtually disappeared, with predictable results.

Crime and drugs? We should be concerned. The *National Goals* report presented data on victimization among twelfth-graders showing slight increases over the past decade in threats, injuries, and vandalism (Figure 2.8). The same report notes that teachers feel safe during the school day, but one in seven urban teachers is uneasy about staying after school. There is some good news—twelfth-graders reported substantially less in-school drug use in 1991 than in 1980—but more than half had used alcohol (the drug of choice) during the past 30 days. The news also depends on whom you talk to and what you ask them. In its 1994 report on sophomores, the National Center for Educational Statistics (NCES) asked tenth-graders whether they felt unsafe at school. More than 50,000 students were surveyed from the 1980 and 1990 classes. In 1980, more than 12 percent of the students felt unsafe; by 1990, that figure had dropped by a third to 8 percent. Jeffrey Owings of NCES commented: "I see the whole atmosphere of schools being more academically oriented than they were in the 1980s." John Ralph, also of NCES, put a different spin on the findings: "It may be that students are subjected to more threats, but they've grown more jaded."

It's hard to find good news in this business, but it is important to balance perceptions with data, and to dispel myths. For instance, Barry O'Neill of Yale tracked down a story about changes in "school woes" since 1940. The story line was that the 1940 concerns were talking and gum-chewing, while, for example, the 1980 leaders were drug and alcohol abuse and pregnancy.[29] O'Neill's findings in the March 6, 1994, *New York Times Magazine* showed another side to the story. The 1940 survey asked school people, "What are your big problems?" The 1980 survey, conducted by T. Cullen Davis of Fort Worth, was a multiple-choice test that asked, "Have you experienced this problem?" Davis didn't ask the respondents to *rate* the problems. The answers you get depend on the questions you ask. The 1993 Gallup polls we cited at the beginning of this chapter show remarkably little change in teacher concerns over the past three decades, with discipline always near the top of the list. This is not to question the serious trends in problem behavior, especially in the high-school years and especially in economically depressed communities. But bad reporting can hyperinflate problems and overlook the good news.

Schools are troubled not only by students but by circumstances. The infrastructure of public schools is deteriorating. In his book *Savage*

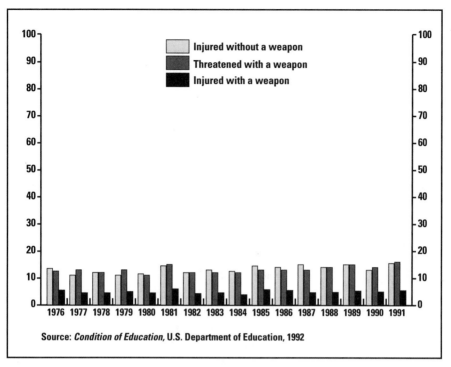

Figure 2.8
Percentage of high-school seniors reporting that they were
victimized at school during the previous year.

Inequalities, which we mentioned in Chapter 1, Jonathan Kozol describes inner-city schools as "unhappy places, . . . their doors guarded, police patrolling the halls, windows covered with steel grates. Taxi drivers flatly refused to take me to some of these schools and would deposit me a dozen blocks away, in border areas beyond which they refused to go. . . ." During a visit to Manierre Elementary School in Chicago's Cabrini Green neighborhood, co-author Calfee picked up the school newspaper, which front-paged Shanay Williams' essay on "My Neighborhood":

> My neighborhood is full of bad things and people. It's harmful because you can't walk up or down without seeing people selling drugs. Where there are drugs there are usually guns, knives, and death. We all know that there are good drugs that get prescribed by doctors to help fight illness, but I'm talking about bad drugs like crack, rocks, weed, and cocaine. . . . Most of the people being

killed are young children and even babies that haven't been able to live a full life. If people would stop killing each other the neighborhood would be a safer place and we might be able to live a full life.[30]

Elsewhere in the newspaper, the "City Update" section reported the killing of a 13-year-old boy by two other juveniles.

Kozol's descriptions and the Manierre stories really are bad news. You might think that we would be investing additional resources in schools serving such communities. Decrepit buildings, tattered textbooks, libraries with few books and no librarians—some things have not changed from the Coleman report. Per-pupil spending in U.S. schools varies over a broad range compared to most other developed nations. Nations with centralized educational systems try to sustain equal funding levels for all schools. In the United States, in contrast, school funding frequently reflects economic conditions in the local community, leading to enormous variations between the richest and poorest schools. Schools serving the neediest students often have the leanest resources, even when federal and state contributions are factored in. These disparities often mean large inequities between the rich and the poor. Urban areas average $900 per student less than schools in the suburbs, according to Michael Casserly of the Council of the Great City Schools.[31] Iris Rotberg, in a 1993 *Washington Post* op-ed piece,[32] noted that average annual per-pupil spending for the 100 poorest districts in Texas was just under $3,000 per student, while the 100 wealthiest districts spend $7,200 per student. In Illinois, district spending ranges from $2,400 to $8,300 per student. Researchers may argue about whether money matters; a fifteen-minute drive from Cabrini Green north to Evanston suggests that it does!

But even under severely deprived conditions, schools are often safe havens for children, places where they are relatively protected from the surrounding drug- and crime-ridden communities, especially in the early grades. Kindergartners are not toting guns, second-graders are not into pimping and prostitution. Even in the toughest areas, most elementary schools are well managed and orderly. It is a daily challenge, but schools are taking up the slack. Kids in ravaged urban areas may come to school with different experiences and different skills from those of young suburbanites, but they still come to school in the early years bright, curious, and ready to learn. And in the best areas, schools provide support and stability for children from homes where both parents are pursuing their careers or where mom is rebuilding life after a divorce.

The Bottom Line

American schools *are* holding their own, on average, despite the whammies and handicaps that society is throwing their way. This conclusion doesn't justify complacency. For one thing, we probably cannot expect teachers and administrators to hold this line forever. Exhorting families to do a better job has not had much effect during the past few decades—not in urban ghettos nor, for that matter, in middle-class suburbs. The school is the primary institution in American society for supporting children. Investments in the early years of schooling have a return rate estimated at five to ten times the original cost. Crime, punishment, and ignorance are expensive.

In the elementary grades, the effective use of language for thinking and communicating is the most significant academic outcome. Tomorrow's agenda must go beyond the basic-skills model of past generations. Schools are holding their own on multiple-choice tests, but these indicators paint weak pictures of what students should be learning. The following chapters portray a new literacy curriculum, one that promotes reading and writing as cognitive competencies rather than behavioral skills, that supports learning as active and reflective rather than passive and rote. This curriculum can work in the schools that we have. It does not require new teachers, new technologies, new schools, or even new money. It does demand new ways of thinking by teachers, administrators, and others who are concerned about our schools and our children. But we begin from the foundation of schools as they are today. Rather than embark on a jihad against a "failed" system, we ask: What can we do with the kids we have, with the teachers we have, in the classrooms and schools we have?

A Closer Look: How Did North Shoreview Happen? 3

U.S. schools may not be as bad as they have been portrayed. But they need to change if we are to prosper in the new millennium. Critical literacy, not the rote learning of facts, is the direction for future education if our students are to handle the demands of an information society. How to achieve this goal in the face of multilingual classrooms, fiscal inequities, and family erosion?

For an answer, let's return to North Shoreview Elementary School in San Mateo, California, which we visited in Chapter 1. At first glance the place isn't especially futuristic. Students live in the local neighborhood. Parents send them to North Shoreview because it's close, and the kids can walk to school. The school looks very conventional. The asphalt playground features a tired jungle gym; no green playing fields at North Shoreview. The buildings, recently painted, are still old and tired. The cramped office, a center of continuously frantic activity, is governed by an unflappable secretary. The classrooms are large and well lighted, but the floors are hard tiles, the desks and tables pockmarked, the textbooks old and tired. A few computers and television sets, some overhead projectors from the 1960s. Technology plays second fiddle. This is a people-oriented enterprise. Ask parents and teachers what the school needs, and they will tell you: "After-school daycare, a preschool program, smaller classes (more teachers), classroom aides."

The visitor is quickly captivated by the children. Their enthusiasm and excitement is infectious, their imagination thriving in a climate that fosters inventiveness and creativity. Yet North Shoreview faces problems that confront all schools in communities on the edge. Many students are dropped off early by working mothers. Others are tardy because no one wakes them up. Children are often sleepy, hungry, sick, neglected, sometimes abused. The secretary doubles as school nurse and triples as counselor. Breakfast is there for those who want it; a jar of peanut butter and a loaf of bread replace an apple on the teacher's desk. North Shoreview teachers are committed to academic excellence, but they must also meet students' (and families') basic needs.

The school does receive special funding: Aid for Disadvantaged Students, Bilingual and Special Education, and grants from the "war on drugs," health education, school lunch, ad infinitum. These funds come at a cost: proposals to write, tests and evaluations, endless paperwork for eyeless bureaucrats—Evelyn Taylor sometimes wonders whether small grants are worth the trouble.

Despite its mundane appearance, North Shoreview is nonetheless a model for schools of the future—at least the foreseeable future—both in what it achieved and how it got there. North Shoreview became a "New American School" without the hype.[1] Teachers employed the tools of Project READ to bring about changes that were conceptual and practical rather than superficial and decorative. The transformation did not take large amounts of time and money, did not require experts and layers of bureaucracy, and did not depend on the magic of a one-in-a-million principal (although that helps) or a selected staff. Finally, North Shoreview is a public school, its doors open to all comers. Its students are special, but they are not specially chosen.

To appreciate what makes a school special requires X-ray vision. Several years ago, an administrative team visited a Project READ school in South Central Los Angeles to evaluate the program. Most team members had not taught for years, and none had taught in at-risk schools. One administrator entered a first-grade classroom, and was immediately grabbed by three little boys who asked if they could read to him. The students knew that the visitors wanted to find out how well they could read and write. The visitor bent over to listen to the young trio, but interrupted: "Do you boys know that your shoes are untied?" They nodded their heads, and went on reading.

After a few minutes, the administrator left the room, remarking to the teacher on the way out: "Do you realize that most of your students can't tie their shoes?" He was apparently unaware that he had seen a miracle. "Everyone knows" that first-graders in South Central Los Angeles are poor readers, and yet in this classroom virtually all students appeared competent and motivated. The administrator would have learned even more if he had asked them to write. And he might have discovered that loose laces were then in vogue.

Project READ made a difference for the North Shoreview teachers because it helped them look at their world from a new conception of reading and writing, and with a new strategy for helping students learn.

"Open Your Books to Page 35"

Let's travel back in time to pre-READ days and a typical fourth-grade reading lesson at North Shoreview. The same scene occurs today in more than 90 percent of the 1,300,000 elementary classrooms around the nation. The teacher sits before the class, a manual in her lap, and reads the following instructions:

> Boys and girls, I've written six words on the board: *admired, dependable, complained, downcast, participate, national.* Let's go around and tell what each word means and use it in a sentence. [Students respond.]
>
> Now, open your books to page 35. Amos, please read the title. [The story is about a bicycle race.] Good. Martha, the next paragraph. Matthew, who is in the race? Who is going to win?

Teacher questions and student recitations continue until the end of the story, when the teacher assigns worksheets for practice. The lesson sketched above, still the norm in most elementary schools, is from a *basal reading series,* the packaged materials issued to teachers to ensure that they follow a uniform course of study.[2] The teacher follows a script, much like a factory worker, one step at a time through a preset list of exercises. The daily routine is the same from the beginning to the end of the school year: vocabulary, round-robin reading aloud, recitation of answers, worksheet practice. Lessons in first grade follow the same procedure as in eighth grade; only the stories change along the way. Even with the most imaginative teacher, the experience rapidly becomes dull and pointless for all involved. High achievers go through the motions, accomplished but bored. The technique is little changed from the era of McGuffey's readers, a time when most people learned to do as they were told, and when most students dropped out by the eighth grade.

In this lesson, what are students being taught, and how are they being taught it? The manual answers the first question. Students are learning *vocabulary* (the list of words), *character analysis* (the question about the racers), and a variety of *skills* (word roots). Unofficially, students and teacher are learning to follow instructions. The objectives are so low-level that it is hard to imagine how tomorrow's graduates could profit from such exercises. Teaching is predetermined by the manual. The teacher gives directions, asks questions, prompts for answers, all following the script—even the answers are in the manual. The teacher's job is to manage; the student's job is to recite.

Implicit in this approach is a concept of literacy as mastery of basic skills, after which students can presumably turn to the real business of schooling. The most important skill is fluent oral reading. By third grade a student must be able to open to page 35 and "read."

Project READ transformed the North Shoreview teachers' conception of reading. Basic skills were replaced by *critical literacy*, a focus from the earliest grades on the literate use of language to think and communicate.[3] This change influenced teachers' ideas about both what to teach and how to teach it. Students found that reading and writing could be worthwhile endeavors for solving problems and becoming team players. They learned to handle printed text, but they also learned that reading was important because it opened the door to meaning. They learned to spell, but also learned that it is important to have something to say. They learned to speak as well as listen, to be active rather than passive. They learned to construct good answers to good questions, and to explain their answers.

What to teach and how to teach it, curriculum and instruction—these questions are central to education. At North Shoreview, Project READ freed teachers from dependency on the teachers manual, slowly at first and then with greater confidence. They began to realize that their intuitions, informed by READ structures and strategies, allowed them to explore student interests without losing sight of academic goals. They began to realize that student-centered instruction meant much more than "anything goes." Curriculum changed from a box of materials to an arena of ideas, instruction from a march through rote exercises to a playful dance of imaginative projects.

This chapter describes the concept of critical literacy. It is a case study in how a cognitive approach to teaching and learning can revolutionize what is taught and how it is taught, what is learned and what it means.

The next section describes the cognitive origins of Project READ, which became the foundation for North Shoreview teachers. The section after that focuses on instruction. Whereas scripted lessons are passive, isolating, and rote, cognitive instruction is active, social, and reflective. The final section lays out the curriculum of critical literacy, a blend of elements of Greek rhetoric and the graphic organizers that are a Project READ trademark.

The integration of reading and writing is an essential feature of the program, along with a developmental approach to learning. Today's textbooks separate reading from writing, each age-grade level alienated from its neighbors. In Project READ, teachers focused on common elements from kindergarten through middle school, a re-creation in modern garb of the philosophy of yesterday's one-room schoolhouse.

The devil, as they say, is in the details. Project READ is not a pre-packaged reading program for students, but a well-engineered strategy of professional development for teachers. It worked at North Shoreview because teachers had a window of opportunity to work together as a team, focused and organized, active and reflective.

Project READ's Origins: Cognitive Learning

The psychology of learning has undergone major rethinking in the past half century, a shift from *behaviorism* toward *cognition*.[4] Behaviorism is still alive; the ideas and techniques work quite well for training. The model describes stimulus-response links as a function of reinforced learning opportunities (Figure 3.1). With practice, an organism emits responses

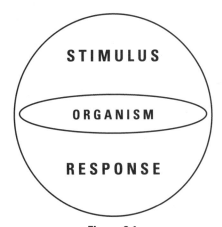

Figure 3.1
Sketch of a behaviorist model of learning.

to a particular stimulus then are rewarded. Behaviorists divide a complex task (reading, for example) into a large collection of specific objectives. Students learn each behavior by practice with feedback. Student differences are handled by adjusting the pace; faster students move more quickly and slower students are delayed, but everyone follows the same path.

A cognitive approach to learning builds on quite different assumptions, emphasizing thought processes (Figure 3.2). Behavior is still part of the equation, but the cognitivist also records qualitative facets of performance, and asks "What are you doing and why are you doing it?" The focus is on the mind as a living organ, driven by purposeful goals:

> The human mind seems to be not at all like a storeroom, a library, or a computer core memory, but rather presents a picture of a complex, dynamic system. . . . In fact, human memory does not, in a literal sense, store anything; it simply changes as a function of experience.[5]

In Figure 3.2, *long-term memory* occupies center stage. Human memory is remarkable in its virtually unlimited capacity; we never run out of storage space! Every healthy human being can remember an apparently infinite amount of information. It is *not* true that some people have "teaspoon-sized" brains while other minds can handle gallons. Anything that captures attention and is connected to previous experience can find a place in long-term memory. Moreover, the mind is a natural organizer. Information is stored in *categories:* narrative images, "how to do it" routines, abstract conceptual "stuff" that comes from schooling. Language allows us to label and connect the elements of experience, to express our thoughts to others, and to talk to ourselves during reflective moments.

The gateway to long-term memory includes perception, attention, and short-term memory. Our perceptions of the world are influenced by our experiences. The artist sees patterns in an abstract painting that the novice misses. The street-wise adolescent spots dangers that elude the visitor to a tough neighborhood. Attention depends on experience, but also reflects interests and styles. The football addict twirling the radio dial picks up the crowd's background noise and tunes back to join the action. Strolling through a mall, men and women tune in to different shops and goods. Without attention, nothing gets in. Those who think of education as *exposure* to cultural information are doomed to disappointment. Learning requires engagement rather than exposure. Students do not connect with a situation unless it captures their interest.

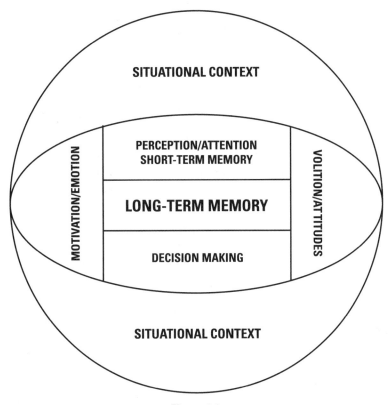

Figure 3.2
Sketch of a cognitive model of learning.

We do our active thinking in *short-term memory*. Functionally distinct from long-term memory, short-term memory is sharply limited in its capacity to store information—no more than five to ten "chunks" at any time. Like items on the cook's menu board, information in working memory changes continuously; nothing is permanent. Organization is critical. If you try to remember a ten-digit telephone number while juggling other mental matters, you will fail. That's why advertisers resort to mnemonic codes; "Call 1-800-MERCEDES" stays in memory as you decide between the sedan and a sports model.

The structure of human memory has important implications for educational practice. Every child can learn anything that attracts his or her attention, but the information has to be organized to be "thinkable." Large piles of disconnected facts are mental chaos. The most natural mode of organization takes shape as semantic networks or *webs*, collections of ideas and events that are clustered around a few nodes.

Storage is easy; retrieving information, though, depends on structure, on connecting with nodes. Multiple-choice tests provide the student with the clues to previously taught material; retrieval is not needed. Life outside school is more like an essay exam. Simply studying is not enough. The student must develop a systematic plan of action for accessing material, and for constructing a coherent response to questions. With complex information, the key is to "chunk" the material by looking for natural lines of division. It is like carving a turkey. The novice easily makes hash of the Thanksgiving bird. The expert relies instead on X-ray vision that goes beneath the surface to the joints. Much the same, teachers need to look beneath the surface complexities of the reading-writing process if they are to make professional decisions about what to teach and how to teach it. Otherwise they are forced to follow the basal scripts. The key in curriculum design is to divide the domain into a few distinctive elements that serve as the course of study from kindergarten through the middle grades.

The human mind is also unusual in that it can think about itself. Language is the foundation for reflective thought, what psychologists call *metacognition.* The capacity to draw away from the task at hand and talk to yourself about what is going on affects both the speed of initial learning and the capacity to apply that learning in other situations. Reflection is an "unnatural act." Today's youngsters often rely on "Ya know what I mean." That's because explaining yourself is a difficult task.

Indeed, one of the most important outcomes of schooling may be the development of reflective thought. Preschoolers lack this capability. They learn by doing, they think what they think, and they assume everyone else sees the world as they do. By the age of four or five, children begin to negotiate meaning among themselves. Language helps communicate wants and wishes. Playgrounds become laboratories for developing skills in explaining yourself. The task is not easy, however, and adult guidance is critical if children are to move beyond "I want!" and "Ya know!"

The final characteristic of cognitive learning is the link to motivation and attitudes. The simplest forms of behaviorism rely on extrinsic rewards to control learning. Beyond doubt, rewards influence behavior. But research shows the greater effectiveness of internal motives in directing and sustaining performance. Critical here is the capacity to reflect on the long-term consequences of actions and choices. Teachers who pose questions and make assignments struggle to motivate students who may see little point. Students who answer preset questions and complete predetermined assignments learn little about handling tasks that require them to frame questions and plan their own sequence of steps. Cognitive learning stresses a balance of skill and will, goal accomplishment and goal setting, specific objectives and large-scale projects.

The cognitive revolution has yet to influence the nation's classrooms. Most reading lessons still emphasize low-level reading and writing skills. While some teachers and students (and an increasing number of parents) chafe at the daily regimen, what are their alternatives? Who has time to think about anything new? These questions led to the emergence of Project READ in the spring of 1980 as a collaboration between teachers at Graystone Elementary in San Jose, California, and a Stanford research team. Graystone students had high test scores, and so teachers could take a risk. The teachers were bored by routines and wanted to challenge their students with more-demanding tasks. They were intrigued when one of this book's co-authors (Calfee) described cognitive learning at a district conference. They wanted to know how to translate the theory into practice. If memory systems, semantic networks, and metacognition meant abandoning the teacher's manual, what was going to replace it? How would teachers decide how and what to teach? Project READ emerged as a school-university collaboration around these two fundamental questions.

How to Teach?

We take you once again to the year 1992, a year in which instruction at North Shoreview looks quite different from the basal lockstep described at the beginning of the chapter. Students are usually busy with team tasks. The teacher spends time every day reviewing the status of projects, providing feedback and guidance, answering questions. There are occasional lessons, but these are seldom scripted, taking shape instead as dialogues, ideas scribbled on large sheets of butcher paper posted around the room as work-in-progress documents. The classroom is generally abuzz with children's chatter, sometimes verging on chaos. The casual visitor is puzzled, because the teacher doesn't seem to be doing much direct teaching. In reality, the teacher is doing the toughest kind of teaching—developing a physical, conceptual, and social environment that supports effective learning.

Decisions about what to teach may be independent of decisions about how to teach, but the student is more likely to get a coherent classroom experience when these decisions complement one another. It makes little sense to teach higher-order thinking through recitation, or, for an exercise on creativity, to require the correct answers. A Project READ lesson differs from existing practice in several ways. First, the typical basal reading lesson includes objectives in vocabulary, comprehension, decoding, and so on—a collection lacking coherence—while a Project READ lesson focuses on just a few outcomes. Second, the basal lesson is teacher-directed—the teacher relies on the manual for both questions and answers—while in the Project READ lesson the teacher asks questions meant to evoke a wide array of responses. Third, basal lessons emphasize content, while Project READ gives priority to process and structure—studying *Charlotte's Web* or the Civil War can be valuable, but more significant is learning to analyze stories and topics. Fourth, the Project READ lesson ends not with practice on worksheets, but with the creation of a "work product"—a composition, a play, a book, an exhibition.

Cognitive instruction. The **CORE** model—**C**onnect, **O**rganize, **R**eflect, **E**xtend—was designed by co-author Robert Calfee at Stanford University in 1988 to help teachers plan learning that is active, social, and reflective (Figure 3.3). Unlike the step-by-step basal lesson, the CORE design is flexible and iterative. The model permits freedom of movement while progressing toward a defined goal, and can be applied to a 20-minute lesson or a three-week project. A given lesson may call for emphasis on any of the four elements. Order is not important. Reflection may come before or after organization. The teacher may begin in the middle of an idea, move around in apparently random order, then stop for a moment to handle a puzzled expression.

Connecting: real questions and answers. Although the CORE model provides a blueprint for instruction, details are everything. CORE points the teacher toward a student-centered mind-set that contrasts sharply with the teacher-directed style dominating current practice. How to make it happen? An easy answer is to let students say their piece. Treat classroom discussion as conversation. Anything goes. Be natural.

But schooling needs to go beyond "natural." Students need to acquire skills and strategies for handling themselves in formal settings, for participating in problem-solving teams, for communication that is explicit and directed. They will acquire these skills more easily if their teacher's classroom questions are real.

What is a "real" question? Real questions connect. School questions are often artificial. The teacher asks the question, the student's job is to answer, but the teacher knows the "right" answer. It's a game. A real question is one where the questioner is genuinely interested in learning

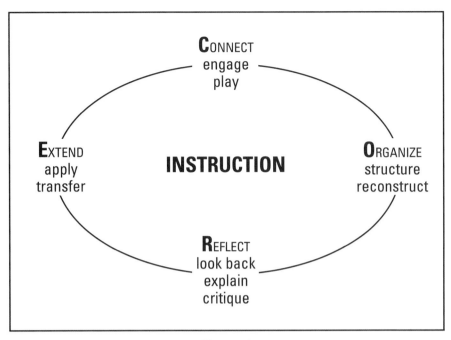

Figure 3.3
The CORE model of instruction.

something from someone else. Think about the exchanges with "Dr. Ruth," the sex expert. No one asks her "test" questions; they want to know what she has to say about something that is important to them. The essence of real discourse is its unpredictability and authenticity.

Real questions call for complex answers. Yes-or-no questions are seldom genuine unless quickly followed by "Why?" When you ask your doctor, "Should I take aspirin to avoid heart attacks?", you want more than yes or no; you expect an explanation. Real questions are an invitation to dialogue: "What did you think about Jane's fiance?" "He's okay" is less interesting than "He seems responsible but rather aloof—what do you think?"

Real questions also call for real listening, which comes naturally when a person has an investment in the situation. If you have experienced heart palpitations, then you are likely to attend to a friend's comments about an article on aspirin and heart attacks; if you are in good health, your mind may wander. A big part of succeeding in real life is being able to listen when it's *not* natural, when you don't immediately connect with the situation, when the need to listen is formal rather than natural. This requirement is critical in high school, since high-school teachers often depend on lectures; the pattern continues through college courses, committee discussions, and meeting prospective in-laws, among others.

Teachers have learned more about talking than listening, as classroom studies show. More than half of the talk is by teachers; when students do say something, teachers seldom build on these comments. This pattern is understandable. Most teachers have spent almost two decades in school settings where *their* teachers talked and they were silent—kindergarten provides more opportunities for genuine discourse than college courses.

The following dialogue from a sixth-grade class in Chicago illustrates the concept of connection. Calfee is conducting a demonstration lesson for several teachers interested in Project READ. The students recently spent two weeks studying the geography of Africa:

Calfee: You guys have been studying Africa? [students nod assent.] Here's a map of the continent, and a globe. What do you remember about the continent? [Long pause.]

Student #1: There's more than 50 countries in Africa? [Hesitant but upbeat.]

Calfee: Great—that's a lot of countries. . . . What's a country? [Long pause.]

Student #2: It's like Chicago or Illinois.

Student #3: No, dummy! The U.S. is a country. Chicago is a city, I think. [Scattered comments about whether Illinois is a country or not, general agreement that the U.S. is a country, but not Chicago.]

Calfee: Hmm . . . Why do you think Africa has so many countries?

Student #1: 'Cause it's so big. There's got to be a lot of countries.

Calfee: How big is it? Can somebody show me on the map how big Africa is? Come up here and show me. [Uneasy comments—"You use the little box in the corner, it shows you . . ." A student finally volunteers.]

Student #4: See, you use this little line here [measures the scale with thumb and index finger], and then you put it on the map.

Calfee:	Show me.
Student #4:	See, you put it down here, and then again, and again, until you get to the end.
Calfee:	How far is it, then, from the top to the bottom of Africa?
Student #4:	Well, let's see, the line is . . . 500 miles, and I did this ten times, so it's . . . 5,000 miles!
Calfee:	Good thinking! [Student returns to desk with relief.] How far is 5,000 miles? How long would it take you to go that far if you had to walk it? What would the walk be like? You guys made these relief maps, with mountains and deserts and rivers—suppose you were an ant going for a walk on these maps.

In the ensuing discussion students convert abstract maps and scales to human dimensions: how long it takes to walk a mile, to walk from the school to Chicago's downtown Loop (about two miles). They struggle to envision barriers (deserts and mountains) and routes (rivers and valleys). As the lesson ends, the class is beginning to transform their papier-mache relief maps into geographic realities, into human settlements, into political constellations.

The critical feature of this lesson was *connection*, often the missing ingredient. While television ensures that most children have seen the earth as a sphere turning in space, linking the images on a 19-inch screen (or a 12-inch globe) with a 5,000-mile hike across deserts and mountains is another matter.

If the point is to transfer information from teacher to students, the easiest way to do it is to tell students what they need to know and then test them for recall. No need to connect. The Project READ goal is to teach them how to learn. The teacher sets up an engaging problem for the class, provides students with strategies and structures for effective small-group problem solving, then steps aside to function as observer, referee, facilitator. The aim is for students to understand the geography of Africa not as a collection of meaningless facts, but as an experience made real by the imagination.

A problem-oriented approach to instruction takes unpredictable turns. Interactions depend not on specific questions and answers, but on the group's overall movement toward a resolution. This may be illustrated by a real example, from a North Shoreview special-education class wrestling with the War of 1812. The textbook material provides the details, but these third- and fourth-graders have problems with textbooks. The teacher suggests an alternate strategy. "Imagine an argument among a bunch of people," she says. "Your job is to find out who is fighting with whom and why, and what's going to happen. Treat the chapter like a story—you've learned about character and plot."

This honest and direct introduction gives the ensuing discussion a purpose that shapes the details. "Was the British Navy bigger than the U.S. Navy?" may be answered by a textbook, but the answer is important only in the context of the overall problem. "Who had the most to win and lose?" is a more interesting question. "Who are the characters?" is a matter of central importance.

The North Shoreview students spend the next hour in small teams examining the text in a concerted (and student-led) effort to try to discover who was fighting whom and why. In this classroom, whole-class activities are not an end in themselves, but an occasion for students to learn how to function in teams. These teams learn explicit strategies for discussing a problem, including roles for each team member (leader, reader, recorder, reporter), a "script" to steer the process (telling teachers how to open a lesson, what to include in the middle, and how to close it for review), and guidelines for group participation (for example, "focus on one thing," "make sure everyone gets involved," "take time to think about what you're doing").

Organizing: structures and strategies. In cognitive learning, structure is critical. The major contribution from Project READ was a simple structure for organizing the entire literacy curriculum, along with a toolbox of *graphic organizers* to handle reading and writing tasks. The discussion of the READ curriculum later in the chapter will emphasize structure, and we need not go into detail yet. The message here is the importance of organizing each activity. The lesson that begins without a clear focus, wanders at random across activities, and ends when the bell rings—such a lesson is incomprehensible for practical purposes. The educated and devoted adult can survive a committee meeting with these features, and maybe even learn something. But for children trying to make sense of the world, coherence is essential.

Organizing does not mean prescribing. The classical outline format illustrates the point. Students are often taught to "organize" their papers as a hierarchy:

I. gzibscl drept
    A. forqcht
        1. solmneeni vok
            a. vok bor
            b. vok wuulsh

This structure is one way to build a composition, but by no means the only one, and seldom the best beginning. It works well as a table of contents, but only after the writer has decided how to approach a topic, and how to communicate with a particular audience for a particular purpose. In Project READ, organization was designed not as a straitjacket but as a Tinkertoy—a set of building blocks to foster creative thinking. Two structures introduced at the beginning of the chapter, *webs* and *weaves*, emerged at the outset as especially powerful (Figure 3.4). Webs, so named because they resemble spider webs, connect a central topic through a small number of nodes to a wide array of peripheral details.

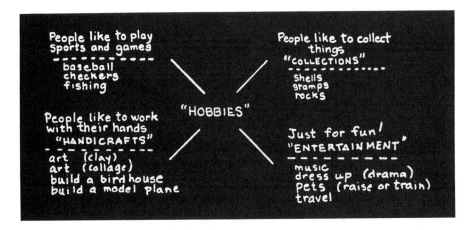

Compare:	Distance to the Sun	Weather	What do you see?	What lives there?	Any other information
Mercury	Mercury is the closest planet to the Sun.	It is very hot. It is also very cold at night.	Mountains, valleys.	Nothing lives here. Too hot.	You should never land here or you will burn up.
Venus	It is the second planet closest to the Sun.	It is very hot, too. It is hotter than Mercury.	Mountains, canyons, plains, craters, valleys.	Nothing lives here. Too hot. No water. Too dry.	They call it the Evening Star. It looks like a bright spot.
Earth	Earth is the third planet closest to the Sun.	It is not too hot. It is not too cold.	Water, trees, birds, schools, houses, clouds, people, plants.	People, animals, plants.	This planet is a good place to live.

Figure 3.4
Examples of graphic organizers for webbing and weaving.

Weaves are matrices, the crosshatch of cells providing opportunities for comparisons and contrasts.

Reflecting and extending: meaningful practice. Reflection and extension are linked here because they play off one another. Reflection is hard work, because you have to think about what you're doing while you're doing it. Like patting your head and scratching your stomach, it strains attention. Extension—developing an idea or project at some length—offers a chance for reflection. The typical fifty-minute lesson is usually crammed with too much to do and too little time to think. And tomorrow you'll be off to something entirely different. That is why Project READ recommends project-based learning. Projects—students writing books, composing plays, designing science experiments, simulating historical events—take time and reduce "coverage." But they also encourage discussion about the meaning of the activity. We will present several examples in the following chapters.

Extension is also important for meaningful practice. Project READ emphasizes the need to go beyond rote memorization to genuine understanding. But practice and understanding are both vital. You may learn the routines for operating a word processor with no insight into the principles, but then you will have problems switching to a new system or handling emergencies. Or you attend a seminar on the latest in word processors, which gives you an idea of how a new system works. But unless you spend time working with the system, you will lack fluency and fail to see the limitations.

Practice works best when purposeful. We have seen the football place-kicker on the sidelines, hammering balls into the net. This event has little in common with the first-grader filling out worksheets. The place-kicker is driven to practice because he knows that he's got to deliver when it's fourth down on the opponent's thirty-yard line, seven seconds left in the game, a tie score.

But practice also works best in context. Kicking into a net is fine, but the real test comes on the field, when the crowd is roaring, the ball is on the far hashmark rather than the middle of the field, a new center has replaced the injured veteran, and rain is pelting down. Place-kickers grab every opportunity to practice under real conditions, because that's when practice helps most.

Reflection and extension are best learned in a social context. Reflection, or talking to yourself, is fostered when students work together on meaningful problems. The task may be as small as drawing a matrix of the ideas from a chapter in the science textbook (Figure 3.5), or as large as some of the thematic projects described in later chapters.

Projects offer students an extended chance to practice what they have learned under real conditions. It's one thing to do an assignment on library skills: "Find a book on whales, read the table of contents, skim the book, and write a paragraph on what you think about the book." It's quite different when your eighth-grade team is preparing a report on the local ecology for back-to-school night, and you want to do it right. You have limited time, the librarian called with the book that you wanted, and you've got to run to the library in the rain. Like the place-kicker, you take advantage of the opportunity and learn from it. Practice can make perfect, if it's the right kind of practice.

What to Teach?

Cognitive teaching opens new possibilities, but the question remains: What should be taught? A *curriculum* is a *course* of study. Both words derive from the Latin *currere: to run.* Imagine a race course—not the

Figure 3.5
Reflecting and extending require teamwork in the earlier grades. These two fifth-graders from an Oakland, California, classroom are constructing a matrix that summarizes a science chapter on animal taxonomies.

high-school track, but the marathon from Athens to Sparta. You need to think about where you want to end, where you will start, and a few benchmarks along the way. It's best to begin at the end. What should be the school curriculum in literacy?[6] In yesterday's world, literacy meant little more for most people than reading and writing one's name. Most students left school before the end of eighth grade. In tomorrow's world, the young person leaving the middle grades requires full command of language in order to handle the challenges of high school and life thereafter. The perspective must shift from the view of reading and writing as *basic print skills* toward one of *critical literacy:* the capacity to use language in all of its forms as a tool for problem solving and communication.

This change in conception has substantial implications. Phonics is no longer the doorway to literacy, but rather part of a larger tool kit. Student discussion is no longer incidental but essential. Comprehension does not mean rote answers to simple questions, but reconstructing a passage and giving it personal meaning. Composition is not an optional assignment but a critical activity from the earliest grades.

The language of the English. Language is the foundation for literacy. This claim may seem obvious but it is not trivial. By age three, virtually every child knows a spoken language. Performance matures through adolescence and beyond, but the essential features of adult language appear in the preschooler: a well-developed phonological system, a large store of words and ideas, the capacity to create sentences and stories, and an understanding of the rudiments of conversation.

The English language is a story in its own right. History is the key to English. Ours is a complex language, its vocabulary larger than any other in the world. Unlike other cultures, we have never said "no" to a word. Rooted in Celtic origins, the language of the British Isles reflects successive waves of invaders who each left an impression. The Romans came around the birth of Jesus, leaving behind their alphabet. The Angles and Saxons followed, invading from the north, spreading havoc and their roughhewn vernacular. They were great in love and war, but not much interested in reading and writing. In 1066, William the Conqueror left the shores of Normandy for England, bringing a well-organized army, but also books, teachers, and spelling tests—all French. Two hundred years later, Middle English emerged as a blend of coarse Anglo-Saxonish and cultured French. The former served for everyday purposes, the latter for cultured settings: *folks* and *parents, love* and *adore, live* and *exist.* Then came the reign of Elizabeth I, the time of Shakespeare and Bacon, Milton and Locke, Newton and Halley, the King James Bible and the British Navy. Words flowed by the tens of thousands into England from throughout the world. Modern English had arrived, a polyglot of remarkable vitality and richness, a language of change, arguably the dominant language in today's world.

Both spoken and written English mirror the multiple origins of the language. The Roman alphabet that is used for written English can be traced back to Egyptian pictographs and the Phoenician syllabary, followed by the Greek invention of a genuinely alphabetic script with both consonants and vowels. Before the Norman invasion, local priests handled written communication, adapting Roman letters to the German-based language, 24 letters to represent almost double that number of phonemes. When the printing press arrived in 1476, English spelling was in a state of turmoil. Things haven't gotten any better since then; linguist John Nist notes: "Present-day English spells post-Chaucerian and pronounces post-Shakespearean."[7]

The Anglo-Saxon layer of the language is built mostly around the infamous four-letter unit—actually three to six letters forming consonant-vowel-consonant (CVC) combinations. Compound words (*doghouse, uplift*) splice these units together to make more complex words. The Romance layer—Norman French, Latin and Greek from the Elizabethan era, and other words begged, borrowed, and built since then—introduces the root-word-plus-affix pattern (*international, hypercritical*), leading to words of considerable length and complexity.

The reader who ignores the history of English sees chaos. Almost any letter can go with any sound, and vice versa. The key to understanding the language, both spoken and written, is to become an archaeologist, moving through the layers to find the patterns from the past.

Formal language and the rhetoric. There is more to reading and writing than meets the eye. The Jewish 13-year-old preparing for his Bar Mitzvah may manage the ceremony by learning to pronounce Hebrew even though he does not understand the meaning. Early reading instruction that emphasizes phonics can lead to the same outcome. In fact, critical literacy has less to do with *medium* and *message* than *manner*.

By *manner* we mean the style of language use, the contrast between formal and natural language. The former is more *standardized* than the latter. Dialects, word usage, and grammar vary substantially across societal groups, but a newscaster in Los Angeles sounds remarkably like her counterpart in Atlanta or Boston. Formal language is also more *explicit* than natural language. With a given audience in mind, the formal speaker tends to say everything needed to make the point clear. In a natural setting, "Ya know what I mean?" is more acceptable. Natural language is for the moment; the tone is more personal and the logic more intuitive.

We who are well educated take our style for granted. We were taught to read and write, but along the way we learned far more. We learned, for instance, to adapt our style to the situation. You take these shifts in stride. In traffic court to argue a ticket, your plea is spoken but your style is literate. You dress properly, you speak clearly, you organize your thoughts to persuade the judge of your cause. In short, you employ formal language. Returning home, you write to a close friend about your day. The note is written but the manner is natural. The words are casual, you don't fret about spelling or grammar, sentence fragments suffice. You don't work from an outline. The contrast in these examples has to do not with writing versus speaking, but with language style.

All children enter school with a fully functioning natural language. They can speak, they can comprehend, they can compose. They do differ enormously in language style, especially in the mesh between their home language and the formal language of school. Children from educated homes know about "school talk." Kindergartners who have not already learned this style are often viewed as "not ready to learn," even though at home and on the playground they are full of chatter. The development of formal language in the early grades is at least as important as learning to decode, and probably more important in the long run. The issue is not proper language. Rather, if youngsters are to prosper in the later years of schooling and in the world beyond school, they need to know how to employ formal language techniques when the situation calls for it—and when to "lighten up."

Critical literacy emphasizes effective communication. Being able to read and write is important largely because it enhances communication. The Greeks practiced literacy long before they invented the alphabet. The foundation for effective communication comes from the *rhetoric*, a set of techniques devised by the ancient Greeks to shape discourse in the Forum.[8] Modern rhetoric appears in college composition texts and "How to Communicate" seminars. It provides structures for framing an argument, for comparing and contrasting two topics, for composing an essay. In Project READ, time-tested rhetorical principles and techniques were clothed in modern cognitive garb and translated into language accessible to kindergartners—*webs* and *weaves, story graphs* and *cause-effect "dominoes."*

The rhetoric also offers criteria for evaluating a message. For the

Greeks, a *critic* was someone who could explain and judge the merits and shortcomings of an event or object. *Critical literacy* entails not only the ability to act according to written instructions, but also the capacity to think analytically, to gain insights and understanding from what has been read, seen, or heard, and to communicate with others about it both in speech and in writing, both formally and informally. Basic literacy allows a person to read instructions to operate the voting-booth lever; critical literacy allows the individual to comprehend issues for deciding whom to vote for and why.

Finally, the rhetoric encourages *meta-talk*, an essential ingredient in critical literacy. A simple but powerful idea like compare-and-contrast allows people to talk about how to talk (and write). It supports the human capacity to use language to reflect.

Learning to read. How does a child learn to speak? The answer is veiled in mystery, but it is clearly a natural event. Expose infants to language and they will begin to talk. How does a child learn to read? The answer depends on what you mean by reading. As noted above, most teachers, parents, and students focus on reading aloud, on basic skills rather than critical literacy.

The debate about how reading is learned—and it is a great debate—centers largely around beginning reading, and what should be taught in the early grades.[9] One opinion holds that *reading occurs naturally.* Expose young children to print and they will become readers and writers. This viewpoint is strongly espoused by today's Whole Language movement, but the contrary evidence is rather substantial. At a common-sense level, if exposure sufficed, then all inner-city youngsters would be literate because they are immersed in print. That doesn't seem to happen.

The *stages* view, embodied in the basal reading series, emphasizes the mastery of specific skills during a succession of phases. The first stage, reading readiness, is often seen as something to wait for. When children reach a certain point in development, then they will have the perceptual and linguistic competence for reading. Others recommend teaching simple skills—the ABCs, visual patterns, colors and shapes, "concepts of print." In any event, the idea is that at some point a child is ready for the decoding stage, when phonics can be taught. This second stage is often referred to as "learning to read." Once students have mastered phonics, then they enter the third stage, "reading to learn."

In the *developmental* view, reading and writing become extensions of listening and speaking. Learning to become literate comes about by building on the language that the child brings to school as the foundation for more-advanced competence in the literate use of language in all of its forms. The process is not natural; the teacher's role is to create situations that lead students toward more-accomplished achievements. Nor does it move from simple (start with letters) to complex (end with books). Rather, the teacher mounts a frontal movement across a broad array of literate activities—words and books, speech and print, comprehending and composing. The teacher does not wait for nature, but neither does he or she ignore it. A developmental view of literacy has been around for a long time, but poorly articulated. Outstanding teachers such as Sylvia Ashton-Warner, who spent her life in New Zealand working to improve English-language literacy among the Maori, have relied neither on nature nor on a prescribed set of objectives. Project READ embraced a developmental view as most sensible for cognitive learning.

Four Key Curriculum Elements

So much for the language and literacy—now to the key question of what to teach. Project READ, building on cognitive principles, began with one cardinal principle: Keep it simple. The aim was to find a small set of distinctive elements—we labeled them *structures and strategies*—as a foundation for critical literacy. Too many elements, and the teacher is overwhelmed. Too low-level a view of literacy, and students' potential is shortchanged. We were looking for conceptual tools to transform the elementary teacher from a factory foreman into a professional who could help students take charge of their own learning. The teacher was no longer the possessor of all knowledge; instead, Project READ passed on to students the secrets for analyzing and synthesizing knowledge—for thinking. We remembered the aimlessness of 1960s "relevance" and "freedom." The goal was a curriculum supporting the highest levels of literacy in an exciting, social, and reflective way, but a curriculum that went somewhere.

We divided the literacy curriculum into four domains paralleling the linguistic analysis of language: 1) *Vocabulary* corresponds to the field of semantics, the study of words and concepts. 2) *Exposition* refers to technical reports and essays. 3) *Narrative* covers stories and personal experiences. 4) *Decoding* means phonics, linking to phonology, the perception and production of speech sounds. We labeled this package the **VEND** plan, a simple acronym for remembering those four elements— elements that, to those with a classical education, will seem familiar. They should be, because they were the foundation of reading and writing in the generations before behavioral objectives came into vogue. Most of today's college graduates, however, moved from kindergarten through the baccalaureate on a diet of behavioral objectives taught piece-meal and tested by multiple-choice tests. The "big picture" that some take for granted was missing in their education. Many of these individuals are now teachers.

Each of these four domains has its own unique set of terms and ideas. The way you talk about narrative is different from discussions of expository writing. This feature of the Project READ curriculum made it possible to design inherently simple lessons. The basal lesson is a collage of behavioral objectives from different domains, lacking coherence and focus. A READ lesson can focus on a single element: "Today we're going to work on *stories* and how they are built—plot and characters."

The four domains also support a view of reading as a developmental process. Rather than teaching in stages—phonics first, then words and sentences, and finally the good stuff—the READ curriculum allows students of all ages and abilities to participate in all four domains. Kindergartners may not know all of their ABCs, but while they are learning them, they can talk about how stories are built, and they can prepare reports for the daily show-and-tell. In kindergarten, the stories are picture books and fairy tales; in fifth grade, chapter books like *Phantom Tollbooth* and *Tales of Narnia*. The kindergarten teacher asks the children to think about the moral of *The Three Little Pigs,* while the third-grade teacher has students rewrite the story from the wolf's perspective. At both grades, story analysis is a major curriculum element and thematic issues are explored. Kindergartners are on track when they can divide the story plot into beginning, middle, and end; sixth-graders are expected to know about problem and resolution, episodic analysis, and character development. At both grades, the concepts of character, plot, setting, and theme provide the tools for analysis.

Differences in ability and background are readily accommodated within this framework. Kindergartners recently arrived from a Spanish-speaking country may be in a bilingual classroom, but they can learn to analyze simple stories using the same tools as the English-speaking kindergartners next door, whom they will join in a year or two. The 11-year-old Russian emigree, still acquiring English, can join the rest of the class in studying *Phantom Tollbooth,* although she will need some help with individual words. The common concepts allow the teacher to adapt the same materials to differing levels of proficiency without watering down the conceptual goals.

Finally, the separation of literacy into four large domains supports integration with other subject matters. A concentration on reading and writing as skills leaves many students wondering, "Why am I learning these things?" Imagine instead a schedule in which literacy fills the entire day, but never in isolation, always in the context of activities in the core disciplines. Reading and writing open the doors to literature, science, social studies, mathematics, and the arts.

For instance, one third-grade teacher told us of her unit on early American history. For two weeks, students rebuilt their classroom as a pre-revolutionary fort. The official focus was history. Opportunities for literacy learning abounded, with questions about significant concepts and terms (vocabulary), reading library books and encyclopedias to find out about New England during the 1700s (exposition), and reconstructing life among the Mohicans (narrative). Students prepared synopses of library work, recorded meetings for designing the fort, and completed a project report. On back-to-school night, parents entered a classroom transformed into a stockaded fort complete with store, stable, bank, and living quarters. As they walked around the room, each setting was accompanied, museumlike, by captions explaining the experience. The project demonstrated students' accomplishments in history, literature, and art. Behind the scenes were contributions from the four domains of critical literacy. The scene is a modern version of an old idea—it was not too many decades ago when rather than being all-consuming endeavors, reading and writing were learned studying the arts and sciences.

After identifying the four domains, the next step in the development of the READ curriculum was divide-and-conquer: identifying a small number of structures and strategies within each domain that were critical for comprehending and composing, for understanding and constructing. The next four sections describe how we handled this job.

The story about stories. The narrative component is a good starting place because it is familiar.[10] Virtually every child enters kindergarten with a "story grammar" in his head. Like sentence grammar, a story grammar is a set of naturally acquired patterns for understanding and creating narratives. Children learn about story structure from experience: listening to fairy tales, seeing cartoons, hearing their parents tell about their day, and explaining how they ripped their jeans ("Billy made me do it").

If children already know about stories when they come to school, what is left to learn? The answer is, quite a lot. Kindergartners (and many of today's college graduates) don't fully know what they know. They may thoroughly enjoy a book or a movie, and yet find it difficult to explain why, other than "Ya know, I really, really liked it!" Instruction in the narrative domain leads students to a deeper understanding of how narratives are built, and gives them a technical language for talking about both comprehension and composition.

As Figure 3.6 indicates, the narrative domain is divided into four elements: character, plot, setting, and theme. These building blocks apply equally to fairy tales and to Shakespeare. The figure shows a sample graphic organizer for each element, showing how it might be structured during a lesson. The *character weave*, a kind of matrix, allows a third-grader to compare Little Red Riding Hood and the Big Bad Wolf. The weave serves equally well to contrast Shakespeare's Hamlet and Othello or Charlotte and Wilbur in *Charlotte's Web*. Weaves can be used to compose as well as comprehend. Fifth-graders can create personalized character profiles contrasting themselves as they are now and as they think they will be at the end of middle school as eighth-graders. The process begins with *webbing*, with free associations: "What words describe what you are like now? What words describe what you would

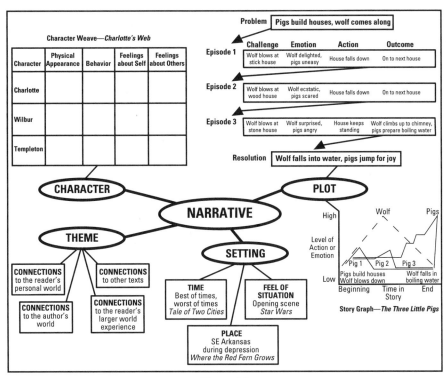

Figure 3.6
The basic elements of narrative comprehension and composition.

like to be in eighth grade?" The weave or matrix then refines the initial associations.

The plot is the lifeblood of a good story—the action. The characters, driven by an overarching problem, move from one event to another in search of a resolution. Readers appreciate and understand the tale as they empathize with the characters, as they are drawn into the roller-coaster ride. Figure 3.6 shows two techniques for bringing the action to the surface through graphic organizers. The *story graph* literally graphs the level of intensity. The teacher leads kindergartners through *The Three Little Pigs*. "Let's draw the story. It has a beginning, a middle, and an end [draws baseline]. Some parts are exciting and some are peaceful [draws left axis]. I've got some gray yarn for the wolf—tell me how he is feeling at the beginning of the story [anchors the yarn at the level chosen by the students]. What happens when he blows down the straw house—where should the yarn go now? [teacher continues to end of story for the wolf.] Now let's do the first little pig—what color yarn shall we use for him? [And so on to the third little pig.]" The colored strands provide kindergartners with a vivid graph of the flow of action, an image that they can call up when, say, they are fifth-graders wrestling with the War of 1812.

Analysis of story plot into episodes works with longer and more-complex stories. An episode is a subplot, with its own problem, reaction, and outcome. The reader can often sense the *boundary* between one episode and the next by a shift in time, place, or situation, the end of one activity and the beginning of the next. Knowing to look for these boundaries helps students in tracking the flow of action, which may otherwise become a muddy river. Again, the aim is to make explicit an understanding that may already exist in some form. In the words of a Sacramento third-grader, "An episode is the place in the story where you can put a commercial." For the first-grader, the boundaries in *The Three Little Pigs* are easy to spot. By making the structure clear and giving names to the elements, the foundation is laid for coping in high school with the otherwise difficult-to-digest *Tale of Two Cities*.

The ideas in Figure 3.6 may seem obvious—surely everyone knows about these concepts. In fact, basal reading systems give only haphazard attention to these fundamentals, which are lost in a cacophony of trivia questions. Today's teachers, unless they were English majors, may not understand the distinctiveness of the narrative form (they often refer to it as fictional writing). They have heard about character and plot and maybe even theme, but these ideas are not central in their instructional planning. Teacher preparation prescribes lists of "good literature" instead of providing tools to help teachers make their own informed judgments or suggesting strategies to guide students toward that same goal.

Graphic organizers such as webs, weaves, and story graphs support higher-level comprehension in two ways. First, they provide simple frameworks that allow teachers to ask good questions without losing their way in the details, even if they are not experts in literature. Teachers can raise open-ended questions that have a sense of purpose. Second, the organizers make public the process of understanding a story. Student reactions, instead of disappearing into thin air, become part of a written record. Thinking becomes external, and the class has a tool for combining individual efforts. Moreover, all students—even very young ones—can appreciate and apply high-level concepts for analysis and synthesis, for comprehension and composition.

Strategies bring the structures to life. Consider this illustration of a lesson using the character weave. The second-grade teacher opens the lesson:

> I'm going to read a couple of stories to you. The first is about *Swimmy*, a little fish who makes the best of a bad day, and the second is about *Frederick the Mouse,* and how he helps his cousins live through a cold winter. While I read each story, think about your feelings for the main character. Whenever a word comes to mind, raise your hand and I'll write down your word.

This introduction sets the stage for the lesson, which focuses on character analysis. It differs from typical story reading in two important ways. First, not one but two stories are used in the lesson. Both are by the same author, Leo Lionni, whose stories are quite popular; most second-graders are probably familiar with both stories. In *Swimmy*, a little black fish escapes with his life when a giant tuna gobbles up all the other fish in his school. He wanders through the wonders at the bottom of the ocean, and then finds another school hiding in the dark crevices of a rock. "Let's go play," he ventures—the other fish are afraid at first, but then Swimmy suggests that they shape themselves into the image of a giant fish, and they are able to venture forth into the ocean. *Frederick the Mouse* opens in late fall as a nest of mice prepare for winter. Frederick appears to be lazy and worthless as he basks in the sun, taking in the autumn's sights, sounds, and smells. Asked to help gather seeds and acorns, he replies that he is collecting other riches for the months to come. At winter's end, when the small band despairs, Frederick offers poems rich with memories of warm days and full bellies. Both stories connect with important issues, but it is rare for them to be brought together for comparison.

Second, the introduction directs students to actively monitor their reactions to the characters. As the teacher writes words on the board, students' thoughts become public (Figure 3.7). The words take shape on the blackboard as a splash of ideas around each of the characters. The students are connecting, and the splash of words begins to take shape as a semantic web, a cluster of ideas that "characterize" Swimmy and Frederick.

Once students have responded to the individual stories, the strategy moves to organize the ideas into a weave: "OK, guys, good work. Now let's make a chart for *Swimmy* and *Frederick*, so we can see how they are alike and how they are different." A weave begins to emerge. "Great!," says the teacher. "Now what are some other ways in which they are alike and different? Who can think of a word that fits both of them? That fits one but not the other?"

A *strategy* includes activities and questions to guide students in building and using *structures*. Unlike the prescriptions of a basal reader ("What color was Swimmy?"), READ strategies employ webs and weaves as a

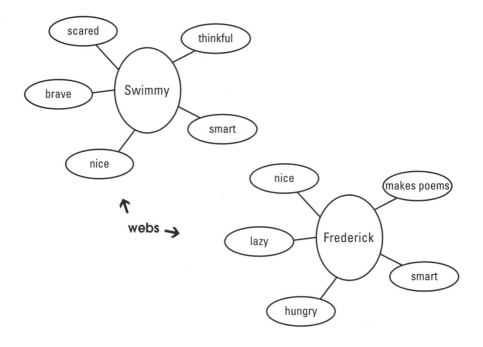

Figure 3.7
Semantic webs help to organize thinking about two children's stories.
Weaves highlight comparisons.

a weave →

	Swimmy	Frederick
scared	yes	no
brave	yes	sort of
nice	yes	yes
smart	yes	yes
thinkful	yes	sort of
lazy	never	sometimes
hungry	no	yes
poet	no	yes

Figure 3.7 (cont.)

jumping-off place. Much like a skydiver, the teacher moves to the top of a hill, a landing spot in mind, but free to soar with the class through unpredictable events. The goal is not just to reach the ground (although that is important), but to explore the currents. For teachers accustomed to following directions, READ strategies can be unnerving at first. If there is no one right answer, then does "anything go?" Of course not. Responses must be explained and justified. If a student says that Swimmy is "dumb," then he or she must convince the rest of the class of this judgment and connect it with the passage and with personal experience. If someone suggests that sea-bottom creatures like sea anemones and moray eels are mythical beings, or wonders whether an anemone can eat Swimmy, the teacher knows where to point the students to find the facts.

As the next anecdote illustrates, the results can make the flight worthwhile. READ structures and strategies apply to writing as well as reading. Young children can compose compelling narratives when given opportunity and support. At a Project READ school in South Central Los Angeles, a kindergarten play opens as a young girl walks onto the stage, looks out upon the audience of parents, and delivers her opening line: "My life is broke!"

This attention-grabber had a history, of course. The class had written the play themselves during the previous two weeks. The project began when the teacher introduced the assignment, asking the children, "What is something really important to you that you would like the people in the audience to learn from the play?" Referring back to Figure 3.6, the teacher was guiding the students toward a thematic focus: to find a moral for the story in their own experiences. The kindergartners "splashed" various ideas into a blackboard web and finally agreed that, for many of them, life would be better if they had happier families. The opening line emerged from these discussions. The next task was to construct a series of episodes. These were kindergartners, and so the events have a *Three Little Pigs* brevity: "The plumbing is broke" (a student leapt from the wings with a toilet plunger); "The electricity is broke" (a student from the opposite side with a light bulb). The final episode—the crisis—comes as the girl announces "And my family is broke" (a boy and a girl, dressed as grown-ups, walk out, sniff at each other, and stalk away from one another). How to resolve the crisis? What would you do? For kindergartners, magic is still possible and often essential. A fairy godmother emerges onstage, offering the girl a single wish. After brief but obvious reflection, the kindergartner chooses: "Fix my family!" The "parents" appear and make up: "Well, I guess we can get along." Then the other characters reappear: "The plumbing is fixed!" "The electricity works!" A simple but moving story, coherent because it possesses a purposeful structure, real because it conveys a genuine message.

Standardized tests have ruled the roost for several decades, but life after school is not a multiple-choice test. The effects of READ structures and strategies on children's creative abilities may not show up in evaluation reports, but it matters, especially in writing. A first-grader in Norwalk/La Mirada near Los Angeles approaches a visitor (co-author Calfee) to share her story: "Me and Juan went to the zuuo. We had fun." The two sentences cover the top half of the sheet with carefully printed words. "That's a nice story—a great beginning. How are you going to finish it?" The child's brow wrinkles—she has filled half a page! "You could add some more events, and it needs a good ending." The girl nods and walks away. Fifteen minutes later the visitor moves to leave. "Mister, I finished my story. But I had to write on the back. . . ." The narrative continues: "We saw the munkees and a lin. We went on the swings. We got some cottn candy. It was a grate day." "What a marvelous story!" And it is. It has coherence and substance. Length is not the issue; structure is.

Figure 3.8, also from Norwalk/La Mirada, is a marvelously cartooned story by a third-grader; it illustrates the imaginative capabilities of young children when they have been given structural supports. This lovely piece speaks for itself: the sense of characterization, the flow of the plot, the snatching of victory from defeat, the engaging art, the visual touches.

Why teach narrative if students already "know it"? The answer is partly motivational. Hiding within virtually every student is a range of stories that can lead them to explore and express their wishes, their values, their hopes. At a time when our society is seeking to re-establish its values and beliefs, literature provides a powerfully legitimate forum for our children to experience and explore what is important as a member of a democracy founded on capitalistic principles. *Dori* (the subject of Figure 3.8) retells Horatio Alger—do your best, and maybe you'll win. We have seen programs for character education packaged as exercises and worksheets. Learning about character values in our society cannot be accomplished through prescription, nor does it come down to "picking the right answer."

Reading about Swimmy, writing about Dori—these and numerous other instances illustrate the potential of the READ structures and strategies to support learning that is active, social, and reflective. The products are impressive in their own right, but equally important is the motivation that children gain for academic work, and their explicit understanding of what they are doing and why they are doing it.

Reading and writing reports. We turn next to exposition not because it is simple, but because it is such a contrast with the narrative. If stories are natural, expositions are anything but.[11] They expound, inform, explain, interpret, define, persuade—they do everything but tell a story. The kindergartner doing his first show-and-tell illustrates the problem. Johnny knows that he must come up with three sentences; that's the rule. He begins his report, hands in pockets:

> I've got a rock in my pocket. [Pause.] My mommy's going to have another baby. [Pause] Daddy's gone on another airplane trip.

The teacher, familiar with the Stanford grad students whose children fill her class, thinks about this disjointed string of sentences. Daddy is on the airplane, which means that he has finished his thesis and is looking for a job. That explains why Mommy is pregnant. Both topics will be difficult for Johnny to develop. "Johnny, tell us about your rock. Where did you find it? What does it look like? What are you going to do with it?" These three questions lead Johnny toward a more coherent report, laying the ground for five-paragraph essays and even persuasive arguments.

The foundations of exposition spring from the rhetoric, the stuff of today's college composition courses. In the Greek art of oratory, *rhetors* served as professional persuaders. In 322 B.C., Aristotle published his

Figure 3.8
The story of Dori the dog.

So it was agreed that she would perform.

7

At first she was a little scared, but she got over it.

8

She did flips, somersaults, cartwheels, spins, whirls, figures, and of course she roller skated.

9

Suddenly, she lost her balance!

10

She fell flat on her back and . . . CRASH . . . she bashed into the wall and fell on her face.

11

Then everybody started laughing!

12

Figure 3.8 (cont.)

Dori got up and bowed.

13

Her nose hurt a little, and she had a headache, but she felt good.

14

Finally the judging came and . . .

15

Dori won!

16

Figure 3.8 (cont.)

rhetoric, a highly analytic work that was decried by critics who preferred intuition and practice over principles. Aristotle organized his rhetoric in three parts: deliberative (analysis of the object), forensic (organization of the presentation), and style (character of the delivery). Most of today's college composition texts (e.g., Brooks and Warren)[12] embody these same three elements in some form or another, often as development of the topic or thesis, selection of a discourse form, and attention to details like construction of sentences and paragraphs.

So what have exposition and the rhetoric to do with elementary reading and writing? Quite a bit! Today's reading programs use stories to teach reading skills. Around third grade, science and social-studies textbooks grow in importance and size, and students are expected to expound upon literary works (they have to write book reports). Nowhere along the way are they taught expository forms, and so they encounter enormous difficulties in handling these assignments. In the middle, high-school, and college years, and in life after school, technical writing is the most important challenge to the literate person. Think about the last time you struggled to comprehend the Internal Revenue Service instructions for completing your income tax.

"Since exposition is difficult, perhaps it should be delayed until everything else is in place"—this way of thinking exemplifies a stage-based and behavioral approach to literacy. In contrast, a developmental and cognitive approach starts with the question, how can kindergartners be introduced to expository structures and strategies that prepare them for heavier exposure in the later grades? Johnny and his rock demonstrate how the teacher can address this question. The starting point is to ensure that the teacher understands the contrast between exposition and narrative, and possesses a handful of structures and strategies to introduce students at all grades and ability levels to expository forms.

Figure 3.9 shows the basic Project READ design for exposition. Underlying all expository writing is the task of informing the reader about the topic under discussion. The basic building blocks are organized in two categories: descriptive and sequential. Within these two categories are listed a small number of structures for organizing the information. Johnny's report on his rock illustrates the idea of the descriptive or "snapshot" structures, which are based on the webs and weaves discussed earlier. These structures are well suited for painting a picture, creating an image, or elaborating on a topic. Consider this excerpt from a Julia Child cookbook:[13] "A fish mousse is a puree of high-quality fish. . . . Its texture is infinitely finer than fish cake because of the cream, and the more cream it takes unto itself, the lighter and more delicious it will be."

The sequential or "process" structures cover expositions as diverse as recipes and the operation of a four-cycle engine. The text may be a list of steps, or may incorporate explanation. Turning again to Ms. Child, a recipe may proceed rather simply: "Cut the fish into 1-inch pieces. Drop the fish into the bowl of a food processor along with the egg, cream, and seasonings." On the other hand, she can also offer more-complex sentences: "If the mousse seems loose and lacking in body, process in bread crumbs by quarter-cupfuls. . . . If too stiff, process in more cream by small dollops."

These design elements are top-level; once the big picture is constructed, then the comprehender and composer must deal with paragraphs and sentences. Most expositions fail, however, because they are a jumble of thoughts. The first task is to pick a topic and decide how to develop it—Johnny's problem. Given a topic like "My Rock" and the goal of informing an audience, the teacher pointed Johnny toward a

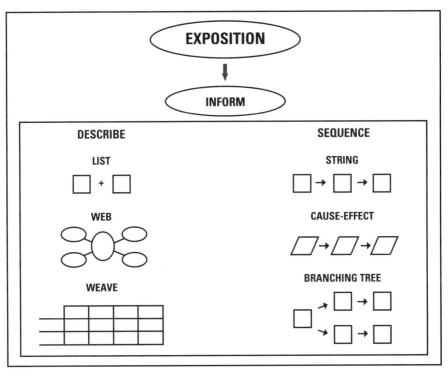

Figure 3.9
The basic elements of expository comprehension and composition.

descriptive approach and a topical net—a web. The figure suggests other alternatives. For instance, if Johnny has collected two rocks, then a compare-contrast strategy—a weave—would have been appropriate. If he showed a plastic container of silkworms munching on mulberry leaves, a cause-effect structure would be more appropriate. The point is that exposition, unlike narrative, requires analysis and construction from the outset. A story may be appreciated with relative little understanding. Expositions require work.

Coherent expositions focus on a single topic and development. Johnny's rock is an example. So is a five-paragraph essay. Unfortunately, students too often encounter in textbooks models that lead them to believe that complicated is good. A middle-school chapter on energy begins with a story about trains, moves to the sun as our source of energy, then dawdles for a while about the complex nature of energy—"Energy will be hard for you to understand." Probably so.

A better text might still begin with an anecdote, although today's students are probably not that familiar with locomotives, and so a comment about the sun's warmth might be more appropriate. Then, how to develop the topic? A descriptive approach might use a variation of the topical net—"Energy appears in six basic forms: mechanical, electrical, chemical, nuclear, gravitational, and thermal." A sequential structure might develop the interplay between potential and kinetic energy— "I'm holding this science book above the desk—does it have any energy in it?" The text (a teacher's presentation) could then explore what happens if the book is dropped (where did the energy come from and where did it go to?) or burned (a less desirable alternative). Or the author might combine these forms, beginning with a story, moving to a topical net which is then displayed as a matrix comparing and contrasting different forms of energy, and concluding with a sequential explanation of the conversion of energy.

Graphic organizers are especially powerful in handling exposition. Science textbooks challenge our students. The problem is partly that too much information is crammed into each page. More stuff about birds and snakes than most middle-grade students can ever remember—and why should they? And then there are the amphibians, fish, and mammals. The day has only so many hours; how to cover all of this material? The usual approach is to assign one chapter at a time for home reading, after which there is "discussion." The results tend to be less than spectacular. Some students can regurgitate the facts, others complete the assignment but nothing seems to stick, and then there are those who simply don't do the reading. The coverage is superficial and chaotic, a stampede of factoids.

What do students need to know about various animal types? Probably the most fundamental insight is an awareness of the power of a taxonomy to compare and contrast different vertebrate classes, to create a matrix. Casual reading may work for stories, but understanding an exposition requires the reader to reconstruct the text, using the elements in Figure 3.9 as Lego or Tinkertoy building blocks. Ideally, the textbook writer has constructed chapters as a coherent design using these parts. The students' job is to take the chapter apart and rebuild it. That's assuming chapters are coherently written, which unhappily is often not true.

A weave or matrix is the best way to compare and contrast a collection of objects. We have seen numerous classrooms in which teachers handled textbook coverage by assigning different chapters to different groups of students. The class project begins with a giant matrix, the chapters as row headings, column headings based on students' ideas about important distinguishing features for different animal types.

Chapter	What kinds are there?	What do they look like?	What do they eat?	How do they get around?	How do they reproduce?
Insects and Spiders					
Fishes and Crustaceans					
Reptiles and Amphibians					
Birds					
Mammals					

The categories above are typical starting points for fifth- and sixth-graders, who are still rather concrete but beginning to be interested in procreation. As reading proceeds, groups add categories based on the text and their analyses, as well as entries recommended by the teacher. The task for each group is to examine the textbook chapter for their animal type and to record information for each category on index cards, which are then taped to the matrix. At the end of the project, each group reports on its work, talking the entire class through that group's row of the matrix. Each cell appears as a collage of "fact sheets," including photos cut from magazines and artwork showing the internal operation of the various beasts.

This strategy is more participatory than the typical teacher-led discussion, and more informative. Students are actively searching for information rather than passively taking in facts, which leads them to actually think about the concept of a taxonomy. In one fifth-grade classroom, a student team grabbed Calfee as he walked among the tables. "We're working on insects and spiders, and this chapter doesn't seem to tell us a lot of things that we need to know. Did we miss something?" The students took Calfee through the chapter, and he assured them that they were right. The textbook writer had apparently become quite enraptured with a few selected species (a lot of material on trapdoor spiders) and had failed to include information essential for comparing and contrasting insects and spiders. Where else might the students locate the missing information? The library seemed a good bet, and so off the group went in search of books on bugs.

It's true that each student group focused on only one or two types of animals. Didn't the other groups miss something by not reviewing all five chapters? We don't think so. For one thing, the entire class experienced the entire matrix, and we suspect that the student reports had at least as much staying power in memory as trudging through the textbook. Second, each group went through the process of reconstructing in depth the analysis of a particular animal group. Do a few things well—and the matrix allows everyone to benefit from the collective efforts.

The comprehension of expository texts covering technical material begins to be a major challenge around third or fourth grade. First, students are encountering brand-new concepts, facts, and relations. The idea of the water cycle comes not from direct observation but from theory. Likewise the relation between geography and history—where and how people live is influenced by land and water. Second, expository structures are not natural events. Family dinner conversations, when there is family dinner, seldom include dialogue like "Let's compare and contrast this evening's supper with yesterday's visit to McDonalds." Many students, even in the middle grades, have not been taught the difference between stories and reports, nor do they have the tools to analyze these two forms. Third, today's textbooks can be virtually incomprehensible; the publishers are driven to include everything but the kitchen sink, and even the best writing breaks down when a passage is overloaded with information (Figure 3.10). Project READ structures and strategies resolve this problem in two ways. First, they clearly distinguish between narrative and exposition. Second, they support learning that is *active, social,* and *reflective,* even in the demanding area of exposition.

Figure 3.10 shows how third-graders at 59th Street School in South Central Los Angeles analyzed a narrative (*Amelia Bedelia*) and an exposition ("Amphibians") to highlight the contrasts in structure. *Amelia* has a cause-effect sequential flow, while "Amphibians" is a weblike description of facts, typical of U.S. science textbooks.

Words, words, words. The first two elements, narration and exposition, pertain to passages. This section and the next deal with what Project READ teachers refer to as "word work." You might think that teachers would automatically teach about words, and many do, mostly by rote practice on word meanings and spellings. The Whole Language movement mentioned earlier virtually prohibits such activities. In this philosophy, good literature—mostly narrative—is the proper vehicle for fostering literacy. Teachers are cautioned to avoid words in isolation; vocabulary and spelling are to be taught on the fly. Seuss-like books open some opportunities for spelling patterns, but most authors of children's literature are interested in telling a good story rather than

Figure 3.10
**Classroom charts showing graphic analyses of a story (*Amelia Bedelia*,
shown above) and an expository chapter ("Amphibians," below).**

in providing occasions for vocabulary and spelling practice. Whole-language advocates mean well; they believe that learning to read should be engaging and purposeful, and we agree. Moreover, some students can figure out how words work on their own, and with help from their families. But many other students will become literate only if the curriculum includes structures and strategies at the word level.

The procedure is actually quite simple. First you arrange the pieces into different groups. Of course, one pile may be sufficient depending on how much there is to do. If you have to go somewhere else due to lack of facilities that is the next step. Otherwise you are pretty well set.

It is important not to overload the unit. That is, it is better to do too few things at once than too many. In the short run this may seem important but complications can easily arise. A mistake can be expensive as well.

After the procedure is completed one arranges the materials into different groups again. Then they will be used once more and the whole cycle will have to be repeated.

At first the whole process will seem complicated. It is difficult to foresee any end to the necessity for this task in the immediate future, but then one never can tell. Soon however, it will become just another facet of life.

Figure 3.11
An example of expository text (after Bransford & Johnson, 1972).
One suspects it is about laundry.

Word work comes in two flavors. Most essential is *meaning*. Words are the core ingredient in language. The visitor to a foreign country needs words far more than grammar. Words link experience, thought, and communication. The fuller and richer a person's vocabulary, the more intelligence we attribute to that person. Knowing a word is more than a dictionary exercise. Really knowing a word entails depth of meaning, precision of usage, appreciation of relations and analogies, and the capacity to play with the ideas. All these notions are part of semantics, the study of meaning. The second aspect of word work emphasizes *print*—the capacity to decode a string of letters to gain access to meaning. This section describes the Project READ curriculum for word meaning; the following section presents the decoding-spelling curriculum.

What do students need to learn about words and ideas?[14] As with stories, kindergartners already know a lot. They enter school with a rich storehouse of words. Estimates range between 1,000 and 10,000 words by age five, depending on what it means to "know a word." Of course, some words are more relevant and appropriate than others for school. The street-smart kid may find some of his or her language

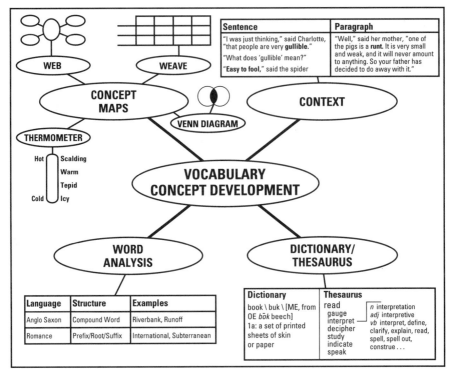

Figure 3.12
The basic elements of narrative comprehension and composition.

unacceptable in the classroom, and for good reasons. Other children not only know what language to use but how to use it. The teacher asks her first-grade class, "What is a dog?" She is asking for a display of knowledge, a formal definition. Children who already know the school game will respond as expected: "A dog is an animal with four legs and a tail that is often a pet." Youngsters who don't know the game are more likely to be confused by the question. Why is an apparently intelligent grown-up asking a question when she almost certainly knows the answer! It's not a real question, so there must be a trick.

And so what do students need to learn about words? Figure 3.12 lays out four elements in the Project READ curriculum. At the upper left is a collection of techniques for helping students talk about words and ideas, probably the most important vocabulary outcome in the early grades. These techniques are an alternative to memorizing words, almost always a lost cause. Learning a genuinely new word can be a slow and tedious task. If students acquired ten words per day from kindergarten through twelfth grade, they would add 25,000 words to their vocabulary—a tiny dent in the more than 500,000 words now in English dictionaries. The key to vocabulary growth is not memorizing but being strategic and organized.

Two structures in the upper-left corner of Figure 3.12 have already been mentioned. In *webbing* or semantic mapping, students (a) brainstorm around a topic, (b) organize the collection into clusters, and (c) expand the collection with the help of dictionaries, thesauri, and grown-ups. The power of this simple technique is that it begins with student knowledge and experience, and builds on this base in an organized way. Asking students "What comes to mind when you think about *dogs?*" is more authentic than "What is a dog?" The range of possible answers is more varied and more informative, and the semantic web provides a framework for portraying the responses. The *semantic weave* is a simple but potent extension of webbing, and is effective for the same reasons. Both strategies are closely related to exposition; the aim in many expositions is to construct webs and weaves among ideas. A *Venn diagram,* from mathematics, is a pair of intersecting circles; like a matrix, the diagram shows how two topics are alike and different. Other structures have sprung from the imagination of READ teachers. The *thermometer,* for instance, uses a familiar metaphor to introduce students to precise word usage. All these techniques encourage playfulness with language.

Project READ strategies tend by design to begin with what students already know. How then do they learn anything new? The answer is that, once a base is built in existing knowledge, then textbooks, dictionaries, the teacher's knowledge, and other resources can be added to the mix. To illustrate: Understanding a story plot requires students to discuss how characters' actions reflect their emotions. Ask students about feelings, and the results are often painfully meager: "Mad, bad, sad, glad." How to expand this impoverished vocabulary? A web worked well in one third-grade classroom we observed. The teacher opened the lesson by writing "Feelings" in the center of the board: "What comes to mind?" As the standard answers emerged, she wrote each in a different quadrant with a red marker. "We're going to be reading lots of stories, and we need to discuss the characters' feelings. We need more words. Let's focus on *mad.* What other words mean about the same?" The teacher wrote student responses with a green marker: "grouchy, mean, furious, tough, angry, infuriated, blasted," and so on. At lesson end, the teacher made a rule: Students could use green words, but not red ones, to talk about feelings. As the year progressed, the web expanded as students added words, the teacher consulted her Roget's Thesaurus, and new words were created—*mad-sad* for situations where you are angry but you understand the other person's actions.

Webs and weaves allow students to make effective use of what they already know, but they can also be tools for helping students see what they *need* to know and how to organize information they find in other sources. While previous examples have illustrated the potential of webs to connect with students' experiences, students need to learn how to tap into new information sources: textbooks, certainly, but also dictionaries, encyclopedias, libraries, the entire "information highway." If a student studying insects doesn't know the meaning of *exoskeleton*, it is reasonable to ask for help from classmates; but he or she also needs to know how and where to search out authoritative information. Once a dictionary definition is located—"An external protective or supporting structure of many invertebrates, such as insects or crustaceans. Compare *endoskeleton*"—the student can use webbing methods to link the new information to what is already known.

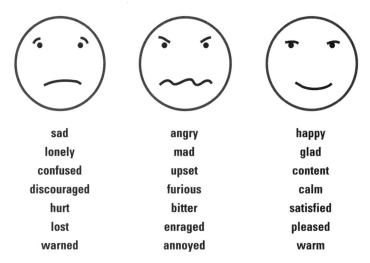

sad	angry	happy
lonely	mad	glad
confused	upset	content
discouraged	furious	calm
hurt	bitter	satisfied
lost	enraged	pleased
warned	annoyed	warm

The teacher should play a strong role in directing students to authoritative sources, and in showing how to connect book knowledge with practical experience (Figure 3.13). Insects come in a variety of shapes and sizes: flies, ants, butterflies, cockroaches. They have certain features in common: six legs, antennae, and squishiness. Teacher question: "What keeps insects from collapsing into a lump, which would happen to a person if you took out the skeleton?" As it turns out, insect bones are not on the inside but the outside. This knowledge comes partly from experience and partly from books. By asking the question, the teacher

Word Splash

*"What comes to mind when
you think of insects?"*

Legs	Blood	Escape
Antennae	Mosquitos	Tiny
Big/Small	Diseases	Trees
Crawl	Malaria	Leaves
Tickle	Tropics	Rain forest
Annoying	Hive	Trillion
Ants	Hole	Larvae
Water	Killer Bees	Bug Bomb
Butterflies	Attack	Leeches
Centipedes	Repellent	Suck Blood
Queen	Itch	
Workers	Bite	
Bees	Spooky	
Insects	Swarms	
Communicate	Clever	

Clustering

*"How can we group
these words?"*

Research Reading

*"What does the book
tell us about insects?"*

Headings from a typical third-grade
textbook, *Animals of Planet Earth:*

Animals are alive
    Living things reproduce
Animals need a place to live and grow
    They need food
Animals can be put into groups
    Fish
    Reptiles
    Mammals
    Amphibians
    Birds
Animals with backbones
    Inside the backbone
Animals without backbones
    Mollusks
    Ringed worms
    Animals with jointed legs (insects,
      crustaceans, arachnids,
      myriapods)

Weave

*"How are insects like
other animals?"*

	What kinds are there?	What are they like?	How are they built?	Where do they live?	How do they reproduce?	What do they eat?
People						
Mammals						
Birds						
Fish						
Amphibians						
Snakes						
Bugs						
Spiders						

Figure 3.13
**Illustration of the development of the concept of Insects from a word splash
through clustering to research and on to a matrix.**

introduces a category that calls for a response. The insect web provides the student with a graphical space for storing the information.

After students have collected the basic information as a web, the matrix is a powerful device for combining information from a variety of sources. Once a student has begun to think about skeletal forms and functions, this category takes its place as one of the features that are important for comparing and contrasting different animal forms. In what ways are the skeletons of various beasts alike and different? What about grasshoppers, worms, octopi, snakes, fish, chickens, dogs and cats, hummingbirds? Students may be able to bring their personal experiences to bear on some items on this list, but books are essential for other entries. The matrix allows students to keep track of what they think they know, what they need to find out, and what they have learned.

Webs and weaves organize collections of words into conceptual networks. Sometimes words have to be handled one at a time. The lower-lefthand segment of Figure 3.12 shows strategies for vocabulary development that depend on word analysis. Most English words are combinations of more-basic forms. As we noted earlier, Anglo-Saxon relies on simple compounding. Grab a couple of basic words, glue them together, and you have a new word; *cribwork, crosswalk, crowbar,* and *cubbyhole* appear at the end of the "C's" in the dictionary. Teachers routinely teach compound words. Students learn to divide a long word into two short words. They often have no idea why they are doing this.

As it turns out, the key to understanding a compound word lies partly in knowing the short words, but the relation between them also matters. How can students come to understand a relation? By playing with the parts. This third-grade lesson illustrates the possibilities:

Teacher: Today we're going to work with some long words. How are these words alike?

sidewalk, bookshelf, firehouse, raincoat, lawnmower, spaceshuttle

Students usually look first for commonality of meaning, but eventually someone pops up with the right answer: "They're compounds."

Teacher: Right! What does that mean?

Student: You're supposed to divide them in two.

Teacher: Why?

Student: [Puzzled] Because. .. .

Teacher: Well, let's play a game. If we divide all of these words, here's what we get:

side	**walk**
book	**shelf**
fire	**house**
rain	**coat**
lawn	**mower**
space	**shuttle**

Teacher: Suppose you pick any word from the left and any from the right, so you make a new compound. What would it mean? What about a *lawncoat* or a *firewalk?*

The activity prompts students to play with the language, with the aim of discovering that words are ideas rather than engravings. A *lawncoat,* partly because it is not in the dictionary, can mean anything you want it to mean. The challenge is to create an image, a concept, an idea. When you can do this, especially when you can draw a picture of the result, you are beginning to understand English from the ground up.

As the word-analysis panel of Figure 3.12 shows, the Romance layer of English employs a different pattern for combining word parts: prefix-root-suffix. Unlike the plain language of the Angles and Saxons, the parts are not simple. Consider *submission: sub* is a boat or a sandwich; *miss* is a young woman or a failure to hit; *ion* is part of an atom. What can students make of this mixture? There is a structure, but much like exposition, it requires not passive memory but active working with the parts. A variation on the compound-word strategy provides an opening. The teacher lays out the following patterns on the board:

[in green]	[in red]	[in blue]
anti- (against)	**-act-** (to do)	**-ion** (state of being)
bi- (two, both)	**-dict-** (to say)	**-al** (describes)
micro- (small)	**-mot-** (to move)	**-ology** (study of)
re- (repeat)	**-ped-** (to walk)	**-ness** (state of being)
un- (not)	**-vid/s-** (to see)	**-or** (doer)

Teacher: What words can we make with these parts? Suppose we make an *antipedor.* What might that mean?

Anyone who has been in New York City realizes that this term describes motorists. What about *microaction?* Seems like a synonym for procrastination. *Bidictor* certainly describes those who speak with forked tongue. And so on. The point of the exercise is to help students see the chunks of meaning buried in long words like *persuasibility* and *metaphysical.*The meaning may not spring immediately to mind, but the reader will appreciate that structure can be found in a string of letters.

The upper-righthand quadrant of Figure 3.12 deals with words in context. A radio advertisement warns the listener—"People judge you by the words you use!" True enough. To increase your vocabulary, the promoters urge you to buy audiotapes to increase your vocabulary with little if any effort. The promotion has a grain of truth. Most readers of this book have enormous vocabularies, partly because you have rich experiences and concepts, partly because you know how to analyze words, but also because you read a lot. And as you read (and listen), you think more or less explicitly about the words that come along. Recall the earthquake story in Chapter 1 (see Figure 1.4 on p. 13)—the ground shakes, and educated people can scarcely wait for the morning paper to find out what happened. You peruse the text, adding to your vocabulary: "The Nazca plate subducted or slipped under the South American Plate. Subduction occurs when one plate overrides another, forcing it down." The accompanying picture shows a plate and a subduction. Comes another earthquake, and subduction rings a bell. You didn't study the word; context did the trick.

Context is a powerful influence, and one that should not be left to chance. The effect goes beyond reading; print is powerful, but so is listening to radio and television, and even lectures. Teaching students to learn from context, sensible as it seems, is rarely done. The student first needs to monitor understanding: Are words coming along that are strange and that I might need to know? Narratives seldom depend on vocabulary because the plot carries the action. You don't need a dictionary to understand Tolstoy's *War and Peace,* and using one can even destroy the story. Exposition, in contrast, requires special attention to new and unusual words. Newspaper articles are excellent sources of exposition and vocabulary development. The writers must use real words, but must explain technical vocabulary to everyday readers. Otherwise, the paper won't sell.

Imagine a class of sixth-graders viewing an overhead projection of the earthquake article depicted in Figure 1.4. The teacher asks, "What words seem difficult or strange?" The question encourages students to monitor their understanding, the first step in the strategy. Next, "How can we discover what these words mean?" Neighboring words and phrases help. A sentence provides clues. The figure comes into play. Sometimes an entire paragraph or passage matters. An example comes from E.B. White's *Charlotte's Web*: "'Well,' said her [Charlotte's] mother, 'one of the pigs is a *runt*. It is very small and weak, and will never amount to anything. So your father has decided to do away with it.'" The *American Heritage Dictionary* defines a runt as "an undersized animal; the smallest of a litter." White's context is richer. Instruction attunes students' ears and eyes to the richness of language, and to the potential of almost any passage to enhance one's store of knowledge.

Dictionaries and thesauri appear in the lower-righthand corner of Figure 3.10 as reminders of the power of our cultural repositories. All too often, today's students learn that dictionaries are useful only for filling in worksheets. Thesauri are seldom covered, although they are far more fun, especially those written expressly for kids, such as the ones by *Richard Scarry*. Once a youngster becomes a word hawk, there is little stopping him or her—learning is active, social, and reflective.

How do you say "ghoti?" No topic in reading instruction provokes as much controversy as phonics.[15] Some educators fervently insist that reading is saying words. Others insist with equal fervor that reading is about meaning. Middle-of-the-roaders can find in Project READ a resolution of this conflict.

Today's decoding curriculum is largely behavioral: Divide spelling-sound correspondences into specific objectives (e.g., f, ff, gh and ph all make the sound /f/). Teach children these objectives through direct instruction and seatwork. Avoid rules, which are untrustworthy. A common rule for vowel pairs is "When two vowels go walking, the first does the talking": vowels in words like *pain, beet, boat*, and *fuel* take the name of the first letter—but the exceptions (e.g., *said, bread, great*, and *language*) outweigh the examples. George Bernard Shaw presented *ghoti* as evidence of the craziness of English spelling; the word is pronounced *fish*, he claimed: *gh* as in *enough, o* as in *women*, and *ti* as in *nation*. Don't bet on it. *Gh* is never *f* except at the end of a handful of Old English words. *O* as *short-i* occurs in just one word. *Ti* as *sh* is always in a Romance suffix like *nation*. *Ghoti* is obviously an alternate spelling of *goatee*.

The fact is that many teachers and parents see decoding, for better or worse, as the first stage of reading, and perhaps all that needs to be taught. Teach phonics, and the child will automatically transfer these skills to comprehension. The skill-based, "bottom-up," drill-and-practice program has drawn fire from some educators, who oppose what they see as an inhumane and mindless curriculum. They propose meaning as the goal of reading: Children will discover what they need to know about phonics if allowed access to good books. The debate has gone on for more than a century, and shows no signs of slackening. Here are a few samples:[16]

- Rudolph Flesch in *Why Johnny Still Can't Read* repeats his earlier argument that phonics is the foundation for reading instruction.

- Stanley Sharp argues with equal vigor that *The Real Reason Why Johnny Can't Read* is the inconsistency of English spelling. Nothing can be taught until we regularize the letter-sound system.

- Psychoanalyst Bruno Bettelheim views mispronunciations as Freudian slips, best ignored. Expose the child to good literature and let spelling take care of itself. Whole-language advocates hold a similar view, but without psychoanalytic overtones.

- Educator Herbert Kohl writes that the real basic skills are "using the language skillfully, . . . thinking for problem solving, thinking imaginatively, understanding fellow human beings, and knowing how to learn something for oneself."

- Psychologist Robert Glushko puts the contrary view bluntly: "Dealing with nonsense is what reading [is] fundamentally all about."

English spelling presents unusual but not insurmountable difficulties. The complexities spring from the nature of spoken English, a polyglot par excellence, and from the evolution of a writing system for this marvelous mixture of languages. Relying on the basic principle that learning should be active, social, and reflective, the READ decoding-spelling curriculum starts from the premise that there really is a system to English spelling and that an important part of word work is to prepare students both young and old to explore the system. The task is not rote memorization but cracking the code. The most important clues for this job are the alphabetic principle and the history of the language.

English spelling is necessarily *alphabetic*. Many languages use letters to represent sounds, but are sufficiently regular to permit learning based on syllables rather than phonemes. You can get along in Spanish with *ma, me, mi, mo, mu*. In English, as noted earlier, the basic building block is the consonant-vowel-consonant or CVC combination. More than 50 different consonants or consonant combinations can be placed at the beginning and end of this pattern, along with more than 25 vowels or vowel combinations in the middle—50x25x50 yields more than 60,000 different possibilities, a lot to memorize.

The basic building blocks of the alphabetic system are consonants and vowels. A simple concept, one that you learned as a child and probably take for granted. Consonants were the basis for early systems of print, the vowels often unmarked. Greeks used vowels to transform Phoenician syllables into Greek patterns. Today's students pick up consonants quickly but still struggle with vowels. They rely on consonants when starting to spell (much like the Phoenicians) and then add vowels (much like the Greeks).

The history of English spelling is about much more than vowels and consonants, however. As successive invasions swept across the land, they left their marks on both the spoken and the written language, on how words are built and how they are spelled. Figure 3.14 lays out the structure. Anglo-Saxon words are the most common. They are relatively few in absolute number, but each receives a lot of use:

> [Every English-speaker] loves his mother, father, brother, sister, wife, son and daughter; lifts his hand to his head, his cup to his mouth, his eye to heaven and his heart to God; hates his foes, likes his friends, kisses his kin and buries his dead; draws his breath, eats his bread, drinks his water, stands his watch, wipes his sweat, feels his sorrow, weeps his tears and sheds his blood; and all these things he thinks about and calls both good and bad.[17]

This clever excerpt, constructed completely of Anglo-Saxon words, demonstrates the short-and-simple quality of the language, and

	LETTER-SOUND CORRESPONDENCES	SYLLABLE PATTERNS	MORPHEME PATTERNS
ANGLO-SAXON	cap stand that set brisk skip pin/pine car beat pinning/ tall crown pining snow	tennis sister napkin hobo cabin hundred	railroad pigtails like bid unlike forbid unlikely forbidden
ROMANCE	direction spatial excellent	inter- intro- -ity	prediction disruptive admission
GREEK	physics chemist	auto- micro-	microscope chronometer physiology

Figure 3.14
Basic elements of the English spelling-sound system.

the building-block character of the spelling patterns. Anglo-Saxon words also provide the grammatical glue that holds sentences together, old words like *a, the, of, through, was, will,* and *so on.*

Simple on the surface, Anglo-Saxon confronts students with two major problems when they try to break the code, as we shall see shortly. The Romance layer presents different obstacles. The Normans mandated French as the official language when they arrived in 1066. The English absorbed the vocabulary but changed the pronunciation to fit their more guttural style. The Normans also brought books and teachers, and so spelling remained constant while sounds changed. Vowels were affected more than consonants, except for suffixes like *sion, cious, tion, tial,* and *cial.* In these patterns, the initial consonant becomes *sh* and vowel combination is pronounced *uh.* Like Anglo-Saxon, the Romance layer of the language poses two challenges for readers and spellers.

Now, the problems with Anglo-Saxon spelling: the first is the nature of sounds and their relation to letters, the second is about the vowels. As noted above, facility in English spelling requires a deeper understanding of the alphabetic principle than is the case with any other language because of the large number of CVC combinations. Learning letters is simple enough. Letter shapes and names must be memorized by rote because there is no real structure. Learning sounds is another matter. The key to learning about sounds is not the ear but the mouth. Figure 3.15 lays out a matrix showing how sounds vary depending on how and where they are made. Close your lips, put a ball of air behind them, pop it out, and you've made a *p.* Make a *t* and you'll discover that it also pops, but this time your tongue touches the ridge behind your teeth. Experiment with the matrix and you can feel the patterns. For the nasals or "nose sounds," try holding your nose while you make the sound.

What has this exercise to do with learning to decode and spell? Quite a bit, it turns out. Some children come to school having somehow figured out something about sounds. They are better at rhymes, at talking about speech sounds, and so on. Many have learned the rudiments of reading at home, which gives them a language for talking about sound. But many other students have no idea what the teacher is talking about when she says, "Listen for the *p* in *pat.*" You may have the same difficulty, but don't know it. Say *spa* and listen for the *p.* Unless you have formal training, you are unlikely to realize that the second sound is not a *p.* Hold your hand in front of your lips, say *spa, pa,* and *ba,* and you will feel much more air released with *pa* than either *spa* or *ba.* In fact, the second sound in *spa* is actually a *b.*

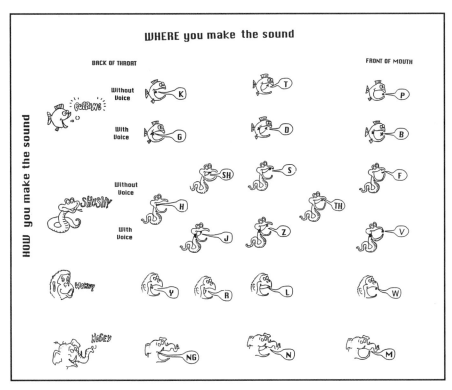

Figure 3.15
The sounds of English—how to make consonants.

Training programs developed for students with reading difficulties increasingly include a "phonetic awareness" treatment. They rely on memorization more than understanding. Students (usually third-graders, because this is when children are "identified" for special education) learn names for each of the patterns in the figure; *p* is a lip-popper, and so on.

In the Project READ decoding curriculum, one element of word work covers speech sounds. The first-grade teacher gathers a group of six to ten students—"Today we're going to study how you make sounds when you talk. This will help you when you want to read and write on your own. Who knows a short word with a *P* in it?" The teacher has already primed the pump for answers to this question by flooding the classroom with print: *Pat* has his name prominently displayed on his cubby, *pencil* appears above the pencil box, and *pumpkin* is in the large Halloween web. The teacher writes the students' words, reviews them with the group, and then asks the critical question: "Let's go back to *Pat*. How do you make the sound at the beginning of this word? Pretend I'm from Mars and don't know how to talk. You've got to teach me." We are always fascinated when young (and not-so-young) children struggle to explain speech. The first response is usually "You do it this way," along with an enthusiastic and splattery demonstration. "I can see what you're doing, and I can hear you, but I don't know what to do. It's coming out of your mouth; what part of your mouth are you using?" "You close your lips and blow." "Like this? I'm closing my lips and blowing . . . " The teacher lets air flutter between her lips. "No! You gotta really close your lips and make 'em pop."

The children's language is imprecise, their frustrations apparent ("Why doesn't this grown-up get it?"), and their intensity obvious. Eventually they succeed in leading their teacher to make a *p* sound for *Pat.* "Can I do the same thing for the other *p*-words?" The children check it out, and it works—even at the end of words like *pop*, where many children typically drop sounds. The children, without knowing it, are improving their articulation and gaining knowledge about public speaking. The lesson continues with *T* and *K* sounds, the first row of the sound matrix. Within a few weeks, students can talk knowledgeably about the matrix in Figure 3.15.

Once students have acquired a language for talking about sounds, they can check both decoding and spelling, and the teacher turns then to the CVC building block. Small-group instruction begins with short vowels. "You've learned to read a lot of words, but now you need to know how words are built. Here are three popping sounds—*P T K*— and the first *glue letter*—*A.* Let me tell you how to build a word. You pick one of the popping sounds, then I'll stick in the glue letter, then you finish with any of the popping sounds. Who wants to build the first word?" Enthusiastic first-graders often volunteer a complete word— "*PAT*"—but understanding requires going through the process one step at a time. First the *P,* then *A* is glued in, and then the *T.* Once the student completes a word, the teacher asks: "What does the word say? Let's check that our mouth follows the letters."

With three consonants and one vowel, students can build nine patterns. Some are real words, others are not. It doesn't seem to matter to most children, who are quite happy with *TAT* and *KAT.* Purists may worry about nonsense words and alternate spellings, but the goal of the lesson is to construct a conceptual understanding. Conventional spellings can be refined later, but the aim is to lead students to understand the alphabetic principle.

The second problem with Anglo-Saxon spelling is the vowels. As

Figure 3.16 shows, vowel patterns fall under three headings. Vowels change when joined with *R* and *L*. These effects are a natural part of speech, and are probably not worth much teaching time. *Cats* and *dogs* illustrate a related effect. The final sound in *cats* is *s* and *z* in *dogs*, but few people notice the difference. The vowel digraphs bear the brunt of many attacks, especially the *ough* combination. These spellings are quite old, early efforts to deal with the mismatch between Anglo-Saxon phonemes and Roman letters. They fall into two classes, one of which is consistently pronounced, the second with two unpredictable pronunciations. (Also Figure 3.16.) They appear in a small collection of frequent words, and warrant little teaching time.

The contrast between long and short vowels, on the other hand, does demand attention. Often referred to as the "short-e" rule, it is actually a marking system of broad scope. William Caxton, who brought the printing press to England in the late 1400s, designed the system to regularize vowel spellings for Anglo-Saxon words. His Belgian typesetters complained about inconsistencies, and so Caxton made a rule. Each vowel had two primary pronunciations, today's long and short sounds. Caxton's rule worked this way: if a vowel is followed by a second vowel with at most one intervening consonant, the first vowel is long. Otherwise it is short.

Sounds complicated, and the logic is indeed complex. How does one communicate the pattern to first-graders? A typical lesson builds on the short-vowel CVC patterns introduced earlier, which means that students are fluent with combinations like *tam* and *mop*. They are reading a lot, and so have encountered lots of long-vowel words like *tame* and *mope*. Time to figure out what's happening here. The whole class joins in this exercise, each student with a large letter-card in hand. "OK—for today's word work, we'll start with a spelling test. The first word is 'tam.'" Three students rush to the front of the room displaying their letters: TAM. "Now, suppose we want the glue letter to say its name, so we get 'tame?'" One student suggests that adding *E* will do the job; that's what his father told him. "Your father's right. Let's bring *E* up here, and I'll tell you what's happening. If *A* can reach around *M* to a glue-letter partner, it can say its name. *E* doesn't say anything; it's just a partner. OK, back to your seats—let's do 'mop' next. How do we change it to 'mope?'"

So far the teacher has added drama to routine phonics. The activity is more fun than worksheet practice, and students work with a broad array of patterns rather than just "long-*A*." The next step differs significantly from usual practice, however. To fully understand the marking

CONSONANTS		
SINGLE	**BLENDS**	**DIGRAPHS**
p g d b c y w l r t f j m n s h k q x y z	<u>initial</u> bl br cl cr dr fl fr gl gr sl pr tr sc sk scr spl sm squ sn str sp st sw tw thr <u>final</u> -ft -mp -nt -lk	<u>initial</u> ch sh th wh gh <u>final</u> -ng -ck -sh

VOWELS		
SINGLE **SHORT LONG**	**r & l CONTROLLED**	**DIGRAPHS**

a: mad   made
e: pet   Pete
i: Tim   time
o: hop   hope
     hops   hopes
     hopped   hoped
     hopping hoping
u: cut   cute
	ar: park lard charm
	or: for horn short
	er: her stern fern
	ir: bird thirst sir
	ur: fur churn burn
	al: hall fall call
	      halter falter
	      walk talk balk
		<u>one sound</u>
		ai/ay: pain, play
		  ee: meet
		  ie: piece
		oi/oy: foil, toy
		  oa: boat
		au/aw: laud, law
		  ew: few
		
		<u>two sounds</u>
		  ea: breath, breathe
		  ei: seize, eight
		  oo: noon, cook
		  ou: round, soul
		  ow: cow, snow

Figure 3.16
Anglo-Saxon consonants and vowels.

pattern, students need to see its full extent. The teacher continues the lesson. "Now suppose we want to change 'mope' to 'moping.' Where's our ING card—come on up." The students form MOPEING, and the teacher points out that the *E* is not needed anymore. The student with the *O* card can reach around *P* and touch *I*, another glue letter. That does the job. "What if we wanted to spell 'mopping?' If we add ING to

MOP, it doesn't work. Any ideas?" A student suggests adding a second *P. O* can't reach around two consonants, and so MOPPING works. A twenty-minute lesson, and students have reconstructed the entire Caxton marking system.

The remainder of the Anglo-Saxon spelling system is a matter of building on this foundation. At some point, usually around third grade, students begin to encounter Romance words in substantial numbers, often in science and social studies. Students who have gotten by with a small "sight word" reading vocabulary are suddenly lost, and even fluent readers wonder what has happened. So many new words, and so *long!* A cognitive perspective asks, "What do students need to know?" The Project READ analysis of English spelling suggests two answers: dealing with the leap, and dealing with the length.

The first issue is actually easy to handle. Once reading becomes a matter of understanding how the system works, students quickly become invested in learning about their language and how it evolved. History places the mystery of the language in a different perspective. Americans come from a wide range of cultures and languages, and the study of our language gives multiculturalism a concrete meaning. The key to handling the leap, in short, is to know that it is there, that you are literally leaping from one language to another. Phonics connects to social studies and to literature.

The second task, handling the length and complexity of Romance words, requires more care. Lessons in roots and affixes like those sketched earlier are one strategy. But development of technical vocabulary is linked to subject matter. By middle school, many teachers are subject-matter specialists: "Outta my way, fella, I'm a scientist," to quote Bill Murray in *Ghostbusters.* Science is important, but if our students are to gain access to the disciplines, every teacher needs to understand language. Eighth-graders memorizing vocabulary for the assigned reading on *reflection* and *refraction* of light need morphological assistance. Besides the two "*R*" words above, they meet *concavity* and *convexity, diffusion* and *dispersion, transmission* and *absorption.* Only if the student knows how to break these words into smaller chunks will they be digestible.

Our coverage of decoding and spelling has been lengthy. We have placed it at the end of the chapter because the other components are more essential to genuine literacy, in our judgment. If a child has "learned to read" but doesn't like books, little has been accomplished. If a student has a perfect score on spelling tests but hates to write, then actual damage has been done. On the other hand, children who enjoy being read to but cannot read on their own need help. And students whose spelling is so chaotic that they cannot read their own papers a week after composing them are shortchanged by teachers who argue that "it's the process that matters." The cognitive strategies that work for comprehension and composition, that foster development of vocabulary and concepts, are equally applicable to understanding the English spelling system. And the results can be impressive. Figure 3.17 displays compositions by three first-graders in a local school that combined the four Project READ curriculum elements. The students are from a variety of backgrounds, on average blue-collar. These are first-graders, and while their handwriting was pretty good, we transcribed their work for ease of reading. The original spelling was preserved. The first piece is a collaborative venture written in January after a local showing of Tchaikovsky's ballet. The second and third pieces are from a May assignment based on another field trip, this time to the circus. Elena's journal entry is typical for this class. Some students wrote more, some a little less. But all were able to create a readable exposition. Michael's work is more remarkable than appears on the surface. This young boy is diagnosed with fetal alcohol syndrome, and he could have become the wild kid in the classroom. Instead, he became the class poet. In September he could read nothing. At year's end, he presented Calfee with a special poem. These works are not yet perfect, but they show the possibilities when students begin to understand the four components of critical literacy. What happened at North Shoreview was not unique.

Is That All? Is It Enough?

"Teach a few things well." The READ model presumes that teachers can lead students to critical literacy by following an instructional strategy with four elements, and a curriculum design that also contains four elements. Surely there must be more to the program than this? And the answer is yes, much more is required. The framework furnished by CORE and VEND provides a foundation for making sense of all the crazy-busy things that happen when 25 to 35 children are placed in the same room with one adult. CORE and VEND provide the conceptual foundation, but bringing Project READ to life depends on the art and wisdom of classroom teachers. In the chapters that follow, we describe how the program has played out in different settings. Unlike the basal reader, Project READ places on the teacher the daily task of making decisions about what to teach and how to teach it, and collaboration among teachers has been an important factor in the success of the

The Nutcracker

Written by Rachel and Mallorie, Illustrated by Nathan and Mickey, Songs by Melissa

One morning it was Christmas. it was a nice moring. the two kid's opened there prasants. the girl's Grandpa gave her a nutcracker   it was pretty. The little girl sang a song. it was called Jungle bell's

Dash-ing through the snow, in a one-horse o-pen sleeigh
Laugh-ing all the way.
Bells on bob-tail ring, mak-ing spir-its bright
What fun it is to rigd and sing a sleigH-ing song to nigHt!
Jin-gle bells, jin-gle bells   Jin-gle all the Way. Oh, what fun it is to ride in a one-horse-o pen sleigy.

The girl thowtht he was so pretty that she like him a lot's

The tree got pretty   So the nutcracker got pretty too.

the girl like's him.

The End

Elena's Journal

One day the circus train came to town.
I lived in the town that they came to.
They had lions & tigers & bears.
Oh, my! Today they are setting up
They are setting up the tents and the actors & clowns are practicing.
The people came to see it. The jugglers are reddy. Every butty is reddy.
The circus people worked very hard for this circus, so you could see it.

Michael's Journal

One day the clown pelple couldn't stat the circus.
A little boy said, "yes, you can."
His dad said,
    "I hava monkey." "you do?"
"yes!" "now, you don't!"
"yes, I do!" The monkey came on the stage.
The show stated, and the kids and the Dads and the Moms were there.
The monkey did some trixs.
The kids stated claping.
I wish that I had a monkey
I would play with thaem and make a bed for him and fed him
and let him woch korttos.

Figure 3.17
Writing samples from READ students.

program. As we zoom back from the classroom to the school, our two crucial themes will be the importance of teacher collaboration and the energy that arises from a sense of community.

It's 8:30 a.m.: What Is Your Child Learning? 4

hapter 3 offered snapshots of classroom learning framed against a conception of cognitive instruction and a curriculum of critical literacy. The aim in this chapter is to describe how that concept plays out in a variety of classroom settings.

Never mind the headlines, the test scores, the theories, and the rest. Prepackaged educational programs lack the flexibility to survive in different contexts. The real stuff of schooling—the daily interaction of teachers and students—is acted out in individual classrooms all around the country. Those classrooms may serve run-down neighborhoods or campuses with manicured lawns and clean streets. But let's overlook these contrasting exteriors and focus on the essence of the educational experience, the *reading lesson*. Some examples in the recollections that follow are not about "reading" in the usual sense—the first scenario is a lesson in high-school economics. But in every instance, the focus is showing how a teacher can transform the daily lesson from an assembly-line experience to one that connects students' experience, knowledge, and beliefs to the academic knowledge and skills essential for survival in an information age.

Telling and Teaching

The most common teaching method at colleges and universities is direct instruction: "telling." A professor lectures to a classroom of students who presumably don't know as much as the professor, and who therefore take copious notes from the expert. The same teaching style is commonplace in the precollege years. Developmental stages and individual differences notwithstanding, teachers mostly talk and children mostly listen. Student reactions are brief answers to stylized questions. Consistent with a factory model of education, students are empty vessels to be filled in assembly-line fashion. A simple index of this phenomenon is the amount of "teacher talk," the percentage of classroom discourse occupied by the teacher rather than students. In the typical college lecture, 95 percent of all talk is by the professor. As early as fourth and fifth grade, elementary and secondary teachers follow the same pattern. While they may intend to foster discussions, teachers ask virtually every question (except for intrusions like "Can I go to the bathroom?" or "Is this going to be on the test?") and student answers tend to be short and literal.

"Today's kids don't know a lot. It's hard to get them to interact." True enough. The omnipresence of television and the diffusion of family life mean that many kids go for days without engaging in a real conversation. This state of affairs does not mean that children have nothing to say, nor that they are incapable of interaction. The CORE technique described in Chapter 2 suggests that the key is to *connect* through authentic questioning. Splendid models can be found in enemy territory: think about the interchanges on television talk shows (Phil Donahue and Oprah Winfrey) or advice columns ("Dear Abby" and "Dr. Ruth").

What students have to tell. Up to this point our examples have been from the elementary grades. Let's go to an economics class at Yerba Buena High School east of San Jose, California. Yerba Buena is in a poor neighborhood, a port of entry for new arrivals from around the world. Several teachers have tried READ techniques with their classes, but most teachers are initially skeptical, especially those assigned to teach the state-mandated economics course.

The biggest stumbling block, according to the teachers, is the textbook; students in the lower tracks were simply unable to grasp the concepts. Twenty students and four teachers gathered for a special lunchtime lesson on the chapter entitled "Business Organizations." According to the textbook, businesses are organized as *proprietorships, partnerships,* and *corporations.* Students are to learn the differences among these three types of businesses. Visiting Project READ director Bob Calfee agreed to teach a lesson on this chapter. The students ranged widely in ability, some from the upper track and others from the remedial group. Unused to sitting next to their teachers, students munched silently on their sandwiches.

Calfee began the lesson by writing several vocabulary items from the textbook:

economics entrepreneur joint proprietorship corporation profit

Calfee: What do you guys think economics is all about? What words come to your mind when I say "economics?" [Long pause.]

Students: Money. Scarcity. Products. Profit. Services.

Calfee: Why do you think we need to know about economics? What's the value? [Silence. Teachers frown.] Have you got an economic system at home? Is your family an economic system? [More silence.]

Brendan: Yeah, I think so.

Calfee: Say more. [Silence.] How do you handle money? Do you guys have anything to do with money at home? [Someone mumbles about money and "decision-makers."]

Calfee: Who decides?

Ngo: Parents.

Calfee: Do you have a job?

Ngo: No.

Calfee: Ever had a job?

Ngo: No.

Calfee: You get an allowance?

Ngo: No. I just ask.

Calfee: Tell me a little more about how that happens.

Ngo: If I need money for lunch or for other things that I want, I just go ask them.

Calfee: Why don't you act it out with someone else—I'll play your father, Sam. [Laughter.]

Ngo:	[Taking up the challenge] Dad, I'm going on a field trip to Berkeley. I need $100 for lunch for a few days.
Calfee:	[Acting the father] A hundred dollars for lunch? That seems like a lot. Tell me why you need so much money.
Ngo:	[Hedging] OK, I'll take $50.
Calfee:	How about I give you $5?
Ngo:	I'll be staying for three days. Three meals a day . . . [Said with little conviction.]
Calfee:	Let's see. Nine meals. How much does a meal cost?
Ngo:	Ten dollars a day—just to be on the safe side . . . [More laughter.]
Calfee:	If we negotiate this and agree, three days, $30, I can afford that. You've got $30!
Calfee:	[To students] Can you deal with that? Have we got scarcity now? Could someone live off $30 for three days?
Students:	[With little conviction] Maybe.
Calfee:	You'd have to make tough choices. But you can take this same language and apply it to big business—which is what the chapter is about.

The discussion continued, students drawing from their own experience to define the words. They found within their own families examples of joint proprietorships and other abstractions buried within the textbook. A young Hispanic student, silent during the early discussion, raised her hand during the discussion of partnerships. "I think my parents are a partnership. They have this restaurant. They work together there for lunch and dinner, and they get home late every night. They don't really own it yet, and on weekends my sister and me help them. But I think that it's a partnership. Is that what they mean in the book?" Her example resonated with both students and teachers, who knew little about the strivings of this young woman's parents, recently arrived from Mexico, to establish a new life in the United States. Calfee led the way in creating a matrix to compare and contrast the three organizational types that were the academic focus of the chapter (Figure 4.1). The textbook defined the columns; the students selected the row categories. The lunch hour flew by. "Is he coming back?" a student asked on the way back to class.

	Proprietorship	Partnership	Corporation
How to start			
Size			
Number of owners			
Type of business			
Workers			

Figure 4.1
Matrix developed by Yerba Buena students to compare and contrast different types of business organizations.

This anecdote shows the contrasts between rote training and cognitive learning. First, rather than beginning with vocabulary to be memorized, Calfee helped the youngsters connect with the topic. The students actually knew a lot about economics—but they did not know what they knew. Patient, persistent, *genuine* questioning was essential to draw out their knowledge. Second, the lesson was organized, moving from a semantic web to a compare-contrast matrix. Finally, the instructor's questions linked the students directly to one another in a disciplined manner; the teacher was not a bottleneck. Students could talk to one another without the teacher's permission. The Chicana student was near the bottom of the economic ladder; none of the students were from well-to-do backgrounds, but most were better off than she was. The dialogue allowed her to tell her own story to classmates, but also helped clarify the partnership concept.

Students are more likely to remember a lesson like this—one connected with their world—than a typical textbook presentation. But the strategy is risky. One risk is *missing material.* The textbook chapter included several objectives not covered in the lesson. The concept of *corporation,* for one, was still fuzzy at the end of the luncheon lesson. For these ninth-graders (and their teachers as well, none of whom had specialized in economics), this remained a remote idea. What should students know about the topic, and how might a textbook best convey it in an interesting and organized way?

Second are the related risks of *time and management.* After the students left for their next class, the teachers ruminated on the lesson. They were intrigued by student reactions; virtually every youngster had opened up during the discussion. But teachers were concerned about time. "You know, it took a while before the students got going. Is that typical? And you took a lot of time to cover just a few vocabulary items." They worried about their expertise in handling open-ended discussion. What if students raise questions that a teacher can't answer? "What is a proprietorship, anyway?" asked one teacher.

Students may sometimes talk too much, but it is even more troubling when they remain silent. Calfee handled the first meager answers by turning to "hot buttons" like money and allowances. When the answer was brief, he asked, "Tell me more," and "Why?", which proved to be effective follow-ups. Abstract concepts were personalized by posing a concrete situation, drawing on students' previous experiences and imaginations, giving them room to play, and then returning to reality. Because the dialogue rang true, attention remained high throughout the lesson. The topic became personally important, so students stayed with it. The discussion was alternately serious and humorous. The questions had no simple answers, so every student could hazard a response and come away feeling successful. But this was a "special lesson"; how can the regular classroom teacher sustain interest day after day?

This high-school session has a different flavor from the elementary-school examples elsewhere in the book. In high school you've "got to cover the territory." High-school teachers feel responsible for moving every student through every page of the textbook. The goal is to ensure that students do well on the publisher's end-of-course test. Though this technique fails many students—even our best students are poorly served by a cover-the-earth approach—teachers are driven by "content coverage." Strategic learning requires understanding and reflection. It means changing schedules so that students can pursue a few matters in depth. It means that the teacher becomes an entrepreneur: "one who organizes, manages, and assumes the risks of an enterprise." At least that's how the economics textbook described it.

A teacher who listened. In today's high schools, teachers who see 30 or more different students every hour for six hours every day—150 to 180 different students—may be forgiven if they wince at the notion of student-centered education.[1] But we have met some entrepreneurs like Yerba Buena High School's Ed Sims. After the economics luncheon described above, we walked down the hall to Ed's social-studies classroom. An imposing (athletic and 6' 3") but personable presence, he was fortunate in that his students thought the world of him. After twenty years of teaching he had become extremely skilled at the lecture-recitation approach, but in 1989 he attended a Project READ institute and began to experiment with graphic organizers. He had already incorporated cooperative groups in his program, and he saw webs and weaves as a tool to build more effective student teamwork.

The class began as students wandered in and assembled themselves into teams of five or six. Sims sat at his desk, greeting individual students and handling special problems. Most students had arrived before the bell rang, but there were a few stragglers. Five minutes into the period, the teams were at work—and they actually seemed interested in latitude and longitude. They thumbed through their textbooks, scribbling notes on large sheets of castaway computer paper. Questions and comments floated through the air. "The highest point on the island has got to be here, because the colors get lighter. . . ." "It's going south. That means the numbers [latitude] ought to be lower. . . ."

Sims finally moved toward the podium to open the lesson.

Sims: Welcome back after the weekend to another exciting day in your favorite history class, and a very good afternoon!

Students: Good afternoon, Mr. Sims.

Sims: A couple of historical notes. On this day in 1859 a famous man was born, John Phillips Souza. He wrote marches—we used to have a marching band at Yerba Buena, and I hear it may be coming back. How many beats to the measure in a march? ["Four."] In a waltz? ["Three!"]

Sims: Great—you guys remember all this stuff. Another important event happened on this day in 1956. A fine young man joined the navy to help defend our country—who do you think it was?

Students: Mr. Sims!

Sims: That's right—and now, let us honor our country as we salute the colors of our flag.

The class stood and repeated the pledge of allegiance with remarkable enthusiasm. Sims had been front stage for three minutes of fast-paced repartee, doing most of the talking, not lecturing as much as engaging the students. They sat down, and he continued:

Today we're going to hear reports from each of the teams on the topic of physical geography. We've got to complete this material in the book, and each team has covered a different topic. Your job today is to teach the rest of us what you've learned. You've used cooperative learning to work together, and Project READ can help with webs and matrices.

Now, hypothetically, imagine that I'm from another planet. I really don't know about this place, and so you've got to help me—help all the rest of us—understand what you've studied. You've got to *explain*. Let's start with Team Five.

A dark-haired young woman, the team spokesperson, walked to the front of the room, chewing furiously on a piece of gum, and took the "magic wand" from Sims. She began her report:

Our topic is the earth in space. Our planet is actually a very small object moving around the sun, and the sun is a star in the Milky Way galaxy. A galaxy is a huge bunch of stars in, like, a huge pancake. Anyway, what's important to know about the earth is how it moves in space. We're going to explain how the earth moves, and I'll make a matrix to show all of these things.

The student drew lines on the board, following notes on her computer paper, and filled in the entries, commenting about each one as she wrote it down:

MOVEMENT	CAUSES WHAT?
Rotation	Day and night
Revolution	Four seasons

POSITION	CAUSES WHAT?
Solstice	Longest days or nights
Equinox	Days and nights are equal

As the report spun out, Sims interspersed comments: "That's a matrix—great!" "Equinox—see the 'equal' in it?" The report concluded, Sims brought the entire team to the front for a round of applause. Team Two followed with a report on landforms, which took shape as a rather complex web. The young reporter took some time to explain plate tectonics, using his hands to show how plates can ride up and over one another, or can "slip-slide." The Loma Prieta earthquake, a powerful temblor that had shaken Northern California a few weeks previously in October 1989, was fresh in students' minds (you can find details in Figure 1.4, page 13). The student continued, "The big earthquake we just had went sideways, and the land near the ocean actually went farther north." Sims interrupted, "Someone told me that the earthquake happened because San Francisco has too many heavy buildings, and it's so heavy that it's starting to sink, and that's why we had the earthquake. You mean that's not what happened?" The student patiently explained once more that the buildings had nothing to do with it— plate tectonics were at work. He then went on to fill in other entries on the web: internal forces (volcanoes), external forces (glaciers, wind, even water), faults and folds.

There was barely enough time for the five teams to complete their reports before the bell rang. We chatted with Sims about what we'd seen. "These kids are in high school, and many of them have been in this country for only a year or two," he told us.

> I think it's important to cover the book, the more so for those who are actually new citizens. But we don't have a lot of time; another couple of years and they'll be graduating. The team approach does a couple of things. First, we cover the material better, even for those students who are still slow readers. And you know what, I think that all of the kids are learning the really important things from the book. And it's a lot more motivating for the kids. They have to work hard on English vocabulary and some really tough ideas, but if they *want* to work on the stuff because they have to report it to the class, they learn a lot faster. One of the most important lessons in social studies is about working together for the good of the whole group. I put it to them this way. "You've all got a lot to learn, but if you work together, you'll all make it. That's what this country is all about," I tell them. And when we finish the book, we still have time for some projects that I think are important. I want them to do research on Santa Clara County, so they get an idea of our history, and how the County offices work and how to figure out the system. That's not in the textbook, but it's going to be important for these kids.

Today's educational reformers call for new blood in the teaching profession, preferring exceptional novices who will follow new paths laid out by the reformers. But the wealth of experienced and committed teachers in the nation's schools is a vital resource whose potential is stifled by assembly-line textbooks and tests. Ed Sims was a good teacher to begin with, and his capacity to connect with students was incredible. He loved teaching, and he respected students across the board. Underachieving students experienced the taste of success under his tutelage.

But the anecdote demonstrates how Project READ strategies complemented his talents and experience, and allowed him to explore openings with his students that a less-secure instructor might have found daunting. Sims passed away in 1993, and he will be missed.

Follow the Script or Build the Imagination?

What is happening to younger children at 8:30 a.m.? In high school, the lecture method dominates because of content coverage and teacher-directed instruction. Surely teachers of young children in the primary grades don't lecture! In actuality, they often become lecturers by default as they follow the prescriptions in the teacher's manual. This situation is strange given the many differences between the early grades and high-school education. Elementary teachers teach the same children all day; secondary teachers see different students every hour. Elementary education is child-centered; secondary education is subject-centered. Elementary teachers are generalists, secondary teachers are specialists. Elementary schooling prepares students to learn to learn, and content is less important than process; high school prepares students for the decisions about college and vocation, and specific content is critical.

At least that's the theory. Those with a developmental frame of mind see the early years of schooling as a bridge between home and school. Kindergarten begins with children's interests and experiences, storybooks and storytelling are the gateway to early literacy. By fifth and sixth grade, adolescents should move toward more-demanding academic tasks. But things often don't work out that way, as we shall see.

The script. The basal reading series described in Chapter 3 provides the foundation for reading instruction in most American schools. These series begin with good intentions. The preface to the teacher's edition of Silver Burdett & Ginn's fourth-grade reader, *Silver Secrets,*[2] proclaims:

> *We believe* that reading is the freedom to explore the ideas of all people, everywhere, past and present. . . . *We believe* that reading is a conversation between a reader and an author. . . . *We believe* that the teaching of reading begins with the child—the child's language, the child's own experiences, the child's world. The art and science of a teacher's work is to provide experiences that allow each child to build upon an ever-expanding body of knowledge and ability.

These beliefs are certainly in the spirit of Project READ.

The student's book in *Silver Secrets* offers a profusion of appealing illustrations and stories by a striking array of authors—Laura Ingalls Wilder, Isaac Bashevis Singer, Robert Louis Stevenson, among others. So far, so good. The problems arise with the pre-scripted lessons in the teacher's manual. In Chapter 3 we displayed a portion of an upper-grade lesson directing the teacher's every move. In fact, this pattern holds at every grade level.

For example, *Silver Secrets* opens with a unit (a collection of lessons) entitled "Imagine That!" Here is what the teacher is told to do:

> Discuss the unit theme: Have students turn to pages 12–13 in the Student Text and read the title, "Imagine That!" Ask them to close their eyes for a moment and imagine themselves riding a flying horse, off on an adventure that is very brave or very exciting. Allow time for volunteers to describe their adventures, pointing out that each person's imagination is a wonderful, rich source of adventure and fun. Explain that this unit is full of selections that will tickle their imaginations and put them in the middle of exciting adventures.

On the one hand, the basic idea makes sense—what better way to introduce children to reading than to capture their imaginations! But the manual, rather than trusting the teacher to decide what best connects with their students' interests, specifies a flying horse. The directions are so bland and stultifying that one can easily imagine teachers cracking up in disbelief. In fact, studies show that most teachers follow these scripts almost verbatim.

Perhaps we are being unfair. After all, this is only the introductory material for the unit. Maybe this initial lesson is atypical? Alas, the prescriptive style pervades the entire manual. The first lesson is "The Cat and the Fiddle" by L. Frank Baum (of *Wizard of Oz* fame). The manual instructs the teacher: "Tell students that as you read the story out loud they may hear new words. Pronounce the following words and write them on the chalkboard. Tell students that the words will help them to understand the story better." The manual then lists the words *and* the correct answers [in brackets]:

VOCABULARY WORD	CORRECT ANSWER
companion	(friend)
mischievous	(delighting in teasing and pranks)
sober	(serious and quiet)
comical	(funny)

The teacher is then told to read the story, and to ask discussion questions from the manual; the correct answers once more are in brackets after each question:

- What words did the author use to describe the cat in the story? [Big, black tabby cat, sharp claws, dainty, long tail, and so on]

- Why did the cow "jump over the moon?" [She was frightened by the cat and the fiddle]

- What made Bobby think that Towser was laughing at the cat? [The dog barked and pranced; he sat panting with his mouth wide open, looking comical]

Silver Secrets is typical of the best-selling basals from kindergarten through eighth grade. The teacher follows a scripted sequence of activities from beginning to end of each lesson: introduce vocabulary, prepare students for the story, go through the story asking questions along the way, and end with practice exercises from the student workbook.

Most lessons make an effort to be attention-grabbing. For instance, in another series' teacher's guide for grade three, a story about jam-making suggests to the teacher:

> Invite students to turn to page 12 and read the title and look at the picture. Lead students to conclude that the people shown are the family they will read about in this story. Next, ask students what jam is. Encourage students who have eaten jam to tell how it tastes. If necessary, explain that jam is a sweet, sticky food made out of fruit, similar to jelly.

Even when it comes to jam making, the dialogue is teacher- rather than student-directed. Learning is rote, individualistic, and scattershot. There are no real opportunities for students to connect with stories and/or topics. The prose resembles the IRS 1040 tax manual.

Oh, yes, the manual suggests here and there that the teacher might adapt lessons to their styles and student interests. But for teachers, confronted by large and diverse classes, it is easier to follow the recipes. Energy begins to flag around the third week of September. Teachers are overwhelmed by the task of classroom management (a euphemism for keeping students from shouting, running through the halls, and throwing pencils). Basal lessons are not intrinsically interesting, which increases management problems. And so, at 8:30, after taking role and pledging allegiance to the flag, most teachers open the manual to the next lesson, write a list of words on the board, and ask: "Who can read this word and use it in a sentence?"

The power of imagination. What does the alternative look like? Let's pick up "Imagine That!" as a theme and revisit North Shoreview Elementary School, where teacher Ed Boell's third-graders are about to fly away on their "Magic Carpet." It is November 1992. As we enter the classroom, students are lying on the floor, each on his or her scrap of carpet, eyes closed, lights dimmed, quiet music streaming from a tape recorder. Boell walks around the room talking softly:

> We've just moved out onto the playground on our carpets, now we're going to move up, so we can see the school, now up some more—see the freeway traffic! Okay, get ready to fly away. Up into the air, not too fast, wherever you want to go. Look down, try to find someone, look for an interesting person: What do they look like? How are they dressed? What are they doing? Who else is there? What does the place look like? What year is it? What are the colors? sounds? smells? Now go back to the person you've spotted. What happened to him or her yesterday, the day before? How is the person feeling now? What are they thinking about? What's ahead for them tomorrow? How do you feel about them? What about their friends? their enemies?
>
> Okay, now we've got to come back to the room. Zoom back into the playground—careful not to hit anyone. Let's line up single-file; everyone ready, now slowly move to the door, into the room, stop by your desk, now settle back down to the floor. Open your eyes—we're back!

To the observer, this event first seems a complete mystery. It appears for all the world as though you are looking at 35 sound-asleep third-graders taking advantage of a slightly kooky teacher to grab a post-lunch nap. No sound, no stirring, only an occasional wrinkled brow to suggest any cognitive activity. But the bodies slowly return to life at Boell's command. He turns on the lights and silences the tape recorder. The students stretch and uncurl, slowly meandering back to their seats.

"Now, let's find out where you've been," Boell continues. "Each table, talk about your Magic Carpet trip for a few minutes so you can report to the class." The tables bubble with conversation as small groups of students tell about their individual excursions. Boell wanders around the room—listening, raising an occasional question, taking the temperature—and finally halts the discussions. "All right, now let's pull the pieces together." He reminds the groups that their reports should focus on characters, setting, and plot—what was going on and what it was like. "We don't need to hear everything that happened," he says. "Pick out the really juicy parts. Who wants to be first?"

The hands go up, and for the next quarter-hour Boell is busy collecting the cream from the students' ventures. He sketches each report on a segment of the brown paper stretched across the chalkboard, his writing scribbled and synoptic, a character-plot-setting grid serving to organize the scribbles (Figure 4.2). Students direct additions and corrections, which Boell cheerfully accommodates. The final product looks like a mess, but it makes sense to the students.

Boell next assigns each team the task of making up a story based on the Magic Carpet trips taken by that table's students. Due in two

The Zoo	Star Drood Wars	Party at Disneyland
Setting	**Setting**	**Setting**
San Francisco Zoo Cold, wet, drizzly day	Outer space galaxy, Starship fighter, Drood machine (giant round black ball with lots of space guns)	Disneyland park, Small World, Fairy land in Small World
Characters	**Characters**	**Characters**
Samuel (student), Samuel's sister and father Lions, monkeys, parrots elephants	Luke Skywalker (LS), Drood Master, lots of little drood fiends, 3-CPO, R2D2	Susan (student), Susan's friends (all girls) Susan's mother Fairies and elves
Plot	**Plot**	**Plot**
• Go to zoo with father • Parrot house with squawky birds • Monkey cage, feed peanuts • Visit elephants, mother and baby • Lions—sister climbs fence, lion roars and chases her • Father rescues her	• LS flying through space, sees the terrible Drood machine • LS shoots rockets at Drood machine • LS uses space shield to escape • Drood Master uses Drood sword to get through space shield • LS and DM have big fight, and LS destroys Drood sword with laser sword • LS destroys Drood machine, but DM escapes	• Susan and friends go to Disneyland, get into boat for Small World • Boat stops at Fairyland, fairy godmother invites everyone to a party • Lots of cookies and cake and Sprite • Fairies and elves come out and dance • Fairy godmother gives everyone presents • Susan and friends get back into boat and sail away

Figure 4.2
Samples of students' story outlines following the Magic Carpet trip.

weeks, the stories are to show how the major character solved an important problem. To the inevitable questions—"Mr. Boell, how long does the story have to be?" "Mr. Boell, will we be graded?" "Mr. Boell, does spelling count?"—come the usual answers: "Long enough to tell the story." "Yes, but everybody can get a good grade." "You bet spelling counts—we're going to put these stories outside the main office."

Boell is a disciplinarian, but he also knows how to capture the imagination of his students. He develops the idea of "Imagine that!" not through a fixed script but by an internal "schema" that keeps him on course in the midst of what might seem chaos. In Magic Carpet, his goal is that his third-graders develop a clear conception of the elements of the narrative form, that they learn to both comprehend and compose. But he wants them to go beyond a rote understanding of these elements to the creation of imaginative stories. In this assignment the students write in teams; later in the year he will give more individualized tasks. Professional authors may write in isolation, but for young children learning the process, starting as teams is more productive and more fun.

A look at the neighborhood. To see how READ structures and strategies release children's imagination in another setting, we move across the country to Harlem's P.S. 194, also known as Countee Cullen School after the Harlem Renaissance poet. The five-story brick building, constructed during the Depression, looms above the dreary tenement buildings that crowd the neighborhood. Mary Muncie, an Alabama native, has taught at P.S. 194 since 1983. In 1987 she took a two-year maternity leave. When she returned to work, she heard about READ techniques from teacher-specialist Ila Johnson, who had introduced the program to ten teachers during a summer institute. Muncie has become a believer in CORE, which she thinks is working for her students—and they need all the help they can get.

Muncie knows only a little about the backgrounds of her second-graders—she assumes that most are on welfare, and thinks that at least two live in nearby residence hotels—because, although the children all live near the school, it would be unsafe for Muncie to visit the families. Nor is it safe for children to roam the neighborhood. They live in a city with incomparable resources; the United Nations, the Metropolitan Museum of Art, the Museum of Natural History, the Stock Exchange, the World Trade Center, Broadway—all can be easily reached by subway. Yet Muncie reports that most of her kids have never been outside Harlem and, indeed, seldom venture more than a few blocks from their homes.

This year Muncie is connecting her students to New York City. A posterboard up on the wall bellows: "A Visit to the Big Apple!"—a stylized apple sectioned to show the boroughs of Manhattan, Queens, Brooklyn, the Bronx, and Staten Island. Muncie has actually taken her second-graders on field trips to each of the five boroughs. The preparations have been challenging—parents don't have cars, and buses are difficult to arrange—but so far they've visited the Bronx, the Statue of Liberty on Staten Island, and most recently Madison Square Garden, where they saw the Barnum & Bailey Circus. "Most of them had never heard of the circus," she says. The posterboard is filled with artifacts collected during their visits.

Muncie began the project by using READ techniques to ignite the children's imaginations. Like kids everywhere, Muncie says, her students have a wealth of experiences and interests—animals, adventures, funny stories, silly words. But they lack strategies to help them retain school knowledge, and they have trouble paying attention. "The first thing is you have to get their attention," says Muncie. "Then they need skills to organize their thoughts and ideas, the information and concepts they read." Otherwise, a field trip is just a field trip.

And so the Big Apple project began with the Apple web shown in Figure 4.3. Muncie asked the students for everything they knew about the City. The figure contains only a sampling of the students' contributions. As they prepared for each trip, they added newspaper articles and photos, brochures collected by parents. The scribbled entries on their first web were remarkable for their complex and haunting quality. They came partly from images seen on the television news, partly from stories from parents and neighbors, but the students added a big dollop of their own thoughts and feelings.

Here in the middle of Harlem, Muncie is helping young children address issues central to their lives, an important job for these 7-year-

What We Know	What We Want to Know	How We Find Out
Big buildings	Why so much killing?	Ask the mayor
Airports	Why racism?	Read news, magazines
Has zoo	Why guns?	Go to library
Five boroughs	Why so many homeless?	Listen to TV news
	Why so many peole don't have jobs?	

Figure 4.3
Student web for project on the "Big Apple."

olds, and difficult to script in a standardized manual. The key in this classroom is a teacher who knows how to lead her students to build on their experiences as a foundation for attaining academic goals. A walk around the neighborhood is an opportunity for developing literacy skills.

How do we know how well Countee Cullen School is doing? According to the principal, test scores were up a bit, but not much. Project READ is still new to Countee Cullen. Ila Johnson, the teacher-specialist, is working with ten teachers, but that's only a quarter of the staff. The principal and many teachers have reservations—can anything really make a difference in New York City? Under these conditions, one cannot expect soaring test scores or dramatic turnarounds in schoolwide problems. But even the casual observer to Muncie's classroom can see students actively involved in their classwork. "Time-on-task," to use a cliché from another decade, is high. The careful observer can see a difference in what the students are saying, in how they express themselves, and in what they write. These students are not following the prescriptive routines of the basal reader. Nor are they lost in the touchy-feely activities of the 1960s. You have to look and listen, but the classroom provides the evidence that students are mastering the elements of critical literacy.

Encyclopedic Prose, or Writing from the Heart?

Writing is making a comeback in America's schools. Beginning in the 1940s, an increasing emphasis on test-driven accountability and behavioral objectives led to the "purple plague": reams of dittoed worksheets assigned for mindless practice on trivial tasks. The worksheets required little more than filling in blanks or matching words or pictures to empty slots. Writing more than a phrase or sentence became rare in the primary and elementary grades. High-school students might be assigned a few paragraphs, but the lack of adequate preparation in the early years of schooling led to a steady decline in student competence despite increasing graduation rates.

Because writing was not tested, it became a lower priority for teachers. In the 1970s, several surveys showed that relatively little class time was spent on writing instruction, and students' writing performance, when it was assessed, looked dreadful.[3] The proportion of students failing the University of California Subject A writing examination increased dramatically, and Stanford University developed a required writing course for first-year students.

The situation began to change in the mid-1970s. At the University of California's Berkeley campus, an educational team began to explore alternatives to the standard "writing assignment" approach. The Bay Area Writing Project, a collaboration of university professors and language arts teachers, emphasized writing as a *process* as well as a *product*.[4] Classroom teachers, many of whom had not done serious writing since college graduation, spent summers writing, recapturing the experience of composing their own work.

At about the same time, several states added writing tests to state-wide assessments of reading and math. The tests left much to be desired. Most relied on a standardized prompt ("Write an essay about the most important experience in your life"), with limited time ("You have thirty minutes for this assignment") and no opportunity for preparation or revision. Nonetheless, writing was tested, and so it began to matter. As a result of programs like the Bay Area Writing Project (now the National Writing Project) and state testing, teachers at all grades now include writing in the daily schedule. But what happens during writing varies considerably, as we shall see below.

Copy the encyclopedia. Real writing is hard work. A student can read a book without comprehending it, but it is virtually impossible to compose passively. Nonetheless, where there is a will, there is a way. State writing assessments typically specify a set of formats or genres—the persuasive argument, the personal narrative, even the five-paragraph essay—to be tested, along with scoring guides and model compositions. Teachers use these specifications and materials as guides. The result is that student writing often amounts to little more than copying the style guides. Many of us learned this strategy when we were in high school. A successful research report paraphrased an encyclopedia entry, and a book report meant rewriting the flyleaf. Copying didn't always work, but it set the stage—writing was from teachers and for teachers.

A test-based approach to writing instruction relies on practice. The teacher develops writing activities around the various formats. "Today's assignment is to write a persuasive piece on *school uniforms*. Pick one side or the other, for or against, and tell why you feel that way. Any questions?" "How long does it have to be?" "Does spelling count?" "Does it matter which side I pick?" The answers to these sixth-graders' questions is predictable: one page long, spelling counts, and it doesn't matter which side you argue.

The students spend the writing period hunched over their desks—they may not have access to encyclopedias, but these don't deal with practical matters like school uniforms anyway. At the end of the period, the papers are handed in, and a day or two later come back with a grade and red marks indicating problems, usually in spelling and grammar.

Students understandably come to believe that writing is about the mechanics. In one Midwestern school, Calfee began a lesson by asking third-graders, "How do you get started when you want to write something?" The students were unanimous: "Indent and capitalize!" Calfee visited several other district schools during his stay, and found that every class was convinced of this proposition. In another program, students had to critique their compositions. This sounded promising, and so Calfee asked several students, "What would make your paper better?" "I need to check my spelling and grammar, and to write more."

We have labeled this section "copy the encyclopedia" to capture the essence of an approach that skates on the surface. Students learn a style of writing that lacks both substance and structure. If the paper is long enough and if the mechanics pass muster, then all will be well. The best students learn to write encyclopedic prose. Less able students learn that they can't write, and simply place their heads on the desk. The following sections show how READ structures and strategies open the door for all students to genuine writing.

Writing from the heart—and head. The major task in genuine writing is developing and organizing ideas and words: mechanical details don't really count until the final version. Most U.S. students know how to *write*; they don't know how to *compose*. What are the elements of an effective strategy for composing a work? The process is certainly important, so is the structure, and the quality of the final product can matter a lot. But college composition books often argue for the importance of a sense of audience and purpose, someone to say something to for some reason. When teachers are the primary audience, exchanges quickly become pointless and boring. "You'll be graded" is one way to establish purpose, but external motivation is generally less potent than internal drives. Once audience and purpose are established, then students need techniques for getting their thoughts out into the open, and for building the skeleton of a composition. As noted in Chapter 3, the standard outline quickly becomes stultifying. Semantic webs and weaves are more flexible and engaging.

Finally, learning to write goes much more quickly and effectively when it is social rather than individual. Students need to learn to closet themselves for writing tests, and a few people become professional writers who write alone. But in the world beyond school, corporate writing is often a group effort, and for the young learner, teamwork is the way to go. Research shows that cooperative learning, when effectively managed, means that students benefit individually while also complementing one another's strengths and limits, and that achievement is better across the board.[5] In addition, students learn to reflect and to work with one another.

To see how the theory plays out in practice, we go to Gale School on Chicago's North Side. Like all too many Chicago schools, Gale looks like it was built after the Great Fire and hasn't been repainted since. Several Gale teachers have attended a Project READ institute, and Principal Edie Snyder has invited Calfee to visit—and to teach a class. Gale is a K–8 school, and the eighth-graders are preparing for the upcoming state test, which includes writing. Ronda Kramer runs a special class of fifteen students identified as learning-disabled, and they are having trouble. Kramer feels confident that the students can handle formats like Personal Narrative and Informational Essay, but they are in turmoil about Persuasive Argument.

Kramer introduces Calfee as "someone who can help you get ready for the test." The students listen to her; they seem to think that she's OK. They aren't sure about Calfee: "You guys don't seem very happy about the test?" Nods of assent, as students slouch even lower in their seats. "Why not?" "We don't know what to write." "I hear that it's Argument that you're worried about." Again, the students nod agreement. The lesson begins:

Calfee: Let's find something to argue about. What are you un-
            happy about here at Gale?
Student #1: We gotta go to school.
Student #2: It's not that bad.
Student #3: We gotta take this stupid test.
Student #4: We don't have enough lockers.
Calfee: Lockers—you've got problems with lockers?
Student: Yeah—they don't have enough lockers, and so we gotta
            share them. . . .

Calfee's wife is a middle-school principal, and he has heard first-hand about the importance of lockers in adolescent life—a place of privacy and security. To share a locker is anathema. A hot topic, and a point of connection.

The next task is to organize the students' thinking. Calfee asks the students how to write a letter to the principal about the lockers. The response is vigorous and emphatic, students up in their seats proclaiming how stupid it is they don't each have their own lockers, and doesn't Ms. Snyder know about all the problems like too many things packed together and people mixing up their things. Calfee records the comments on the board.

"Suppose we wrote a letter to Ms. Snyder about lockers and how stupid she is not to fix this problem. Now, suppose you're Ms. Snyder and you get this letter? What would you say back?" The students think for a moment, and then answers begin to emerge. "She'll say we don't have enough lockers because we don't have any money to buy any more lockers." "The halls are already crammed with lockers, and there's no room." Calfee writes these items on the board.

There is a lull in the discussion, and Calfee asks, "Do you think Ms. Snyder would help with lockers if she could?" A pause, and then scattered comments to the effect that the principal has lots of things to do, but is by and large a reasonable person. Calfee proceeds:

> OK, I'm not sure that it can make a difference, but let's build a Persuasive letter to Ms. Snyder about lockers. An argument or persuasion is like a boxing match—do you guys know about boxing? [Most do.] First you climb into the ring and agree to the rules—you pick a topic like *lockers*. Then the bell rings and you come out for the fight. One person takes a swing, and then the other counterpunches. And it keeps going like that—punch and counterpunch—until you try for the knockout. An argument is like a matrix [Calfee knows that Kramer had introduced this label to the students as one of the writing formats], where you have "pro" and "con" columns. You take a punch—"We need our own lockers!"—and then *you* have to make a counterpunch for Ms. Snyder—"We don't have money or room." Then back to your turn—how to handle the problem of money and room?

As the lesson spins on, the pro and con columns begin to take shape (Figure 4.4). The students may do poorly on tests, but they have plenty to say about lockers, including some rather optimistic aspirations—maybe parents or local businesses can help with the money; a side hall has unused wall space. Calfee continues to write.

The hour is almost over, and Calfee is concluding: "I'm not sure what you guys can really do here, but you've certainly made a good argument. When you start the test, think about something that really matters to you, and then get into the boxing ring—punch and counterpunch. And remember, you have to play both sides to make it work."

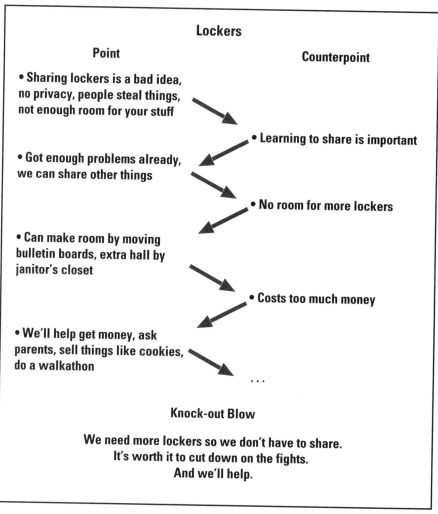

Lockers

Point	Counterpoint
• Sharing lockers is a bad idea, no privacy, people steal things, not enough room for your stuff	
	• Learning to share is important
• Got enough problems already, we can share other things	
	• No room for more lockers
• Can make room by moving bulletin boards, extra hall by janitor's closet	
	• Costs too much money
• We'll help get money, ask parents, sell things like cookies, do a walkathon	
	. . .

Knock-out Blow

We need more lockers so we don't have to share.
It's worth it to cut down on the fights.
And we'll help.

Figure 4.4
Graphic organizer for locker argument, Gale School in Chicago.

The door opens, Principal Snyder enters, and the room is silent. She studies the chart on the board for a moment, and then turns to the class. "I know you are really unhappy about the lockers, but this is a good argument. You have lots of ideas that might help us do something. It's already March, though, and we won't get any new lockers before you graduate. But if you wanted to help next year's class, I'd be willing to use your help in talking with parents and with the local stores."

We don't know how this story turned out. Principals are busy people, and the students' aspirations may have been unworkable. Our main point is the potential of graphic organizers to help students create a composition—and the importance of a sense of audience and purpose for energizing them to do the hard work needed for this task.

Before we leave Chicago, let's briefly visit Disney Magnet School, viewed by many locals as one of the more-privileged schools in the city (as we shall see in the next chapter, not everyone on the Disney faculty agrees with this judgment). Kelly McKee's sixth-grade Disney class is quite a contrast with Ronda Kramer's at Gale—more students, and clearly above-average ability. For Black History month, McKee's class has surveyed a variety of literary works, from *To Kill a Mockingbird* to *How the Leopard Got Its Spots*. The latter, an African folktale, appears better suited to younger children, but it was part of a collection that McKee had put together. In fact, it turned out to be a favorite in her class.

Writing often spins off from reading—the encyclopedia need not be a wasted effort, nor should a folktale. The lesson begins:

> We've read quite a few books this month, and you really like the story about the leopard. I've got an idea. Suppose we were to make this story into a play for the second-graders downstairs. What would we have to do?

Over the ensuing hour, the students explore the task of reaching a younger audience to communicate—what? What was the story really about? The teacher, not completely sure where the discussion will go, nonetheless keeps it moving. Several students—usually rather quiet—volunteer that staging and artwork might be important. Then a boy comments, "You know, this story is not like a lot of other fairytales that those kids know about. Usually the bad guys get killed. But here the leopard doesn't die—he changes and gets better. I think that's the message we need to try to tell. Of course, those second-graders are pretty small, and they might not get it, anyway." This very capable sixth-grader is developing a sense of audience and purpose. Motivation is the energy that fuels the effort, and the READ structures and strategies help to organize and build.

McKee's students work with stories, but down the street at Agassiz Elementary School, Leah Fietsam's third-graders have begun to master the writing of sequential exposition, compositions that lay out the steps in a process and explain how one connects with the other. This type of writing is difficult to understand and to create and is seldom included in the elementary curriculum. Fietsam's class has created "The Great How-To Book," displaying a wide range of sequential compositions. Each student selects a task or activity from a large collection:

"Making a phone call," "Throwing a football," "Cooking pancakes." The first draft sketches the exact movements in the task, along with the important vocabulary words, using either a "linear string" or "falling dominoes" structure (see Figure 3.9 on page 88). The linear string gives a list of steps in a process: "Go to the hardware store, then the produce shop, and finally the florist." The falling dominoes add cause and effect: all of the above, along with "That way, the fruits won't get hot and the flowers won't wilt." The second draft takes shape as a rough composition, which teacher and students critique and edit. The third draft is a polished version appropriate for the "Book." Figure 4.5 shows a couple

---

How to read a book

First, you find a book you want to read. You can find a book by reading the back cover. Or read a recommended book by a friend, or a librarian, or even a book you just bought.

Secondly, go into a quiet room so you can concentrate better. If you go into a noisy room you won't be really knowing what's happening in your book.

Then put on some comfortable clothes so you won't be uncomfortable. Also in that room find a good chair to sit in.

To begin open your book to where you are at or if you just started start at page one. (you also can get a snack.)

Now start reading and make sure you understand before you get far. It is better if you would look up a word you don't know.

How to babysit

I love to babysit and I can teach you. Here is how you do it.

First someone calls you on the phone and asks you to babysit their child or baby. Then they invite you to their house.

Before you go to their house you have to know where they live, wher they are going, what time you should be there, what time they are leveing, what time they are coming back.

An important thing to know is when you babysit for someone you need to know what type of area they live in, if the house is secure, and if you don't trust the person please do not babysit for them.

The restaurant

• Take a shower and a bath. I am dressd up. We go in the car. We get out of the car. We walk in the door. We wait. Order food. We eat. Pay bill. Go home. Go to bed now.

• You have to get dress up. Lets go git in the car. I am eating in a Restaurant. I am got a cop of weter. Lets go

• The hostess ask us how many people I said 4 we got our menu. we ortered pizza and 2 diet cokes a orange ande 7.up.

Figure 4.5
"How-to" compositions from fifth-graders at Agassiz School in Chicago;
first-grade "restaurant" papers from Norwalk–La Mirada.

of examples of fifth-grade work from Agassiz, as well as a few similar compositions from a first-grade classroom in the Norwalk–La Mirada district in Southern California.

Not all student writing needs to be serious, of course. Nor are the READ structures the only possibilities. The guiding principle is that students are more likely to engage in authentic writing if they have a purpose in writing and structural frameworks to help them organize their thoughts. In Morris Houck's fifth-grade classroom at North Shoreview, poetry is a favored activity. Houck uses a variety of methods, but the model in Figure 4.6 is notable for its simplicity and its effectiveness. His aim in this activity is to encourage students to play

---

A THING [start with a noun]

DOES SOMETHING [verb in the middle]

WHEN, WHERE, WHY [ending phrase]

The flag Shakes When the wind attacks	The volcano Burst with laughter and lava When it was tickled
The Statue of liberty Smiles When people come into the country	The smoke Detector Screams with fright When the house has bad breath
A volcano Is like a cut That is bleeding	A crayon Is like A part of the rainbow
The volcano Threw up When it ate rocks	

Figure 4.6
Poems by Maurice Houck's fifth-graders, North Shoreview School.

with word meanings, with metaphors and shades of meaning. The model relies on free-verse triplets that begin with a noun, add a verb phrase, and conclude with a final phrase; as you can see, Houck slips in a bit of painless grammar along the way. The playfulness of the verse shows a remarkable command of the language on the part of students who would normally be considered at risk for academic failure.

Marriage in the fifth grade. Our final snapshot comes as we walk up to the fourth floor of a depressing brick school in the Bronx and enter Inez Ferguson's fifth-grade classroom. A hamster crouches in a large cage. Student writing decorates the walls. Students work away at clusters of tables. Then there is Ronald, sitting at a desk next to Ms. Ferguson. Ronald, an outgoing boy with merry eyes, an infectious grin, and (Ferguson reports) an unstoppable mouth, has this special seat "for his own good."

Ferguson's fifth-graders are doing "A Family Affair." Earlier in the month, Ferguson had assigned the social-studies chapter on the Civil War. As usual, most students "didn't get it." Rather than moving on to the chapter on Reconstruction, Ferguson decided instead to stop and try the CORE model. How could she connect the Civil War with her kids' families in an organized and reflective way? And how to use this connection, once established, for academic outcomes?

A brief segment in the Civil War chapter describing the dreadful separation of slave families struck Ferguson as especially poignant. She noted a link to a later section that told about the divisions between families North and South during the war. The Civil War—like current problems of poverty, crime, and drugs—disrupted family life. In Ferguson's class, a total of two students were from traditional households. Many others were living with single mothers or grandparents. The topic of family life would be worth pursuing for a few days, and it might bring the Civil War to life.

Ferguson began with a word splash, the simplest form of a web described in Chapter 3. "What words come to mind when you think about *family*? What are families like? What kind of family do you hope for when you grow up?" The questions were straightforward enough, but the answers were unsettling. The children seemed to know more about television families than their own. Ferguson asked students to ask their mothers for wedding photographs; one child brought an album to show the class. She persisted: "What do you think about doing a project on families?"

The students expressed some interest—why not. Most spent their off-hours inside apartments, and they knew relatively little about each other's families. How to collect useful information? Wedding albums were scarce, but how about other family photos and documents? The project began. Students pestered relatives and grandparents for artifacts, and the classroom walls gradually sprouted with snapshots of soldiers from World War II (ancient history), grandparents in hand-tinted portraits, relatives at the beach in antique bathing suits and rubber swim caps. Family Bibles, immigration papers, handwritten letters, birth and death certificates— stationery boxes, desk drawers, and even a few suitcases yielded up a multitude of treasures. Ferguson suggested webs and weaves to help students organize around various themes—recreation, foods, dress, transportation, architecture. Exploring their roots was giving students an appreciation of history far more lively than the textbook.

Three weeks after it began, the project culminated in a "family wedding" ceremony. Names were drawn from a hat to select the bride, groom, and honor attendants. The entire class worked on the event: the ceremony, the guest list, and even honeymoon plans. Ronald, the talkative boy with the big grin, drew the part of groom. "I was shocked," he recalls, suddenly and uncharacteristically bashful. "Everybody was looking at me—I'd never done anything like that before." The class promoted the wedding in a major way. Relatives were invited, and many came. Ronald was ecstatic; his grandparents, uncle, mother, father—even his sister, who was in another class at the school—all came.

Ronald, speaking about the event a month afterward, is proud. "It made me feel happy—it made me feel part of everything." Students seldom experience the luxury of a project like "Family Affair." In particular, children like Ronald who are identified as low-achieving have their noses kept to the basic-skills grindstone. Ferguson designed the activity to develop high-level skills in planning and in teamwork, and in the bargain provided the class with a bridge to better understand the world of which they are a part.

What about the Civil War? And Reconstruction? These students are, after all, in fifth grade. What if they miss a chance to learn about Gettysburg and carpetbaggers? This tension pervades our entire book. In the textbook, the battle of Gettysburg was mentioned in one sentence, and Lincoln's address didn't make it. Carpetbaggers got an entire paragraph. Perhaps the studious youngster reading the two chapters would appreciate the significance of these events—and the possible insignificance of other content. But maybe not. Virtually every college graduate has read about the relation between seasonal changes and the Earth's polar inclination. But studies have shown that even Harvard grads don't really understand this relation. We all remember incredible sunsets, the sun slowly slipping below the horizon. But we have all "learned" that the sun doesn't set; the earth turns.

Academic content is important, for all students. But unless the context of learning connects and organizes, then the details will end up in the recesses of memory. More important, instruction that emphasizes the transmission of knowledge does not provide students with strategies or motivation for future learning. These generalizations apply across the board. The more-capable students may pass the tests on a diet of

facts, but the research shows that they are actually the greatest benefi-
ciaries when instruction opens the way for guided discovery.

For Ronald, we can only wonder about the long-term effects of this
experience. Ronald exuded a sense of accomplishment. Could his mock
wedding carry over into adult life, breaking the transgenerational
patterns that afflict him and many of his classmates? Ronald has the
stigmata of a problem child: a candidate for discipline and isolation, a
regular visitor to the principal's office. At least this one time, Ferguson
was able to weave him into the fabric of the classroom, channeling his
loquacious energy into productive outlets—and for a while he actually
enjoyed school.

What Can a Teacher Do?

The preceding snapshots, each focused on an individual classroom, are
tributes to the competence and creativity of teachers working under
tough conditions. Large classes with needy students are a challenge,
but even more difficult is the task of shifting from the factory model to
strategic instruction. Teachers in schools with small classes and advan-
taged students can get by, so they often have little motivation to do
anything other than what they are already doing. "Nothing succeeds
like success." But, like most adages, this one has its limits. Even the
most capable teacher cannot guess what lies over the next hill unless he
or she makes the trip, which can be both risky and rewarding.

Graystone Elementary in San Jose is scarcely an "at risk" school.
Pam Matsuoka was a successful teacher when Project READ began to
emerge as a collaboration between Graystone and Stanford University
in the early 1980s. Already something of a nonconformist, Matsuoka
made little use of prescriptive manuals and worksheets, and she found
it natural to add graphic organizers to her repertoire.

Matsuoka soon volunteered to demonstrate READ techniques to other
teachers. Her second-graders seem comfortable with the situation,
figuring that it's "kinda neat" to have grown-ups watching. On this
particular day, a dozen teachers from a downtown school sit in the back
of the classroom. The children form a semicircle on the carpet around
Matsuoka. The topic is "Ocean," a webbing activity in preparation for
a field trip to San Francisco's Steinhart Aquarium. Matsuoka writes
OCEAN in bold print on the blackboard, and as students volunteer
responses she writes them in clusters: flora, fauna, and environment,
and a space for "weird" terms and phrases that don't mesh with her
predetermined organizational scheme (Figure 4.7). Within several

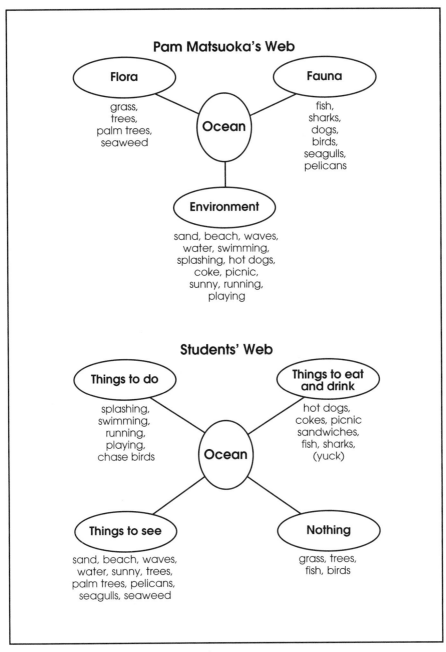

Figure 4.7
"Ocean" webs by Pam Matsuoka's second-grade students;
the upper web is Matsuoka's structure, and the lower web is
how her students decided to organize the seashore.

minutes she has filled the board with student words and phrases.

Matsuoka then asks: "Now, why do you think I put the words together in each of these groups?" Silence—not the best response for a demonstration lesson.

A student raises his hand; "I can't figure it out. . . ." Matsuoka answers, "I have a good reason for the groups. What do you think it is?"

"I wouldn't do it that way!" another boy intervenes. Not the "right" answer, but Matsuoka responds with respect: "How would you do it?"

This reply, so natural outside of school, is seldom found *in* school, where teacher's answers are sacred. The students reactions are fascinating: "Well, I'd put together those things that you can play with." "Yeah, and then some of the things you can eat—at least some people eat them." "Some people even eat seaweed." "And sharks!" "And a lot of the stuff isn't worth anything—it's just there."

Recognizing that the students' classifications are based on nature rather than science, Matsuoka rewrites OCEAN on the neighboring chalkboard, and transfers words from one chart to the other. The lesson has stretched the second-graders to discuss classification schemes, a much higher-level lesson than she had intended. Matsuoka takes the risk that the lesson won't go as planned—and it doesn't. But because she has been responsive to the students rather than to her preparations, she gets superior results. Project READ contributes to this event by offering an instructional strategy—CORE—that serves as a springboard for Matsuoka's natural inclinations. Project READ provides graphic organizers that allow her students to make public their implicit conceptions.

Teachers can move from the tried and true to become explorers and experimenters with their young charges. Classroom walls are a daunting barrier. Elementary teachers live lives of quiet desperation, isolated from one another by a lack of a common professional language, lacking time for collegial interaction. Most stay on the job because they value the connection with students, not because of the pay and working conditions. Genuine reform, if it is to come about, will start with the "engine" that drives schooling, the daily lessons. The job ahead is to rebuild this engine so as to create a new professional atmosphere and motivation, one that influences the entire school. It is to this task that we turn next.

Wanna Trade Places With Mrs. Ward? 5

What is it like to be a teacher? We know a lot about the school as a workplace. Elementary schools are more tolerable than middle schools, and high schools are difficult places for everyone. Elementary schools are generally small, almost homelike: one or two teachers at each grade level, a principal, the school secretary, the custodian, a few "resource" teachers to handle students with special needs—twenty or so adults tending 400 or so children.[1]

Teachers in U.S. schools spend more of their working day in the classroom with students than in any other developed nation. They may mingle at the beginning and end of the day, but their minds are usually preoccupied with preparing for class. Midday brings a half-hour break for munching a sandwich while handling yard duty. The principal arrives early and leaves late, the day full of phone calls and student and parent problems, the evening taken up with committee meetings and bureaucratic papers. The secretary holds the fort while the custodian keeps the place liveable (imagine cleaning bathrooms for hundreds of children).

Adults see one another only in passing. The periodic faculty meeting, one of the few times when everyone gathers in the same room, means a bevy of announcements, an opportunity to gripe, and a chance to grade papers. Teaching is a life isolated from adults and filled with crowds of children, day after day, week after week, year after year.

The physical environment of schools varies enormously throughout the country. Some schools are a delight to behold: brightly colored, one-story bungalows set among green lawns and inviting playgrounds; entry halls lighted by picture windows and brightened by patches of student art; quiet, inviting staff rooms where teachers can find a cup of coffee and a corner couch during the brief moments when they are not with children.

Other schools offer much less attractive prospects. In Chapter 2 we quoted Jonathan Kozol's book *Savage Inequalities* about the unsightliness of many urban schools. The situation is no better inside these schools: "Hallways dark with light bulbs missing or burnt out. . . : 'You can smell the urinals a hundred feet away. . . .' One hundred ten students in four classes, but only 26 books. . . . Classrooms so cold in winter that students have to wear their coats to class, while others swelter in a suffocating heat that cannot be turned down."[2] Kozol lambasted these inequalities because of how they afflicted students, but teachers live under the same roofs. If schools are to become better places for students, they also need to become better places for grown-ups. When Evelyn Taylor became principal at North Shoreview, her first act was to improve the physical environment. She issued a barrage of work orders. A burnt-out portable classroom was removed from the school playground, the buildings were painted, the teachers' workroom was carpeted and decorated with bright colors. She appealed to local stores for peanut butter and day-old bread. She took care of basic needs first, and after that turned to the task of creating a professional environment for her staff.

You Can't Hide Here

In the 1970s, Chicago schools embarked on an experiment in Mastery Learning, the ultimate in behaviorally engineered education. A new curriculum was constructed around "objectives-based tests," which expected students to master little isolated bits of knowledge, and teachers were tightly scripted to instruct students on the objectives. School days were a succession of prescribed worksheets and multiple-choice tests. Auditors visited classrooms to ensure that teachers were hewing to the mandates. The experiment eventually ended with the arrival of a new superintendent. Teachers returned to basal textbooks, a breath of freedom after Mastery Learning.

In the late 1980s, Chicago schools came under the unpitying glare of the media spotlight when a *Chicago Tribune* team published an award-winning, in-depth series of articles on schools that Secretary of Education William Bennett trumpeted as "the worst in America." *Tribune* Editor James D. Squires wrote of a system "so bad that nothing short of wiping it out and starting over can save public education in one of the nation's great cities." A citywide coalition cobbled together a reform agenda and persuaded the Illinois legislature to turn school governance over to the people. Local School Councils were elected in each neighborhood with authority to hire and fire principals, determine the budget, and review the school management plan. The results of the experiment remain uncertain; some Councils seem to be working effectively, but there are also horror stories. To make matters worse, the District opened the 1993–94 school year faced with a $300 million deficit. The cost of training the new school council members and the other educational players had stretched an already tight budget almost to the breaking point. What about student achievement? It actually dropped a bit during the reform years.[3] The State of Illinois managed to bail out the city schools, and the 1994–95 school year started on schedule. Despite repeated threats of early school closure and a deficit in the hundreds of millions, the Chicago schools managed to complete the year. As of this writing, the Illinois legislature is considering another major reform of the Chicago schools, and benefits for student learning are yet to be seen.

Walt Disney School, on Chicago's north side, represents another experiment. To the east lies Lake Michigan and spacious Lincoln Park, to the west the skyscrapers of uptown and, less visible, a collection of impoverished neighborhoods eventually verging on Cabrini Green, a housing complex that epitomizes the devastation wreaked by poverty, crime, and drugs. Disney, a squat, three-story, concrete-and-tinted glass cube, looks more like an office building than a school. The facility is enormous, providing space for students from preschool through eighth grade. The Communication Arts Center serves as a reminder of Disney's original role as a performing-arts school. Each school morning, a stream of yellow buses disgorges more than 1,700 youngsters from the northern third of Chicago.

Disney was created in the late 1960s as a magnet school designed to promote racial integration, in response to court-ordered desegregation. The goal was to achieve a mix that was about 30 percent black, 30 percent white, 30 percent Hispanic, and 10 percent Asian. Because of its status as a magnet school, parents must request assignment to Disney. This procedure is simple, according to Principal Raphael Guajardo—"all the parent has to do is fill out a form." It is true that parents must have enough on the ball to understand what Disney has to offer, and to figure out how to work the system—a new immigrant intimidated by paperwork in a foreign language or a poorly educated parent who doesn't realize that quality varies from school to school might not submit an application. In fact, the system appears to be working reasonably well. Two hundred fifty kindergartners were selected at random from the 3,600 applicants for the 1993 class. The demographics of the entering kindergartners generally mirrored those of the city at large. Sixty-three percent of the students were from low-income families compared with 80 percent in the school district as a whole; one out of eight students was "limited-English-proficient," three out of four were nonwhite.

As for resources, Disney is currently in about the same boat as other Chicago schools. In the 1970s, with roughly the same enrollment as at present, the school had almost twice as many teachers, including specialists in science and mathematics, art and music teachers. District-wide cutbacks in per pupil spending have continued in recent years, leading to larger class sizes and fewer specialists. The performing-arts teachers are concerned about the changes, reports Gail Ward, the floor leader (the equivalent of principal) for the third-floor middle-school team, which handles fifth through eighth grades. Ironically, the performing-arts teachers were the original raison d'etre for the school.

"Do you realize how much this real estate is worth?" asks Ward as she drives into the underground garage. She breezes down the hall on her morning rounds, weaving through the maze of pods and halls, negotiating the adolescent throngs. An able teacher and administrator with twenty years' experience, she could easily find a position at a more prestigious location. She lives in Evanston, and is tempted to switch districts. But she has stayed in Chicago.

Disney is an open-space school, giving the first-time visitor a sense of chaos. As one teacher puts it, "You can't hide here!" Each floor comprises seven large "pods," three of which are instructional areas, each designed to accommodate 200–250 students in a "flexible space" arrangement—no walls anywhere. (See Figure 5.1). The original theory was that the open space would promote collaboration among teachers and students. Teachers could combine classes for floorwide events and homeroom activities. Open space would allow flexibility to meet changing needs and avoid claustrophobic classrooms. Like most efforts that use external manipulation to change how teachers teach, it didn't work.

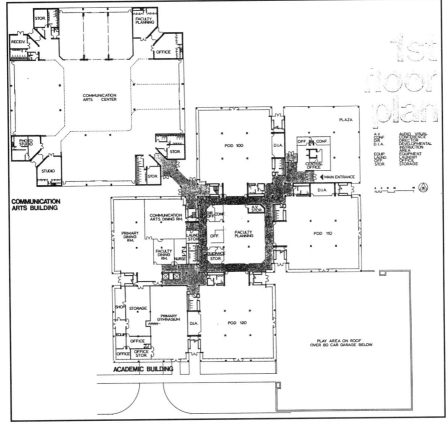

Figure 5.1
Floor plan of Disney School.

The real legacy of the open-space experiment here at Disney is pandemonious noise. Bookcases and standing chalkboards wall off the classes, feeble efforts to dampen noise and reduce visual distractions.

When the Disney staff first encountered the Project READ idea during a two-day workshop shortly before the 1991–92 school year, the teachers were asked, "What is most distinctive about this school?" "Noise!"—the answer sprang spontaneously from one mouth, but virtually every head nodded in agreement. Ward, a born optimist, commented afterward, "It's like a marriage, only you don't get to pick your partners. Everyone is visible—you can see them all day long. It's a lot of stress, and sometimes you're just not in the mood." The teachers worried that Project READ wouldn't do much to reduce the noise; in fact, READ structures and strategies would most likely *increase* student talk. But this time, it could be hoped that the talk would be meaningful and educationally productive.

Ward always opened the school year with a team-building exercise, which had previously met with limited success. While the open space meant that teachers were constantly aware of one another, they didn't really see themselves as team members. Each teacher taught a different grade and subject matter, and they didn't think of themselves as having a lot to talk about.

Project READ served as a catalyst for team building. At her first staff meeting, Ward unrolled a large sheet of butcher paper and led the teachers in a webbing exercise on the topic of trust (Figure 5.2, top). By the time the hour was over, teachers had a glimpse of the potential of graphic structures for wrestling with professional issues. It was not that a great deal was actually written down on the paper, but that the web structure opened the door to genuine discussion. Following the TRUST web, each pod team experimented later in the day with graphic organizers to vent their own issues and resentments, including the problems of noise and open space. The discussion slowly shifted from finger pointing to problem solving. Later in the week, when students returned from summer vacation, many teachers experimented by starting their classes with a web on *trust*. The idea of an open-ended discussion left many teachers uneasy, and so they began with an activity that they had experienced themselves. The students' responses surprised them; the adolescents had a lot more to say about the topic than the teachers had (Figure 5.2, bottom).

Webs, weaves, and story graphs began to blossom around the pod walls during the fall and winter of 1991. Project READ relies heavily on graphic organizers, and the visual impact was immediate. Students (and teachers) could *see* the evidence of student progress and work throughout the open space. As teachers experimented with webs, they began to ask probing questions about teaching—questions that began to tie their work together into a common whole—and a professional network was born: "How did you do that?" "My kids don't say much when I try to brainstorm." They addressed each other's concerns: "Start with a topic they're interested in, like food, until they get the idea that it's OK to say whatever's on their mind. Make it messy. If you worry too much about making everything 'right' you lose the flow. I've been using Post-Its so every kid can stick their ideas right on the board. That way I'm not the bottleneck." Teachers made time to talk to each other about instructional concepts and practices. The fifth-grade team met ten minutes early every day for breakfast—not much time, perhaps, but ten minutes more than they had managed before.

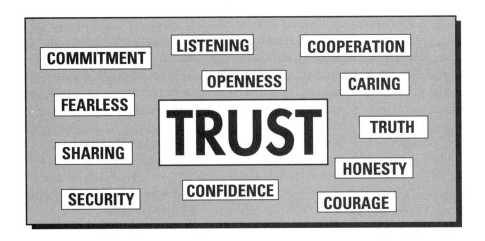

Figure 5.2
Webs on the topic of TRUST. Top panel by teachers from
Gail Ward's third-floor middle-school team at Disney.
Bottom panel by middle-school students at Disney.

The Project READ umbrella stretched over many matters as teachers realized that the techniques could work for adults as well as kids. As always, teachers were concerned about discipline, and so Ward brought in consultants on conflict management and character education. The consultants offered suggestions, but the READ structures provided the tools to support student discussion. Coaches visited from California every few months—at first an irritant, but increasingly an occasion for teachers to talk about long-term issues of curriculum and instruction. In most schools, arranging for a team of teachers to gather for a demonstration lesson is a major undertaking because every teacher is in his or her own cell; on the third floor of Disney, all that was needed was to collect teachers and students in the middle of the pod—open space offered some advantages after all.

The changed circumstances were welcomed by the third-floor team. After its promising start in the 1960s, Disney had fallen onto hard times. Ward had been appointed floor leader in 1985. Morale was low; discipline policy was unclear, and a new generation of students had begun to challenge the limits. "My first day," Ward recalls, "kids were smoking marijuana in the bathrooms." When she intervened, students asked, "What are you talking about? All I was doing was taking a hit in the bathroom." "There were gang signs on the walls, no doors on the bathroom stalls. It wasn't unusual for students to taunt teachers with 'F--- you' and worse." On her second day she had to handle a bathroom fire and a stolen VCR.

Ward saw her chief responsibility as providing leadership: bringing people and programs together. She realized that this was not something she could achieve with a chair and a whip. Project READ attracted her because it supported what she saw as one of the most important goals of schooling—to help students *and* teachers become more effective at thinking and communicating. Project READ connected the goals of a coherent literacy curriculum with strategies for helping adults work together more effectively. Disney was fraught with tensions, reflecting the politics of an ethnically diverse population and the high expectations placed on a magnet school. An easy out was for teachers to close their (metaphorical) classroom doors, complain about the noise, and keep students moving through the chapter. With its graphic organizers, open-ended discussions, and questions designed to help provoke students' thought and not merely force them to recall data, Project READ gave teachers a new voice, which brought with it a new sense of community and empowerment.

The techniques opened the way for individuals—students and teachers—to express thoughts and feelings. Sometimes the attempts came close to backfiring. Ward recalls an incident in which a "monosyllabic" student suddenly left the classroom without saying a word. The teacher was understandably upset, and when the student returned asked for an explanation; "I wanted to say goodbye to my student teacher." Unremarkable on the surface, but this student's vocabulary was little more than "F--- you" during previous years. He was not inclined to cooperate with other students, let alone to feel enough kinship with a student teacher to *want* to say goodbye. (When Ward checked up on the claim, it proved to be true, not just a clever leap through a loophole.) The student might have simplified life by telling his teacher about his plans. And the teacher might have routinely sent him to the office for misbehavior. But teachers as well as students had become more accustomed to "discourse," to talking through issues, to explaining themselves and asking for explanations. Says Ward: "What I notice now is that when kids come to me with discipline problems, they are better at communicating. They can think on their feet—and they can write!"

Self-expression by both individuals and groups is a visible part of Disney's third-floor environment. The "Author's Wall" displays dozens of student compositions that change every month. A highlight of the 1992 school year was the "Letters to the Mayor" project. The mayor and school superintendent had proposed student uniforms, and the third-floor team took advantage of the uproar to lead students through the process of designing persuasive "pro" and "con" essays. The writing that followed was organizationally sound; as we noted in Chapter 3, the READ graphic organizers provide students with skeletons that make it easier to write a coherent piece. The essays were lengthy because the students had something to say. And because the teachers had created audiences as well as assignments, students took care to polish those writings that went on display. They checked spelling, grammar, and other mechanical details, and they used word processors for the final version.

Under Gail Ward's energetic leadership, and with the support of the school's principal, Disney's third-floor team implemented Project READ with unusual vigor. Word about the project spread to neighboring schools. In 1992 and 1993, the team conducted READ summer institutes, hosting teachers from several schools, including four from the infamous Cabrini Green housing development. In the spring of 1993, the Chicago Foundation for Education sponsored a teacher fair. As part of the program, READ teachers from Disney and other collaborating schools displayed their wares, demonstrating how strategic, cognitively oriented instruction could enhance a program like Character Education. Respect for other cultures was an important part of this program; one school devoted the better part of a week to studying the diverse cultures that made up the student population. "Multi-culture" projects were taken on by each class in the school; the only guidelines were that the projects had to cover the full range of cultural groups, and they had to use graphic methods to organize the presentations. Figure 5.3 shows one example of a class project organized as a matrix. By the end of the fair, it was clear that teacher isolation was becoming a thing of the past. The group of twenty instructors from Disney lingered after the conference, discussing plans for exchange visits during the coming school year, and arrangements for another summer institute. Disney teachers no longer needed or wanted a "place to hide."

	People & Culture	Gov't.	Dance & Music	Population	Language	Religion	Flag	Arts	Family Life	Folk-tales	Ways of Living
CHINA											
EGYPT											
NIGERIA											
PUERTO RICO											
BRAZIL											
AUSTRALIA											
INDIA											

Figure 5.3
Multicultural matrix produced by students at Agassiz School in Chicago.

Building from Strength

Several urban school districts have adopted a "tracking" approach to school reform. The school board and district administrators place low-achieving schools in a special category, where they are alternately supported and threatened. In Los Angeles, for instance, the 1986 "Ten Schools Project" identified the "ten worst schools" in the school district for special attention and support. In return for additional funding, the schools were placed under close scrutiny, required to administer multiple-choice tests every quarter, and ordered to send teachers to special workshops on teaching academically troubled students. The technique parallels the practice of ability-grouping, in which low-achieving students are assigned to prescriptive remedial tasks.

A contrasting strategy begins by identifying schools that are doing well but want to do better, strengthening these institutions, and connecting them with other schools as partners. "If it ain't broke, don't fix it" is a tempting slogan for high-achieving schools. On the other hand, schools like San Jose's Graystone Elementary (where Project READ began), when given opportunities for risk and experimentation, have the potential to transform other schools.

Falk School: out of the laboratory. A pleasant, 1930s gabled-stone building atop a verdant knoll overlooking the University of Pittsburgh, Falk School is one of the nation's 100 or so laboratory schools: private schools on university campuses maintained for educational research and for the convenience of university faculty and staff. "When an institution like the University of Pittsburgh supports a laboratory school, it expects that the school will support research, teacher education, educational outreach, and innovation—and also provide the best possible education for the children who attend," notes Falk's principal, Roy Creek. In the next breath, he adds: "Education is always about kids. If you don't do that well, nothing else matters."

Falk is a tuition school, which provides a funding base, but at a cost. If the parents are not convinced that the school is worth it, then the school will be shut down. Creek is blunt: "Parents have to think that our programs are successful." But because it is a lab school, success is also gauged by School of Education researchers. As part of its research program, in the 1960s Falk implemented a nongraded plan in which from kindergarten onward, every class included students from two or more grade levels. The arrangement, by allowing students to stay with the same teacher for two or three years, gave teachers time to become more familiar with individuals' emotional and intellectual development.

The program seemed to be working. Evaluations by the School of Education showed that social cliques were less likely when class groupings were more fluid. Peer interactions became more commonplace in the multi-age classrooms. Decisions about retention and promotion were not bound to an assembly-line mentality. Students who elsewhere might have failed a grade no longer had to be separated from their age peers. The fluid arrangement of classes, which reconfigured student groups every year, had fewer negative consequences for the student who happened to have a bad year. Responses by students, teachers, and parents were positive.

But that was the 1960s. By the 1980s, the board felt that Falk had lost its momentum as a laboratory school. The faculty members were individually superb, but they had lost a sense of shared vision. Falk was still an excellent school, but it was expected to stand out as the showplace for the best and brightest of educational ideas and practices; otherwise, why should the University sustain the school? By the mid-1980s, this question had become central for the Falk board and faculty.

Professor Rita Bean of Pittsburgh's School of Education had taken her sabbatical at Stanford in the early 1980s, and invested considerable time with the Graystone staff during the initial year of Project READ. Bean, whose research focused on the professionalization of elementary teachers, had been fascinated by the transformation of the Graystone faculty during the development of a manual-free approach to teaching reading and writing.

Bean, who was on the Falk board, mentioned her Graystone experience to Falk staff in 1986 as they discussed their school's future. She saw in Project READ the possibility for combining the best features of whole language, with which they were becoming familiar, with analytic strategies that they knew were important for their students' academic progress. Reading and writing were of increasing concern to the teachers. The student body had changed, the result of programs to enroll students from low-income backgrounds and increase the representation of ethnic minorities, with a resulting growing number of students from homes troubled by divorce and overworked parents. They could no longer take family literacy for granted.

With mixed feelings, the faculty arranged to meet with a Project READ coach, co-author Robert Calfee. On a bright, crisp fall morning, a team of Falk teachers met at Bean's home for Sunday brunch. After pleasantries, Calfee opened with a question: "Tell me about Falk School—I'll be there on Monday. What should I look for?" Initial responses were guarded, but a web of thoughts and experiences began to emerge: pride in the institution and its history, concerns about board pressures to innovate, aspirations to "be the best." Teachers had done their homework, and they asked thoughtful questions about Project READ: How was it different from whole-language programs? Would it help their students write better? What about materials? Could it be adapted to a nongraded situation?

Calfee first sketched several READ strategies. Teachers nodded; they were already familiar with webbing and story graphs; other READ organizers—weaves and episodic analyses—were new to them. They quickly picked up the connection between organizers and cognitive processes.

Calfee then asked for questions. Project READ was consistent with the philosophical orientation of whole language—children were more likely to become literate when there was an obvious purpose, when tasks were meaningful, and when learning was participatory. But Project READ added concrete skills and strategies to the philosophical mix. It is well and good to talk about "interest" and "excitement." But for the student who lacks the skills of decoding and spelling, who can neither analyze nor organize a piece of writing, interest and excitement are likely to dwindle around third grade, if not before. In Project READ, reading and writing were integrated. Calfee also talked about the separation between reading and writing instruction that had occurred during the 1940s. He described ways in which students could improve their writing by improving their reading, so that what they read could serve as models for how to write. He mentioned research that showed how student writing improved when it was organized.

Materials? Management? Project READ was not a package but a set of ideas that could be applied in a wide range of organizational settings. Project READ was probably a good match to Falk, Calfee suggested, because a nongraded program confronted teachers with daily decisions; they relied not on textbooks but on professional judgments. These answers seemed to make sense to the teachers, who also commented that the methods would be applicable to a wide range of subject matters and grades, offering a way to build staff unity.

The Monday visit went well. The cadre had spread the word that if a revolution was in the works, it would be a quiet one. The meeting with the full faculty was a rerun of the Sunday brunch. Bean and her team of researchers supported further staff development during the winter and spring. By the following April, graphic organizers blanketed classroom walls and spread into hallways. The staff expressed feelings of revitalization stemming from a common language and sense of shared purpose. They began to talk about themselves as an "Inquiring School."

The concept of an inquiring school goes back to a 1965 address to the Dewey Society by Roy Schafer called *The School As a Center of Inquiry*.[4] Schafer's point was that schools ought to think about what they were doing. He pointed toward the behavioral sciences as a foundation for inquiry. It was a promising idea, but nothing had come of it.

As teachers at Graystone, Shoreview, and Disney reflected on their vision of education, it began to appear to Calfee that the most effective tools for inquiry in elementary schools might spring not from the behavioral sciences, but from the rhetoric—from structures and strategies like those in Project READ. Calfee had talked about the concept of an inquiring school during his first visit, and Falk adopted the label. They used READ structures and strategies, *and* they were an Inquiring School.

By whatever name, READ/Inquiring School prospered at Falk. Evaluations by the teachers and the University of Pittsburgh School of Education showed a renewed sense of enthusiasm by teachers. The students were already at the top of the scale on standardized tests, but the Falk Board of Directors was impressed by teachers' reports of student progress in their own performance tests, in grades, and in student discussions. The Board decided to encourage the teachers to establish an outreach program. This activity was certainly in the spirit of a lab school. Bean invited several districts in the city of Pittsburgh and the nearby Mon (Monongahela) Valley to send teams to meetings arranged by Falk teachers and Pitt grad students. Four schools joined the Inquiring School program during the first year. The Falk staff became circuit riders, visiting local schools for demonstration lessons and consultation. By 1992, the program encompassed over twenty schools and more than 200 teachers throughout Western Pennsylvania.

Falk School had hit the road. "Teachers teaching teachers" has a ring to it but is tough to bring off. Schools are just as isolated from one another as teachers within the same school typically are. The Falk staff took on this challenge, reaping benefits for themselves as well as their students. Creek comments, "The teacher-presenting-to-teacher strategy dissolves the usual skepticism that comes in response to 'experts who don't know a thing about our school.'"

The Inquiring School has become a meaningful concept at Falk, according to Creek:

> The evolution of a common vocabulary and shared understanding [has built] a professional culture in which teachers are increasingly inclined to see constructive criticism from colleagues and to assess their own teaching. . . . This agenda generates new knowledge about teaching, it supports intellectual growth by teachers, and it develops an inquiring attitude by students.

So much for the view from Falk. What does the situation look like from the perspective of their clients?

The view from Mon Valley. Recent surveys have bestowed upon Pittsburgh a reputation as one of the nation's outstanding cities. From the winding highway that descends from the mountains toward the city, the nighttime traveler can see bright lights highlighting arched bridges and riverside restaurants huddled against a background of shimmering glass-and-steel skyscrapers. When the iron and steel industry went into local decline in the 1980s, the city's corporate leaders didn't wait for good times to return—they renewed the economic base by shifting to light manufacturing, environmental services, corporate facilities, advanced technology and, most notably, medical technology.

Up the river, the Mon Valley has not shared in Pittsburgh's progress. Until the 1980s, the Valley's belching steel mills and foundries illuminated the entire south bank of the river. Too old to fix, too costly to rebuild, the factories closed down; as of the early 1990s, the Valley had still not recovered.

McKeesport, ten miles south of Pittsburgh at the entrance to the Valley, is typical of the new hard times. Thirty years ago, the town bustled with Pittsburghers doing their weekend shopping. Workers, mostly white, held good jobs at riverside foundries. During the 1960s, a high-school dropout could make $12,000–13,000 per year in the mills (by comparison, a starting teacher's salary was $6,600). Those heavily unionized, high-paying factory jobs are gone. Vacant mills with shattered windows stretch for miles. The Holiday Inn is boarded up. The unemployment rate is several points higher than the national average; the only major employers are the hospital and school district.

George Washington School dominates a residential neighborhood of two-story brick houses, heavy columns against a neoclassical facade, the founding date of "1923" carved into the cornerstone. The setting combines comfortable and tired, old and drained. The 630 students attending the school reflect the setting. Teacher Richard ("Rocky") Beach talks about the economy's toll. "I have 28 kids in my room, and half are on free lunches," he notes. "That number is pretty consistent throughout the school. In the morning, when the children come in for free breakfasts, sometimes parents sit with them and carry food out in napkins. This school has to do more than teach. We're a social agency."

Beach has spent his entire 23-year teaching career in McKeesport. "When I came, McKeesport was thriving—three mills in a five-mile area. Then U.S. Steel announced it was going out of the steel business in this region. The Duquesne works went first, then Homestead, then National Tube. The city started to decline. McKeesport was once *the* place to shop. Now . . . " he pauses. "The suburban school districts are doing pretty well. The teachers there make more money than we do. There's not much equity for teachers. Not much for the children, either. The suburbs can update their physics labs. Not here. . . ." Why does Beach stay? Job security matters during a time of cutbacks and layoffs. For Beach, in any case, leaving was never a serious option: "Seniority doesn't follow you in Pennsylvania."

But Beach has also become a local. He is proud of his contribution to a community in need, and he speaks positively about the District. "It's always had a reputation for trying new things. It doesn't bury its head." McKeesport has become one of three Mon Valley Inquiring Schools. Teachers and administrators in these schools seem convinced of the positive effects of the program; this is the finding by Bean and her colleagues from evaluations in more than thirty schools and twelve districts throughout Western Pennsylvania. The evaluations include classroom observations, focus-group discussions with teachers and principals, and standardized tests of student achievement. She has reported the results in technical articles and convention papers,[5] but Bean's primary audiences have been the Mon Valley schools and the Falk faculty, and her primary concerns have been how to convey the findings to them and convert their feedback into program improvement.

READ graphics have worked well for this purpose. For example, Figure 5.4 shows a READ "thermometer" for findings from classroom observations. If you are experienced in reading this graphic, the results are quickly apparent: observers found that teachers (a) were effective in using graphic organizers to represent students' work; (b) clearly stated the lesson purpose and connected the topic with the students' previous experience and previous lessons; and (c) posed questions that prompted active student discussion. They were less effective in promoting summary discussions and reflective conversations.

Bean and her colleagues' evaluations also found that reliance on basal manuals and ditto sheets decreased during the school year as the program took effect, while cooperative activities and writing projects increased. Teachers and principals also reported few behavioral problems during READ lessons. Student achievement gains on multiple-choice tests were comparable to or higher than non-READ control groups. Student writing improved markedly as students began to draw on READ structures to organize their thoughts while composing. Project READ-coached students organized their essays as general statements with supporting detail, whereas control students relied on "shopping lists." READ students were able to explain the decision making required for a well-organized composition—they had become "meta-writers."

The Inquiring School model did not "take" in all the schools. Why not? Answers to this question are not always easy to come by. But in Bean's studies, classroom observations, focus-group discussions, and individual interviews turned up school- and districtwide differences that were important for understanding why READ/Inquiring School worked better in some instances than in others. Public schools are not

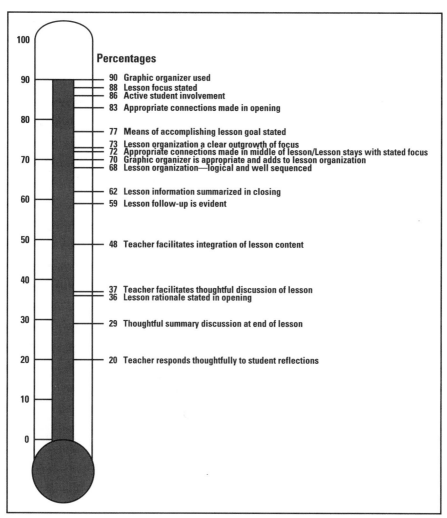

Percentages

90 Graphic organizer used
88 Lesson focus stated
86 Active student involvement
83 Appropriate connections made in opening

77 Means of accomplishing lesson goal stated
73 Lesson organization a clear outgrowth of focus
72 Appropriate connections made in middle of lesson/Lesson stays with stated focus
70 Graphic organizer is appropriate and adds to lesson organization
68 Lesson organization—logical and well sequenced

62 Lesson information summarized in closing
59 Lesson follow-up is evident

48 Teacher facilitates integration of lesson content

37 Teacher facilitates thoughtful discussion of lesson
36 Lesson rationale stated in opening

29 Thoughtful summary discussion at end of lesson

20 Teacher responds thoughtfully to student reflections

Figure 5.4
**Thermometer graph from Rita Bean's evaluation of Inquiring
School sites in Pittsburgh.**

always that "public," and evaluators depend on the collaboration of administrators and teachers to understand what is happening. And so the data come from impressions rather than hard facts. The impressions, nonetheless, mesh with other research findings. Principals are important. Where the Inquiring School model proved most effective, the principal was not only supportive—he or she was involved not only as a "cheerleader" but as a participant. These administrators could walk into a classroom and conduct a webbing lesson. They used READ structures in faculty meetings. They were enthusiastic about language and literacy. They were also undoubtedly susceptible to criticism that they weren't giving enough attention to other matters: math and science, technology, parent programs, and so on. Schools are political organizations, and principals take a risk when they focus on one constituency or topic. When the public expects all things of all schools, principals are caught in the tension of conflicting demands.

In ten of the schools where the program seemed to be working best, the evaluators found other common threads. Teachers played major roles during workshops and faculty meetings. While grateful for university assistance, they emphasized that they had a great deal to offer one another. These teachers took the initiative in presenting the program to school boards and professional groups.

The Inquiring School concept changes the balance of power between principals and teachers. Unlike many other school-change programs, the Inquiring School begins with classroom instruction as the point of departure, and in this area principals are seldom as expert as teachers. For some principals, this shift led to uneasiness. But principals in the ten most effective schools, by taking the time to become familiar with the pragmatics of webs and the principles of CORE, became educational leaders. One delivered these remarks to the local Rotary Club:

> The Inquiring School brings to our faculty new knowledge about the art of teaching, a framework for sharing information with colleagues, and the development of an inquiring attitude in our students. The model stresses problem solving and thinking skills, frees the teacher from relying on published textbooks, encourages students to think about the way that they think and to determine what works best for them. . . . Education [in our school] isn't what it used to be—it's much better!

The institutional impact varied with the individual, of course, and with the individual's stage of development as a professional. For one second-grade teacher, READ/Inquiring School provided her with visual organizers to enhance her teaching, but her reflections stayed close to the surface:

> I felt [after a science lesson on plants] that my objective was met because the kids did very well with the visuals, and they did very well with the test. I kind of checked myself. When we read the next part of the science book, the students did worse on the test when I didn't use the visuals. Definitely worse. So I feel real comfortable that I would use this as a way to teach next year.

The teacher was willing to experiment and to change her methods based on the results, but her vision focused on concrete topics and the immediate realities of her classroom.

A fifth-grade teacher viewed Project READ from a broader perspective. She involved her students in a variety of challenging and unusual activities. For example, at year's end, they wrote a play for fourth-graders about what to expect in fifth grade. In another project, after disappointing results in teaching parts of speech, the teacher organized student teams to act as artists, actors, or models, analogies to nouns, verbs, and adjectives. After recounting to the evaluator her excitement that students actually seemed to come to an understanding and appreciation of grammar, the teacher described her own professional development in these words:

> For me, Inquiring School means more than webs and weaves. Many times I don't use any of these structures, but I feel that they are Inquiring School lessons. The learning is student-generated; I lead the students up to a point, and then through inquiry they grasp the objective. The structures help them organize. . . . I can see by how they design their charts that they can connect to the task in an organized way.

A commitment to excellence: Meramec Elementary. Teachers at the Meramec Elementary School in the western suburbs of St. Louis connected with the program when first-grade teacher Harriet Spilker participated in a Project READ workshop at a national reading convention. Meramec serves children from an affluent community. The three-story brick building nestles into large oak trees that shelter the magnificent homes in this neighborhood. The teachers are proud of their students' accomplishments and work hard to stay in the very front ranks. Student test scores are always in the upper-90 percentiles, the top of the range. The Meramec teachers monitor the scores, but they emphasize other outcomes. Student writing and projects are regularly presented to the school board as evidence of student achievement. Moreover, the teachers take pride in their role as consultants to other schools in the district and elsewhere in the region. They are in a privileged position compared with many other schools and can afford to experiment with new ideas.

Spilker presented Project READ to her colleagues on her return, and they expressed interest in building a more challenging environment for their children. Principal Ruth Mach talked with the faculty about establishing a schoolwide program. As in the Falk situation, an extraordinary school experienced a renewed vision and sense of professional community. VEND and CORE offered a common set of concepts and labels to support their work as a professional team.

And like the Falk teachers, Meramec teachers became circuit riders, visiting other schools in the region to demonstrate graphic organizers and the CORE model. In 1991, the Missouri Reading Association met in St. Louis, and with Mach's encouragement the entire school proposed a daylong preconference workshop. They encountered a logistical problem: the workshop fell on a regular school day. Mach was nonetheless determined that every teacher have a chance to participate. She brought teachers, students, and parents into the planning—for example, of how to organize the school day so that half the teachers could be free during the morning and the other half during the afternoon. Through their combined efforts, librarians, gym teachers, reading specialists, and even Ruth Mach managed to cover the classes, and the workshop became a reality, demonstrating to packed sessions how literacy could encompass a broad range of subject matters—reading and writing, but also science, social studies, the arts, and even sports.

At both Falk and Meramec, the Inquiring School concept opened new opportunities for teachers to take on more-professional roles, to serve as resources to others, to demonstrate the range of their talents. The teachers were initially uneasy about conducting demonstration lessons with troubled students from poor homes. After all, what if the lessons failed with low-achieving students? They nonetheless pushed ahead and to their surprise discovered that these students, while quite different in background and style from the middle-class children they were used to, had a lot in common with their home-base kids. Given the opportunity, all students were responsive to CORE lessons. Most students wanted to succeed, and most could learn.

Fighting Against the Odds

Five blocks from the Watts Towers in South Central Los Angeles, 102nd Street Elementary literally arose Phoenixlike from the ashes of the 1965 riots. Its modern design is mirrored in the nearby daycare-facility-and-senior-center combination. But the time of troubles had not ended for this Phoenix. In the fall of 1991, fences barricaded burned-out street-corner lots, mute witness to the fury of the Rodney King conflagration a few months earlier.

102nd Street Elementary serves families and children from economically distressed areas in South Central Los Angeles. A large school, with over 1,000 students and a staff of more than 60, it was earmarked in 1987 for the Ten Schools program; the Los Angeles Unified School District identified ten schools that fell at the bottom of the pile in meeting the academic needs of African-American students. The District provided both carrots and sticks. Participating schools received supplemental funding for materials, staff development, classroom aides, and the like. They were encouraged to innovate, to experiment, to look for effective programs. However, they were also mandated to test students every three months, with an external evaluator keeping close tabs on progress. After each test administration, the ten faculties met at District headquarters to hear about the results. The news was seldom good, leading principals to renew the emphasis on tests. Each test covered a set of specific objectives: consonants and main ideas in the fall, short vowels and vocabulary in the winter. In most schools, classroom charts displayed upcoming objectives, and the visitor could see students busy with worksheets for each skill. The testing emphasis dampened enthusiasm for experimentation. While the District encouraged high-level learning, the bottom line was mastery of low-level skills.

For the 102nd Street faculty, entry into the Ten Schools program had been a mixed blessing. On the positive side was the promise of additional resources. Of course, they had little control over these resources: budget cutbacks had become merciless, and each district region, not the schools themselves, called the shots about how to spend the cash. But money was money.

On the down side, the pressure to improve test scores was no longer yearly but quarterly. Teachers scarcely digested one set of results before the next list was posted—a few weeks on long vowels and main idea, and then a shift to syllabification and sequence. The tension was unrelenting. Like many inner-city schools in Los Angeles, 102nd Street Elementary was in session all year around, so the school could never take a break.

When Cynthia Dugan arrived as principal early in the summer of 1990, the mood was uneasy, to say the least. An embittering teacher strike in the spring had put an edge on personal relations. Teachers were increasingly frustrated by the testing regimen. And now, a change in administrator. A new principal brings change, and change can bring trouble. Dugan had spent the five previous years as principal of 59th Street School, another South Central Los Angeles school a few miles north of 102nd. She had introduced Project READ at 59th Street School in the late 1980s and had been pleased with the results. When she arrived at 102nd Street Elementary, she discussed with the faculty their reactions to the new California Language Arts Framework (a set of guidelines for public-school teachers) and its emphasis on literature-based literacy and increased writing. The unspoken (well, occasionally spoken) response was: "What matters *really* is what's on the test."

Workshops were commonplace at 102nd Street Elementary, and Dugan caused scarcely a ripple when she arranged for a group of teachers to attend the five-day 1990 Stanford READ institute at the Dominguez Hills campus of California State University. Folded into ravines overlooking San Pedro Bay five miles to the south, sheltered by overarching eucalyptus groves, the campus is a peaceful respite to the troubled inner city lying just over a low ridge to the north.

To their surprise, the group discovered that the institute faculty included not just Stanford coaches but also colleagues from other South Central schools. The agenda allowed them time to compare notes with themselves and with others, time for reflection. A grant from the Weingart Foundation provided basic support and even the luxury of lunch. Most participants stayed beyond the official 1:00 p.m. closing to mull over issues practical and political. The 102nd Street Elementary team continued to wrestle with the inconsistencies in the District's position: mandating the testing of basic skills, while encouraging whole-language techniques. Teachers had worked on skills, and test scores had gone up. But they were concerned because students, especially those in the later grades, were unmotivated. Preparing for multiple-choice tests is not exactly a peak experience. As the week progressed, the 102nd Street team began to see in Project READ the possibility of combining the best features of whole language and skill development.

On the final day of the institute, seven 102nd Street teachers sat on the sun-drenched grass mulling over the week. Calfee joined the group. Time for them to return to reality, and the quarterly tests were back on their minds. READ strategies would steal time from practicing for tests. Implementing a literature-based program was risky. The principal seemed supportive, but principals come and go; teachers are forever. With some apprehension, the teachers made a pact to go for broke. They committed themselves to a team meeting every Tuesday morning twenty minutes before the official start of school, hoping that the union representative would not notice (the contract settlement discouraged teachers from participating in any activity not required under the contract).

Team members kept their commitment, staying the course through the winter months and into a spring made dreary by a series of pay freezes and staff cutbacks. Discussions roamed far afield from Project READ. Three primary-grade teachers developed an integrated primary program in which each teacher took responsibility for a combined class of kindergarten and first- and second-graders, using READ structures to design a developmental curriculum for young children. Upper-grade teachers worked with the Stanford team to develop a project for strategic test-taking: Rather than assigning students to worksheet practice, they stressed collaboration. The strategy seemed to be paying off; their test scores were still below the district average, but while scores in the school district as a whole were declining, the quarterly scores at 102nd Street Elementary were improving. And teachers felt that student interest and motivation were rising. The year passed quickly.

And then, in May 1991, South Central Los Angeles erupted in flames. All six Project READ South Central schools were in the fire zone.

Ten days after the riot, the Chicken Shack across the street from 102nd was a burned-out shell, along with several nearby homes and businesses. The sky was overcast, the air acrid. Amazingly, and unreported by the media, every single South Central elementary school remained unmarked—no physical damage, no graffiti, just frightened children and uneasy teachers. The elementary schools were sanctuaries for children in the midst of rampaging chaos. 102nd Street teachers jettisoned the regular curriculum—tests and all. Classrooms were spackled with webs expressing student reactions to the events that had overtaken their lives. The concern and care of teachers for students was palpable.

A *real* test came when the TV crews arrived. Reporters roamed the school, interviewing teachers and students on camera about the disorders. For the nation it was only a sound bite, but 102nd Street students starred in one 30-second spot. A fifth-grader's snippet required no editing: "I know that people here are mad about the Rodney King thing, but we need to figure out how to show folks what's wrong without hurting ourselves. We talked about this in our class, about how to help ourselves without hurting others. It doesn't help to hurt people." A powerful and well-organized essay, in our judgment.

Life goes on. Two weeks after the disorders, teachers passed out standardized tests to their classes, following the District directives. Three months later, when the yearly tests were reported, the teachers learned that, incredibly, student performance at 102nd Street Elementary had once again improved. In fact, 102nd Street, formerly at the bottom of the pile, was now outperforming every other school in the Ten Schools group as it implemented Project READ (Figure 5.5). The coming June READ institute at California State University was fully enrolled, the 102nd Street team featured on the agenda.

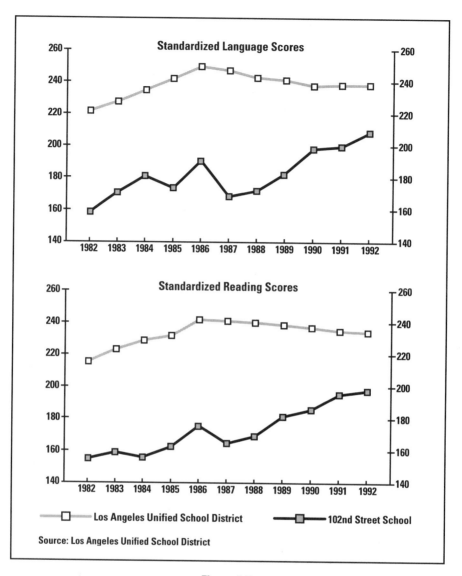

Figure 5.5
Reading scores from 102nd Street School in South Central Los Angeles.

Now to August 1993—two years after the King riots, Los Angeles teachers have taken additional pay cuts, there has been substantial staff turnover (one of the integrated-primary teachers reluctantly departed for higher pay and better working conditions in a suburban district, while the other two team members continue with the project), and kids keep coming. Dugan has asked Calfee to meet with the staff as part of a three-day session before the start of school. The teachers have spent the morning on a science workshop, and equations are scrawled on the chalkboard.

Calfee begins the afternoon by asking the teachers to do a word splash: "Write down all the things that are working for you in reading and writing, and all the problems from last year. Stick with reading and writing." After several minutes of brainstorming, the teachers write their reactions on a large chart, one side for good things and the other for not-so-good things. To the teachers' surprise, given all the turmoil and turnovers, reading and writing are going pretty well at 102nd Street. The chart shows far more positives than negatives. One teacher remarks, "I didn't realize we were doing so many good things. The problem is, we never have a chance to talk with each other"—so their successes go unrecognized, even among themselves. Students are writing more and better, in the teachers' judgment. Spelling, still a problem, is improving. But most importantly, students seem motivated to read and to write, even in the upper grades.

Calfee displays Figure 5.5, showing the trends in standardized achievement. The teachers are astonished. They typically look at a single year at a time, and always score below the district average. Even though they have begun to give less priority to worksheets and objectives, students are doing better on the tests—and are also doing better where it really counts: in challenging reading and writing assignments. Student performance at 102nd Street Elementary now ranks at the top of the Ten Schools, where it had once occupied the cellar.

As this book goes to press in 1995, 102nd Street Elementary continues to fight against the odds. The Weingart grant has ended, and the teachers can no longer count on the Stanford coaches for assistance. They are on their own. But READ strategies and structures are still in evidence in the school. Teachers from 102nd Street, along with colleagues from several other South Central schools, have formed a READ network that meets irregularly for mutual support. The Los Angeles school system has a teacher shortage because of the difficult working conditions, and so has established an intern-training program; a college graduate can get a teaching job if he or she agrees to enroll in after-school courses provided by other district teachers. Interns receive a teaching credential if they complete the two-year program. Project READ teachers from 102nd Street and 59th Street schools have become leaders in the intern program. The READ concepts and practices are surviving in a very difficult situation.

Changing the System

Advocates of educational reform confront an inevitable tension. Policy makers prefer to manage change through external pressure, directly by mandated programs or indirectly by established requirements. Formal research and practical experience show that locally initiated change is more effective and self-sustaining. The problem is that locals often tend to "do their own thing," unguided by any research or information.

As with most such tensions, the resolution requires flexibility on both sides, guided by workable models that demonstrate the possibilities for compromise. We present two in this section; both show how a structured program can be adapted to meet local needs without sacrificing the integrity of the design. The key is a simple, well-articulated plan, and a school that moves beyond superficial compliance.

Ripples from one school. Charles Mack Elementary stands in a suburban community south of Sacramento, the neighborhood straddling two freeways that channel traffic through the San Joaquin Valley to Southern California. In the 1970s, apartment complexes and small single-family homes for blue-collar families displaced farmland. In the 1980s, the neighborhood fell prey to unemployment, family break-ups, drugs, and crime. Mack School confronted increased enrollment, decreasing financial support, and plummeting test scores. By the 1990s, the school was in serious trouble: low test scores, poor morale, dissatisfied parents.

In autumn 1992, Bob Trigg, superintendent of the Elk Grove School District, put the pressure on Mack. Gillian Johnson moved from assistant to acting principal. During several previous "school improvement" meetings, the faculty had developed a list of obstacles to account for poor achievement and parent dissatisfaction: large classes, poor attendance, excessive tardiness, spotty family support, disruptive and irresponsible students. Nothing had changed, and now the teachers were being asked once more to conduct a self-study. Project READ was presented as one possibility for improving reading and writing; the faculty decided to review the program.

Calfee paid a daylong visit to the school. Classes were quite large— 27 to 30 per teacher in kindergarten, 30 to 35 per teacher in the upper grades. The curriculum diverged wildly from one classroom to another. Some classes relied on textbooks and worksheets, others pursued "open education" practices from the 1960s. Some teachers emphasized writing, others skill development. There was little common ground.

With guidance from Calfee, teachers spun a web around "What Mack School is like today." They organized thoughts into five categories:

curriculum, instruction, assessment, the institution, and things we can't do anything about. Next they built a second web around these same categories, but the topic shifted to "What Mack School might be in three years." The coach explained, "That's far enough downstream so that you can dream. But be realistic; don't assume different students or lots more money. Finally, we'll pull these two webs together into a time-weave" (Figure 5.6). With the big picture in view, they then began to think about priorities. What were the most important things to change in the short term—i.e., the rest of the current school year? How could they begin moving from where they were to where they'd like to be?

Calfee divided the teachers into four groups and gave them 45 minutes to work on the task. Each group included teachers from several different grades and specializations (bilingual, learning disabilities, and so on). The process took a while to start; serious talk about educational

	NOW	Three years from now [Theme: All students can learn]
Curriculum	• No common curriculum • Different textbooks	• K–6 integrated curriculum • Articulated curriculum matrix • Focus on comprehension and composition • Oral-language development
Instruction	• Don't know • Haven't seen other classrooms	• Consistent strategies and expectations • CORE model—connect
Assessment	• Standardized tests • "Monster" tests • Teacher tests	• Test preparation • Continuous teacher assessment • Teacher log book • Schoolwide assessment plan
Organization	• New principal • No time to meet	• Use our expertise in different subject matters • Common terminology • Build in common planning time • Grade-level teams; cross-grade teams • Parent involvement in planning
Other Things	• Student Behavior • Class size • Attendance/Tardies • Parent responsibilities • Student responsibilities • Student motivation/social skills • Diverse student needs	. . .

Figure 5.6
Time-weave produced by faculty at Mack Elementary School during restructuring activity.

issues is rare in most schools. Initial reactions tended to be in the "things we can't do anything about" category. Gradually, though, the other categories began to fill in. When report time arrived, all four groups were amazed to discover that they had constructed parallel scenarios. Consensus emerged around three issues. First, the Mack teachers agreed that curriculum—a common vision about what to teach—was the key to school improvement. Second, they agreed that they were in a position to enhance student achievement despite limited resources and increased demands. Finally, they expressed worries about external barriers to action: What if the new principal had other ideas? Also, the seemingly radical changes in methodology embodied in Project READ would require planning time by teachers; would the District support them? The program would take time to affect student achievement; would the District be patient?

Later in the month, following informal conversations and a faculty meeting, the Mack teachers planned a two-day session focused on the reading-writing curriculum. What should students learn from kindergarten through sixth grade? Like most schools, Mack depended on textbooks for curricular direction, but this strategy was not working. They decided that they needed to create a schoolwide curriculum plan that made sense to them. Because neither the District nor the students could afford to let every teacher take two days off, the faculty chose eight teachers spanning all grades to work on the project.

Two weeks later, the group gathered in the school library, where the original time-weaves still covered the walls. They reviewed their task, and by midmorning the group had focused on two features of the READ model: narration and exposition. Half the group took on narrative, the others agreed to wrestle with exposition. At day's end, the teams presented rough drafts to the rest of the faculty (Figure 5.7). The curriculum was developmental; students would move along a continuum where every teacher was responsible for student learning rather than specific objectives for each grade. In the more typical assembly-line model, all second-grade students are expected to "create new characters" whether or not they were ready for the task. In the developmental model, second-grade teachers began the school year by reviewing goals introduced during the previous year ("Let's review what you learned last year about comparing characters") before moving ahead to new goals like "creating characters." Then they could stretch students to try out more-advanced goals ("How are the characters you've created for this story linked to what they say and how they act?"). These ideas may seem obvious, but the isolation of teachers from one another and their

Narrative

Characters   K 1 2 3 4 5 6

1. Identify characters
2. Describe characters' traits (looks, acts, feels)
3. Compare/contrast
4. Identify major/minor characters
5. Create new characters
6. Describe characters' motives (thoughts and feelings)
7. Relate personally to characters and interaction of characters
8. Discuss character development through: dialogue, action/reaction, conflict/resolution
9. Discuss influence of character on plot/theme development

Setting   K 1 2 3 4 5 6

1. Define where/when
2. Identify/describe
3. Create new settings
4. Distinguish between past, present, future
5. Describe influences of setting on other components of story
6. Identify multiple settings
7. Relate how author develops mood through setting

Plot   K 1 2 3 4 5 6

1. Predict (into, through)
2. Determine real/make believe
3. Identify events/episodes (what happened)
4. Summarize (beginning-middle-end)
5. Sequence
6. Identify conflict/resolution
7. Note relationship of cause/effect
8. Identify sub-plot within main plot
9. Discuss influences of plot on setting, character, and theme

Theme   K 1 2 3 4 5 6

1. Relate lesson learned from story
2. Describe how the story affects the reader as a person
3. Link to values
4. Describe how theme is shaped by characters, setting, and plot
5. Exhibit knowledge of multiple themes in one story
6. Identify author's own motivation/purpose

Figure 5.7, Panel A
Developmental chart for narrative curriculum
constructed by Mack School teachers.

Expository

Gathering Information

	K	1	2	3	4	5	6
1. Gather sensory information		▬▬					
2. Identify and locate resources (reference/interviewing skills)			▬▬				
3. Identify point of view, source and audience				▬▬			
4. Identify relevant facts				▬▬			
5. Distinguish between fact and opinion				▬▬			

Organizing Facts/Information

	K	1	2	3	4	5	6
1. Exposure to various organizational strategies		▬▬					
2. Use organizational strategies to organize information				▬▬			
3. Choose and use appropriate organizational strategies						▬▬	

Making Interpretations/Evaluations From Text

	K	1	2	3	4	5	6
1. Distinguish between fact and opinion		▬▬▬					
2. Develop the skill to form an oral opinion/judgment		▬▬▬					
3. Identify causes for problems		▬▬▬▬					
4. Identify causes and their effects/consequences			▬▬				
5. Express a written opinion/judgment				▬▬			

Application

	K	1	2	3	4	5	6
1. Compare and contrast two or more pieces of information		▬▬					
2. Draw analogies to connect and apply information			▬▬				
3. Apply information in concrete format			▬▬				
4. Draw analogies to connect information to novel situations						▬▬	
5. Apply information in abstract format						▬▬	

Figure 5.7, Panel B
Developmental chart for expository curriculum
constructed by Mack School teachers.

dependence on textbooks are major barriers to such continuity.

By the fall of 1993, Mack School had begun to change. Gillian Johnson had been appointed principal, a District decision that met with faculty approval. Narrative-Expository charts, posted in every classroom, had become focal points for both teachers and students, for both teaching and testing. Teachers had begun to develop thematic projects (Figure 5.8), and when the students' day ended, teachers at each grade gathered in teams for further curriculum planning.

In February 1994, Superintendent Trigg asked the Mack staff to report their progress to District administrators and interested principals. Johnson opened the session: "Not too long ago we focused on our students' circumstances—many are from poor families and broken homes, and we couldn't expect them to learn. Now our commitment is to make sure that all our students succeed—that's our responsibility as a school." Other teachers then discussed how this new emphasis affected what they taught, what they tested, and how they handled students with special needs. They stressed two themes: "We are working as a team. And our students are benefiting."

To support these claims, the team displayed grade-level curriculum plans and student writing samples. "We weren't sure that the State testing would show what the kids could do. Those tests don't give students time to think, and they don't connect with topics that the students know about. We're talking about fourth-graders who are starting out behind, but *we* have evidence that our students are learning to read and write." The California testing later in the spring turned out to be a mess (a story for Chapter 6). And the teachers were probably right in their judgment that standardized tests were not the best way to assess the new curriculum. Nonetheless, they were encouraged by the results from District tests. Scores had declined for several years, and in the 1993 testing Mack students had scored at the 30th percentile. But in 1994, the tide turned, and significantly so—Mack's reading achievement had jumped to the 37th percentile.

A few weeks later, the Elk Grove District, impressed, asked the Mack staff to develop a summer institute, in collaboration with Stanford coaches, to relate their experience with Project READ to other interested district schools.

Schools with large numbers of at-risk students often find themselves on the horns of a dilemma. One reform strategy is to install a prepackaged program developed by someone else. Relying on outsiders, however, undercuts professional growth and responsibility, and if the program doesn't work the teachers can claim it's not their fault. The second

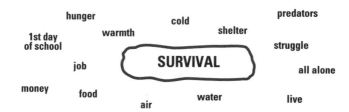

SURVIVAL

BEGINNING

hunger   cold   predators

1st day
of school   warmth   shelter

SURVIVAL   struggle

job   all alone

money   food   water   live

air

MIDDLE

Title	Main character	Setting	Resources available	Adversity to be overcome	Realization
Diary of Anne Frank					
The Mixed-Up Files of Mrs. Basil E. Frankwieler					
Sign of the Beaver					

END

Student-produced survival guide

Figure 5.8
**A graphic depiction showing the development of literature-based thematic
project by a class at Mack School, from initial word splash through
literature matrix to student-produced "survivial guide."**

approach is to develop a completely local program. If successful, the locals can take the credit, but the risk is that an overworked faculty will spend a lot of time reinventing the wheel—and failing to have any effect. Mack's experience shows how structural concepts like those in Project READ can provide an effective jump-start for local development and rebuilding. The webs and weaves helped the teachers see where they were and where they wanted to be. It helped them to set priorities and to create a plan of action. It focused their attention on the core elements of the educational enterprise—curriculum, instruction, and appraisal. And it *worked* for them. Their own assessments have shown improvements in student achievement, in student motivation, and in satisfaction among parents and recognition by the District and colleagues in other schools. The rising test scores provided external confirmation of their progress.

Spreading the word: New York City's teacher consortium. For a contrasting example, consider the *New York Times*'s description of a professional-development conference for teachers in Bridgeport, Connecticut:

> No school for Bridgeport children today . . . Teachers and principals crowded corridors, stood in lunchroom lines, squirmed in uncomfortable classroom seats. . . . Attendance was compulsory. . . . Many meetings were led by consultants from textbook publishers and other educational suppliers. . . . Consultants emphasized the city's goals, especially improving scores on the Connecticut Mastery Test, which are among the lowest in the state.[6]

As the *Times* noted, the experience was "eerily similar to what students experience, right to the final dismissal at 3 p.m." The *Times* added that there were "important differences for the teachers," but these are hard to find in the story. The Inquiring School model is grounded in the notion that teachers should not be told what to do, but should be supported as professionals who need opportunities to connect with one another at the local school level.

How to accomplish this goal when the task is to change hundreds of schools in a large urban context? Can the Chancellor of the New York City Schools afford the luxury of allowing individual schools to reconfigure themselves? During the 1980s more than twenty schools scattered throughout New York City rebuilt themselves as "inquiring" schools, not with great fanfare but through teachers working in professional communities.

On a hot, humid Saturday late in May 1990, 200 teachers attended a teacher fair sponsored by the United Federation of Teachers and held at the UFT Bronx Center. They were the lucky ones; more than 100 other applicants had been turned away for lack of space. The fair was a rousing success. Many attendees taught in the toughest neighborhoods in New York City. The speakers were regular classroom teachers from eleven elementary schools in these same neighborhoods. A year earlier, the same teachers would never have considered publicly exhibiting their craft. Now they had designed and conducted a large-scale conference— and they had succeeded.

The 1990 teacher fair at the Bronx Center capped a yearlong READ program conducted by the Teacher Centers Consortium, a UFT project. The centerpiece of the Consortium's activities is the *teacher-specialist*, an experienced classroom teacher who sets up a "center"—a classroom displaying innovative instructional programs, a place where other teachers can talk about educational matters with the specialist and with other colleagues. The idea is not to "sell" any particular program, but to respond to staff needs and interests.

In August 1989, as a kickoff event for Project READ, the Consortium had conducted a weeklong institute for 100 classroom teachers from ten schools throughout New York City. The teachers had volunteered a week of their summer vacation to learn about graphic structures and strategies. Each school was represented by a cohort of ten teachers and their teacher-specialist. Old-timers described the institute as the first professional-development activity for elementary teachers in their memory.

The August institute was enthusiastically received by the teachers, who appreciated being treated as professionals in attractive surroundings. In addition, they knew that the specialist would be there to help after the institute had ended.

Accustomed to the drudgery of late-afternoon workshops, teachers embarked on a heady week of intense concentration on educational practice and opportunities for small groups to work on curriculum improvement. The chance to interact professionally and socially with colleagues recaptured a sense of community. The small-group sessions on curriculum improvement were not schmooze sessions, but were focused tightly on the practical issue of "what to do next Monday."

As the week came to an end, the specialists were essential in helping the school teams devise their plan of action, in sustaining enthusiasm, and in encouraging experimentation. Each school team arranged to report back to their colleagues (a challenge, given the size of most New York City elementary schools). The specialists worked with the school teams on practical tasks, such as designing an agenda for describing to colleagues what they had learned during the institute, or rehearsing their presentations—small matters, but essential for elementary teachers with little experience in giving presentations before adults.

As the year progressed, team members took on responsibilities for staff development along with the specialists. They performed demonstration lessons and conferred with colleagues. Specialists played a major role in assisting (and reassuring) teachers in these roles: connecting one teacher with another, helping with graphics and lesson design, following up initial visits, posting lesson graphics in their centers, in hallways, outside the principal's office. But as fall turned to winter, more and more individual teachers warmed to their new professional responsibilities. A Bronx teacher made a presentation of the READ curriculum to a faculty meeting. Quiet, somewhat timid, typically reluctant to share her ideas, she told why she had agreed to make a formal report: "I was allowed to join in at my own pace. I felt respected. I trust the specialist and my colleagues, and I know they will support me."

The teacher's presentation was well received, and was an important event in her professional life. For elementary teachers accustomed to the four walls of their classroom, moving outside to work as a professional was new and, for many, somewhat unnerving. Most have limited experience with professional presentations. Their days are spent with little children. They may say a few words to parents at back-to-school night, but they have few occasions to stand before an audience of colleagues as experts.

In early spring, Project READ teachers began to talk about conducting a teacher fair. Teachers at nine of the ten schools formed a planning team that quickly grew to more than two dozen people. Teachers prepared plans on their own time, after school or informally over lunch. They met at the Consortium office to polish the final program, refining lesson scripts, reviewing materials and small-group activities, and preparing handouts. They culled samples of student work from their classes and colleagues, reading and writing, science and social studies, marvelous art projects.

The fair was scheduled to start at 9:00 a.m. on a Saturday morning. At 8:00 a.m., teachers began to filter through the parking lot pushing carts loaded with visuals and handouts. Inside the UFT building, the air was tense with anticipation and anxiety. For the teacher-presenters, being a leader was no longer an abstract idea. Long accustomed to the security of their individual classroom, now just becoming comfortable addressing colleagues at their local school, they were about to appear on stage before strangers.

The fair began at 9:00 a.m. as scheduled, with more than 200 teachers and a sprinkling of principals in the audience. After opening comments, the audience broke up into groups for the program, two or three READ teachers meeting for an hour with clusters of 15 to 20 attendees. Each Project READ team explained and illustrated strategies and structures; they showed off streams of wall charts bearing student work, video segments bringing the classroom to the fair, sample lessons that gave the participants a firsthand experience. In one room, a team demonstrated a thematic project on multicultural literature, showing how students had connected themes in *Julie of the Wolves, Roll of Thunder, Hear My Cry, And Now Miguel,* and *Sounder* with stories from their own neighborhoods.[7] The projects included artwork, murals, and dramatizations.

Another team focused on exposition. They displayed several projects, including a matrix created by students to compare and contrast the planets. Student groups assigned to each planet had started with textbook material, along with materials received from NASA and the Museum of Natural History. Each row of the matrix included standard information about size and distance from the sun. The students drew their own pictures of each planet, the usual as-seen-from-space but also what they imagined to be a view from the ground. The class then transformed the completed matrix into their own *Book of the Planets.*

A teacher of learning-disabled adolescents discussed techniques for transforming simple plays into video presentations. *Soup for the King* began as a third-grade reading assignment (synopsis: the king likes soup, the queen doesn't; the tailor's wife cooks marvelous soup, the tailor doesn't eat soup). The students shaped this simple tale into a "Sixty Minutes" special, a complete account of recent turmoils in the castle kitchen. Each of the dozen students played a starring role in their video.

The fair, which took place in May 1990, was but one happy effect of the summer institute of a year earlier. Teachers began to share projects and problems with colleagues in different grades and subject matters. A Harlem school went even further, adopting a nearby school a few blocks away—a short but treacherous distance. But the fair itself was, for the attending teachers, perhaps the single most influential progeny of the cycle. For the thirty-plus READ teachers in the program, it was concrete evidence that their knowledge and talent was valued outside the four walls of the classroom. And this transformation had taken place during a single school year.

What Do These Stories Teach About School Change?

It is not easy to change a school, not in ways that are educationally significant. New paint restores morale, a banner proclaiming adoption by a local business offers hope, a new computer lab opens the way to the "information highway," a change in curriculum materials refreshes the classroom. But U.S. schools seem riven by deep forces that are resistant to change—the lockstep curriculum, age-grading, ability-grouping, teacher isolation, hierarchical management, standardized testing.[8] More than a half-century of research and scholarship testifies to the detrimental effects of these and other practices, but they have remained unchanged.[9]

What should be changed? What should the priorities be? Teachers ask for smaller classes, even though the evidence suggests that the benefits do not justify the costs.[10] Parents ask for smaller schools, especially in the adolescent years, while simultaneously demanding richer curriculum offerings. Policy makers call for higher standardized-test scores, asking at the same time for a guarantee of "high-level thinking." Employers want graduates who read and write, who think and communicate, but who are also responsible citizens and capable team players. How is a school to respond to the never-ending onslaught of demands? The answer, all too often, is a new paint job, a new slogan, a call for greater efforts by families, communities, and voters. Simple solutions to a complex problem. Install a new program. Appoint new committees. Raise a new banner.

The stories in this chapter speak to the ways in which changes in classroom practice can be supported by changes in the way the school operates. Today's school reformers have begun to emphasize *systemic change*.[11] This strategy starts at the top: state and federal programs regulate mandates for teacher training and testing, for curriculum requirements and textbook adoption. The idea is that the effects will filter down to the local school and eventually reach teachers and students at the classroom level. The idea of coordinated change makes sense. But everything seems to affect everything else. Where does one begin?

Our experiences in the Inquiring School network suggest that reforms initiated by the federal and state governments seldom influence teaching and learning; rather, *the school is the most effective level for promoting change*.[12] What should schools change? Reformers have a long shopping list—teacher autonomy, smaller classes, enhanced assessment, elimination of tracking, classroom phones and computers, more parent involvement. These and other improvements in school conditions may be desirable. But they often require resources and influence beyond the control of the local school. Moreover, the higher student achievement resulting from these changes takes a long time to develop and is hard to guarantee. Accordingly, we propose that *the focus for school reform should be the improvement of classroom instruction.* In a nutshell, schools ought to be given local authority and responsibility for improving student achievement.

These conclusions go against the grain of many current reform efforts. Goals 2000, the current federal initiative for school reform, relies on tougher tests and higher standards to "force" improvement.[13] The federal government faces one rather significant problem: states control the public schools, and so the feds must exert influence indirectly. State-level reformers have mandated tougher tests (some of them quite good), developed curriculum frameworks that call for higher-quality instruction, challenged publishers to produce better textbooks, and established more-stringent graduation requirements. None of these actions have seemed to make much difference one way or another in student achievement. (To be sure, none of these calls for action have been accompanied by substantial increases in funding.)

At the local level, elementary schools, particularly those in at-risk communities, are caught between a rock and hard place. They have reacted in a variety of ways: remedial programs specifically aimed at improved test scores; entrepreneurs who manage a "change process": privatization, vouchers, charter schools, "New American Schools."[14] None of these strategies focus on curriculum and none build on cognitive instruction. In addition, it is difficult to find examples where reform programs produce improved outcomes for students and teachers over the long term, especially if one looks at achievement results in the years *after* the program developers and the special funding have disappeared.

The emphasis on local responsibility and accountability makes sense for a couple of reasons. First is the unique role of the public school in a democratic society. If the aim of American schooling were conformity, then top-down strategies might work. But children's elementary-school experiences seem to us the best place to develop individual responsibility and respect for others—the bulwarks of democracy. If we are to recapture the "town meeting" spirit, then every individual must become competent in group problem solving and effective communication. The Inquiring School model aims at both literacy and empowerment—for students *and* for teachers, and within the context of the elementary school. The Inquiring School returns control of schools to teachers—not to assume administrative burdens, but to take responsible control of what they teach and how they teach it; not to develop a new curriculum or develop new instructional strategies, but to adapt existing resources and materials; not to spend time on grant proposals or parent networks, but to collaborate in ensuring that students receive the best possible education during their time in school. A further benefit of focusing from the outset on enhancing student achievement is the payoff for teachers, who derive great job satisfaction from the opportunity to help students become successful learners.

A second reason for promoting local responsibility and accountability is the importance in our diverse society of adapting instruction to local conditions. This book's authors have visited schools and classrooms throughout the country, not for brief snapshots but for extended observations of and conversations with administrators, students, and teachers. We have tried to capture this contextual variety in preceding chapters. Our two fundamental recommendations—establishment of a professional community at the level of the local school, and implementation of a curriculum of critical literacy—apply to all settings. These principles play out differently in large schools versus small schools, in schools with strong administrative leadership versus laissez-faire directors, in rich schools versus poor schools, in schools with declining test scores versus those that are topping out, in schools welcoming change versus those trying to preserve the status quo. But our experience suggests that these two principles are important in every case.

What ought the role of administrators to be? Principals are exhorted to be "educational leaders." Easier said than done. Everyone wants a piece of the principal: parents (you can't turn away a mother on your doorstep), District administrators (multitudes of meetings), students (broken arms require immediate attention), and, of course, teachers. Then there are forms, forms, and more forms. Instructional leadership is important, but what does this label mean? In some schools it means that the principal mandates textbooks and instructional practices. In other schools it means that the principal protects the teachers from external interference while they "do their thing." In both these situations, the school's educational program depends on the principal.

One fact is certain: principals are not forever. Any faculty that depends on the principal to provide resources and ensure protection will be vulnerable when the principal leaves. A fine balance is needed to create a situation in which teachers have the time and encouragement to create a professional community and to develop explicit ways of supporting that community in times of need.

Districts are another important element in supporting educational reform. We have seen instances where District support for staff development seemed enlightened and effective, and other instances where it was heavyhanded and negative. Teachers gain little benefit from monthly meetings in large auditoriums where experts tell them how to do their jobs. Districts usually control most of the money available for staff development, materials, and special personnel. The regulations and restrictions governing the use of these resources can easily stifle program development, either directly or indirectly (sometimes there are so many pieces of paper to fill out that it's just not worth it).

District administrators control the placement of principals and teachers. As we shall see in the next chapter, promising programs can be undercut by abrupt changes in personnel. Circumstances may make such changes understandable, but unpredictability discourages teachers, leaving them with a sense that they have no voice in important decisions, that today's "white knight" will ride off tomorrow. Districts probably have more capacity to destroy a school program than to establish one. While districts, like state and federal governments, can provide leadership and support, the local school is the primary arena for effective reform. And in the elementary grades, the most critical reform objective is the improvement of the character and quality of classroom instruction.

In this country, school reformers—politicians and academics—place little trust in local schools and teachers. In other developed countries, teachers are treated with more respect, are viewed as professionals whose judgment is trustworthy, and are given the time and resources to consult with one another. What is behind the different attitude in the United States? We cannot answer this question here. As we noted in Chapter 2, parents and community members think more highly of their local schools than they do of schools in general. But as we conclude this chapter, it seems worthwhile to return to Gail Ward's web—our teachers need to recover a sense of trust in one another, and our communities need to establish a sense of trust in their local schools. We are not talking about blind trust—to the contrary. The Inquiring School emphasizes both community and communication as foundations for improving student achievement *and* professional development. We think that school reformers—both federal and state—should support local efforts along these lines.

What Can You Do? 6

Although U.S. schools may not be declining as gauged by standard measures of student attainment, neither are they improving. Despite the reform rhetoric, despite what we have discovered about high-level learning, despite the increasing importance of schools as advocates for our children, and despite socially significant demographic shifts in families, today's classrooms are largely unchanged from decades past. The success of the Project READ/Inquiring School model shows that innovative instruction is possible and practical; it also highlights the difficulties in attaining this goal.

We assume that you are concerned about the well-being of American children, and want to see our schools improve. But how? Some observers foresee a future of private voucher-supported schools or home-based education. Perhaps, but we predict that public schools will remain the bulwark of a democratic society. Indeed, they may come to play an even more vital role as centers of family services. Assuming that most children will attend neighborhood schools with teachers and principals, classrooms and playgrounds, books and pencils, what can you do to understand and assist in improving tomorrow's education?

You Can Make a Difference

First, what you choose to do matters. The frustration of powerlessness is endemic today. Whether stalled in freeway traffic, fighting IRS tax forms, fumbling with a VCR clock, or struggling to explain a problem to the mechanic, people are overwhelmed by the complexities of apparently simple problems. Technologies designed to make life easier (ATMs, keyless locks, computers) can instead increase our sense of time urgency and isolation. People who are "there to help" often merely underscore our helplessness and confusion.

Speaking of complexity, schools have become more complicated in recent decades. The education code for California's schools, for example, has swollen to over 6,700 pages. Forms, regulations, committees, meetings—small wonder that citizens feel entangled when they enter the schoolhouse door. Parents have little choice; they either yield up their children hoping that all goes well, or else enter the fray as best they know how. Small wonder that many people stand on the sidelines if they don't have school-age children. Life is already too demanding, there are many other things to do, and our time may not be worth the effort.

But you *can* make a difference, and individual efforts are vital to changing schools. Polls suggest that a substantial proportion of the population, especially those for whom education has worked, want to do something. What that something should be depends on your view of public education. This chapter is concerned not with the politics of "who controls schools," but with the essentials of education—curriculum, instruction, assessment, teachers, students—in individual classrooms and local schools.

Chances are you are well educated and have managed life successfully. Schooling made for good memories. You can probably recall some downers, but also a number of outstanding teachers. You made the system work for you.

You "know" about schooling because you have been there. But familiarity can breed contempt; it can lead you to see things that are not there and miss things that *are* there. You visit a sixth-grade classroom where the teacher's scintillating comparison of *Phantom of the Opera* with *Romeo and Juliet* enthralls students. Surely this performance epitomizes the best that education can offer. From another perspective, however, the lesson may entertain, but does it lead students to develop their own searching comparisons? When they attempt to draw contrasts on their own, say between *Forrest Gump* and *Midsummer Night's Dream*, then the lesson has a genuine payoff. In contrast, your morning with a boisterous group of second-graders rehearsing a class presentation for an upcoming assembly (the issue is whether second-graders should have a representative on the school council) may seem at first an exercise in chaos. Then you see the final presentation, impressive in the passion and clarity of the final argument and the group's capacity to work together as a team. It takes X-ray vision to explore the deeper meanings that lie beneath the surface activities. The guidelines in this chapter are designed to give you that vision.

If you are a parent or grandparent, you have an immediate interest in your local school. If you are an educator, a teacher or principal, then you are in the front lines. You may be a past, present, or future school board member; leadership in public education seems a heavier burden than in decades past. Or you may simply be a citizen concerned with the well-being of children and families. If you fit any of these categories, then our recommendations can direct your efforts or perhaps illuminate directions you are already taking.

On the other hand, you may not yet have children or may be undecided about a family. Your children may have long ago left the nest, breaking any direct connection with schools. You may have declining interest in the entire institution of public schooling. You may be busy building a professional career. If you fall into any of these categories, we hope this chapter will arouse and revive your enthusiasm for action. Our nation's future depends upon our individual and collaborative efforts to ensure that all children achieve their full potential.

Some people envision a future much like the past, in which the socially dislocated are a remote concern lacking personal immediacy— somebody else's problem. This view is undercut by rising crime rates, ghettos creeping into suburban neighborhoods and rural areas, and social problems invading even the most secure enclaves. We have been thrust into a world where everybody's future affects everybody else. You can no longer draw a circle in the sand and say, "We're okay in here!" Only a small band of the most affluent will be able to build fences high enough to keep out the others, if that is what they wish to do. Meanwhile, the rest of us had better learn to look out for each other in a way that is more truly democratic than any social thinking we have so far been able to find. We are talking about the citizens of tomorrow. Given the current birthrate, the proportion of citizens below-decks relative to those at the top will be greater than ever before. The issue is no longer one of altruism, but of survival.

Reading the Reports, Testing the Tests

Our first word of advice is that you become a more knowledge-able consumer of information about schooling in this new era. Most people learn about schools from the media, from friends and relatives, and from occasional school visits. None of these sources is especially trustworthy at present; they overwhelm but do not enlighten.

Education is an inherently political enterprise. In an earlier era, politics were more local than in today's world. This includes the politics of the local school, now overrun by district, state, and federal mandates and regulations. As noted in Chapter 2, schooling looks quite different when parents are asked about their local school and when citizens are asked about schools in general. How can we make sense of what the media say about schools?

The most accessible sources of information about education come from standardized tests. State bureaucrats convene press conferences when the yearly findings are finally calculated, and the media come when called. While standardized tests have limitations, they do correlate with other, more trustworthy indicators; they mean something and should not be dismissed out of hand. Here are four criteria you should apply to reports of standardized-test results; the "it" in all but the third instance is whatever the test measures:

- Does it matter?
- Does it last?
- Who took it?
- Was it taught?

Does it matter focuses on the numbers that measure the level of performance, the changes from one year to the next, and comparisons among schools or districts. Standardized instruments are very precise, and the margin of error is quite small. Reproducible numbers, but what do they mean? Test results are typically reported in percentiles or standard scores, which mean something to psychometricians. These indices, however, do not allow the lay person to answer simple questions such as "How many more (or fewer) questions did this year's class answer correctly, compared with last year?" The stage is set for tempests in teapots while cyclones go unnoticed. In 1992, the National Assessment of Educational Progress (NAEP) evaluated state-by-state reading achievement and found that New Hampshire fourth-graders scored highest at 229 (not quite "Proficient"), while Mississippi fourth-graders were lowest at 200 (decidedly below "Basic"). The difference is statistically significant. And it fits with "common sense," or at least with prevailing stereotypes. But how well can a Proficient student read? A Basic reader? What can a typical New Hampshire fourth-grader do that the average Mississippi student cannot? The reports do not answer such questions, nor does *statistical* significance translate into *educational* significance. As we noted in Chapter 2, the Government Accounting Office has raised serious concerns about these issues.

Does it last refers to the stability of long-term trends. Bad news captures the reader's attention more quickly than good news. A temporary drop in scores makes headlines, even though the ten-year trend may be upward. Improved achievement seldom makes the front pages. Haphazard reporting of achievement data may be the foundation for the general impression that U.S. schools have declined in recent decades; as we have already discussed in this book, a comprehensive view of standardized-test scores suggests that average achievement has remained relatively stable.

"Sound bite" reporting of student achievement is fostered by public policy and bureaucratic practices. State and federal agencies usually require yearly reports. They sometimes ask for comparison with the previous year, but rarely is a meaningful report issued over an extended period. More typically, candidates for state superintendent or for local school boards wax eloquently about gains or declines in test scores from one year to the next (if the trend fits their cause) and ignore the long-term changes.

Educational accounting practices follow the reporting requirements. Districts and states computerize standardized achievement on a yearly basis. Combining records across years for student cohorts is therefore difficult if not impossible. If someone wants to keep track of the class of 2000, they have a gigantic task ahead of them. Schools maintain individual student records on paper, but these are seldom used to keep tabs on student progress. Students who move around a lot fall through the cracks, although the federal system for tracking the children of migrant workers shows what can be done with current technology.

Long-term trends are especially important for evaluating the impact of innovative programs. The media tends to give every new project its fifteen seconds of fame: "New reading technique increases test scores!" When you encounter such reports, check out the generality of the results in time and space—how many years, how many schools, how many places?

Who took it focuses on the students. Like it or not, some students are more likely than others to flourish in the existing system. We have long known that low socioeconomic status, a non-intact family, poor parental education, etc., are correlated with poor student achievement. These statistics have been commonplace for a half-century. Children from families marked by poverty don't do as well in schools, all other things equal, as children from more-advantaged backgrounds. We know that these detrimental conditions are more prevalent today, and also that these factors are often correlated—children who are poor are more likely to have nonintact families, parents who are poorly educated, and so on. Knowing this, you should be skeptical of simple conclusions such as "School success depends on the family" and "Immigrant children can't learn because they don't speak the language and don't understand the culture." Newspaper analyses don't take into account the multiplicity of factors that may be disguised by a catch-all category. Taken one at a time, surface-level factors may predict without explaining. When you read about simple explanations—"The data show that X is the cause of school failure"—ask yourself whether the report considers alternative explanations. Take the term "one-parent family": Mightn't family status be a proxy for poverty? for social instability and conflict? Are we talking about unwed mothers, or the traumas of the recently divorced? Is "immigration" a proxy for social class? Are we applying the same academic expectations to the child of a Nicaraguan refugee doctor and the Chicano child whose parents have never been inside a schoolroom?

When you read a report about *average* achievement, you should ask yourself: Who makes up the "average"? We noted in Chapter 2 the Simpson paradox; every ethnic group has improved on the SAT over the past several years, but the overall average has declined because of changes in the representation of different groups. It is well established that students from poor homes have lower achievement scores. When newspapers report that test scores have declined, ask about changing demographics. When you are told that District A has higher achievement than District B, ask about family backgrounds.

At the same time, educators are sometimes too quick in placing the blame for low test scores on demographics. As noted in Chapter 2, nationwide achievement has remained stable and actually increased during the past few decades for some populations, despite increases in the number of children from impoverished homes and communities.

Look at the performance of specific groups. Suppose a district has instituted a whole-language program of reading instruction, and reports increased reading scores as a result. Did all students benefit equally from the program? Parents of higher-ability children are often concerned that heterogeneous grouping helps less-advantaged students but at a cost to their children. What does the newspaper report tell you about this matter? Another district has installed a basic-skills program. Same questions.

Was it taught may seem obvious, but it's not. When you read that a particular school or district or student group does well or poorly, ask yourself about precisely what is taught and how it is taught. Many students attend schools that are poorly equipped to handle their academic needs. Fundamental fairness would suggest that all students should have equal opportunity to learn, but this ideal has proven difficult to achieve in practice. In the 1960s sociologist James Coleman issued a report, *Equality of Educational Opportunity*,[1] which concluded that student achievement depended largely on background factors like demographic status. At the time schools were still segregated under the policy of "separate but equal." The survey showed that schools attended by black children were substantially inferior to those for white students. Coleman's researchers didn't actually visit classrooms to observe teaching and curricula. They sent questionnaires to administrators, and compared indicators that were easy to measure with standardized-test scores. They found that academic achievement was statistically tied to socioeconomic status, family and community well-being, and so on. In general, poor children went to poor schools and tested poorly. The researchers didn't look for instances of successful ghetto schools, nor did they ask why privileged children sometimes fail.

National surveys have now begun to assess curriculum and instruction along with achievement, often in superficial ways. For instance, the 1992 NAEP fourth-grade survey of reading achievement asked both teachers and students about the frequency of two practices that affect the quality of classroom instruction: worksheet assignments and writing activities. Worksheets ask students for low-level, fill-in-the-blank responses. These tasks are boring and unchallenging; they keep students busy but stifle thinking. Writing about reading, in contrast, is a more demanding task that reflects higher-quality instruction. Figure 6.1 shows that teachers and students have different perceptions about the amount of time spent on these two tasks. Only a third of the teachers report daily worksheet practice, but more than half their students checked this category. The pattern is reversed for writing; three out of four teachers reported that writing occurred at least once a week, while 40 percent of the students said that they wrote less often than that. We think it unlikely that students were *underestimating* the amount of writing! Our point is not that students are right and teachers wrong, but that we need reliable information about instruction if we are to make sense of the

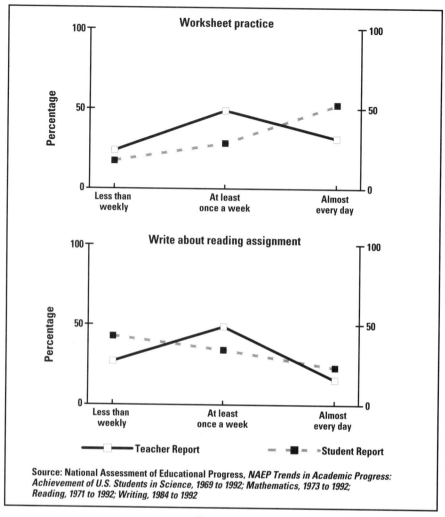

Figure 6.1
Teachers' and students' perception of frequency of
worksheet practice versus writing assignments.

"nation's report card." Even these skimpy data are buried in the technical report. NAEP has not highlighted this information, nor have the media explored them. The information about opportunities to learn is scant to begin with, and we don't even use what we have. What does seem to be indisputably true is that high-achieving students receive a challenging curriculum, which undoubtedly boosts their performance; children identified as low-potential study worksheets and memorize simple facts.[2] The result is that within-grade variability in standardized-test scores typically increases over time; the spread between the top- and bottom-performing groups, small in the early grades, becomes very large for high-schoolers.

We need better information about the factors behind student achievement. The family situation is an important factor, but numerous case studies show students succeeding in school even though they lack a statistically proper family structure, socioeconomic status, or ethnicity. Be skeptical of reports that do *not* describe school conditions and opportunity to learn. The nation has been considering a federalized testing program—the *Goals 2000* of Presidents Bush and Clinton—whose aim is to establish high standards of student achievement and whose results will have high stakes for college entry, scholarships, and employment. The program has explicitly rejected any effort to describe opportunities to learn; many states were uneasy about including such indicators in the mix. The result is likely to be the sound of one hand clapping. Inequalities in schooling persist throughout the nation, and they affect both teacher effectiveness and student achievement. If concerned citizens are to put their shoulder to the wheel, they need to know which wheels matter: preschool programs? support for families? school improvement? tougher tests and higher standards? We should demand information that lets us make these choices intelligently.

Better Pictures

The information-age society that lies just ahead of us will require more of students than success on multiple-choice tests. Graduates need to be productive, creative, and collaborative. Educators are now looking into a variety of alternative assessment methods that better fit these criteria: portfolios, exhibitions, performances. Districts, states, and national programs are exploring and even mandating these alternatives for accountability purposes, for gauging how well students and teachers are doing. Many states now require students to actually write essays (!). Portfolios—collections of student work—are used to assess achievement in Vermont, Kentucky, and several other states.

The virtues of innovative assessments are twofold. First, they force students to demonstrate that they can actually do something. Second, teachers are more involved in assessment; many teachers find it difficult to identify with standardized tests, but can relate to performance tasks. On the down side, these innovative assessments can be expensive in time and money. Compared with standardized tests, they are costly to administer and evaluate. A multiple-choice test takes less than an hour for students to complete, and it can be scanned and scored for pennies in milliseconds; a well-designed writing sample takes more than an hour to draft and polish, and at least a few minutes and perhaps a dollar to read. In Vermont, where teachers have been highly supportive of writing portfolios, they are nonetheless bowing under the added burden on an already crammed-full school day. Reliability can be a problem; scorers do not always agree on the merits of a performance. Finally, when teachers are allowed a say about assessment, they tend to adapt testing to the local context. They ask students to write about topics of immediate interest and relevance. They adjust time and support depending on their judgments about students. They look for ways to optimize chances for success rather than finding ways to trip up their students.

California offers a case study in the opportunities and risks of alternative assessment, in the mingling of extraordinarily innovative approaches with amazing strategic gaffes. Because many other state and federal programs are moving along similar tracks, the California experience offers lessons for everyone who is concerned about school improvement.

We begin with CLAS—the California Learning Assessment System, now in limbo and probably defunct. CLAS is a collection of tests that require students to demonstrate high-level thinking and competent performance. In the reading-writing test for fourth-, eighth-, and tenth-graders, for instance, students analyze a lengthy passage, discuss their analysis with several other students, and then write individual compositions on a related topic. In one version of the test, tenth-graders begin with an excerpt from *The Woman Warrior: Memoirs of a Childhood among Ghosts,* the autobiography of Maxine Hong Kingston. The excerpt recounts Kingston's early period in U.S. schools, when, she writes, "my silence was thickest—total—during the three years that I covered my school paintings with black paint." While reading the excerpt, students are asked to describe the author's thoughts and feelings, and to contrast schools in China and the United States. Following this task, groups of four students discuss their previous school experiences for half an hour; they are encouraged to take notes during the discussion. In a third session, students write individual essays recounting an autobiographical incident from their school days.

Opposition to CLAS centered initially around certain controversial reading passages. Other citizens protested that reading and writing should be taught as basic skills, and that students should not be asked to write about personal thoughts and feelings. While teachers were generally enthusiastic about the test design, many complained that feedback to them about student performance was incomplete and late in coming and that they were not given scores for individual students. The final blow came with a technical analysis criticizing the test's reliability. In the fall of 1994, California governor Pete Wilson vetoed funding for the entire state testing system.

While many complaints about CLAS ring true, the baby has been thrown out with the bathwater. The test's shortcomings are all fixable, and the basic design of CLAS has many positive features: It requires genuine performance by students and is a test worth "teaching to." It blends standard conditions with a degree of open-endedness. It has been applauded by teachers for its authenticity. And it represents the kind of test that merits public attention; if CLAS scores improve, citizens are assured that students are getting better at handling demanding tasks, and if they decline, then the public should be worried.

In addition to the one-shot CLAS test, California has experimented with portfolios, collections of student work assembled over the course of the school year and then submitted for evaluation. The basic idea of portfolios is sound, because it goes to the heart of what reading and writing are really about. Unlike standardized examinations, portfolios provide information over an extended time about students' plans and progress in performing a variety of tasks. For example, a portfolio might begin with students' fall writing samples, followed by several collaborative and individual projects and culminating in a spring exhibition. Portfolios also include evidence about instructional support. For instance, a portfolio filled with worksheets and quizzes is evidence of limited support compared with a portfolio that shows a steady progression from fall to spring in the development of increasingly complex compositions.

While some California school districts support portfolios and many classroom teachers have adopted portfolios on their own, these activities have been unsystematic. By contrast, in states like Vermont and Kentucky, portfolios are now a major element in statewide assessment. Unlike California, where both CLAS tests and portfolios are shipped to central locations for scoring by "strangers," in both Vermont and Kentucky local teachers assess their students' work, with validation checks to ensure consistency. The process of collecting and evaluating this information is expensive, but surveys suggest positive effects on instruction. Teachers are directly involved in the process, and they get immediate feedback about their students—and so do parents and interested community members.

Innovative assessments can play an important role in statewide accountability, but the local school and district remain the focal point for action. How can the results of exams and portfolios move to center stage at the local level? At present, newspaper reports of statewide standardized-test results appear each year to the delight or despair of school boards and local administrators—a "blip from on high"—and then interest quickly subsides. The local school or district is a passive recipient of the information and seldom has any real opportunity for input or reaction. As it turns out, California has in place a mechanism to remedy this situation. An annual "School Report Card" must be prepared for every school in the state with information about various programs—number of library books, attendance rate, test scores, and so on. We use the passive voice because most districts treat the Report Card as a bureaucratic exercise, one more piece of paperwork. The district evaluation office gathers the data, prepares a narrative, and sends a copy to the school. The Department of Education does not review these reports, nor do we know of any instances where a local board has relied on them for reviewing schools.

Imagine a system in which the School Report Card was taken seriously—how might this device better inform parents and community members? Consider this purely hypothetical, four-part scenario:

The *Program Section* of the Report Card presents the school's educational program. What are the distinctive features of the school? What are the teachers like? What does the school emphasize in its curriculum? What is the policy on discipline? on student government? on faculty government? The school's job in this section is to sell itself. In Palo Alto, California, for instance, Ohlone Elementary is a magnet school that must annually justify its "open-education" program—classes are multigraded, the curriculum is flexible, student discussion and teamwork are emphasized. Across town, Hoover Elementary provides an alternative program stressing traditional academics. Both are open-enrollment public schools—which means that they have to sell their programs to parents continuously in order to attract students. For more than twenty years, both schools have been effective in doing just that.

The *Client Section* describes students—their backgrounds, their interests, their aspirations. It also portrays parents and families—what do they do, and what are their aspirations for their children? This section is important for understanding the context of education in a particular school—cultures and languages, stability and change.

The *Outcome Section* highlights student accomplishments and achievements. It contains test information of various types, including displays showing trends over time for different student groups. Here is where the school reports attendance, attitudes, and tardies, and where you learn about special awards and attainments—in academics, but also in the arts, in sports, and in community service.

Finally, the *Futures Section* reports the school's reflections on its accomplishments and challenges—what is working and what needs fixing? What is the three-year plan of action, in which the teachers collectively lay out their satisfactions and concerns, their priorities for the years to come?

This design for a School Report Card can be linked to a public process that involves all those with interests in the school—students, families, citizens, school board members, the business community. It belongs to the local school but also provides for district and state accountability.

So far, so good—but where are schools to find the time and energy required to create such a document? As it turns out, California schools already conduct a self-study called the Program Quality Review (PQR) every three years, providing the foundation for the Report Card. Schools take the PQR quite seriously, not as a bureaucratic activity but as an opportunity for the local school to take stock. Faculties organize into committees to review student achievement, scrutinize curriculum offerings, examine policies for discipline and conflict resolution, update professional-development programs, and evaluate relations with parents and community groups. The resulting self-study is generally comprehensive and soul-searching. Once the report is completed, an external team of teachers, administrators, and parents conducts a two-to-three-day site visit. They are free to investigate any other facets of the school's program that they choose. The team then prepares an independent report of strengths and areas for improvement.

The PQR requires a great deal of work, but it provides an extraordinary professional experience for California schools. It seems quite natural to link the PQR report to the School Report Card. In practice, however, the two activities fall under different legislative categories and are totally separated from one another. While most schools conduct the PQR with fear and trembling—what if they are not perfect?—the report actually receives little attention beyond the local school itself. The district forwards the report to the State Department of Education, which does little more than acknowledge receipt. The main value of the effort is in providing an impetus for faculty, administrators, and parents to take a long, deep look at how they are doing.

We need better and more trustworthy pictures of our schools. If schools did a better job of portraying themselves, of telling their stories clearly and seriously, then communities would be far more understanding and supportive in many instances. Whatever your role—parent, citizen, student, teacher—you have the right to press schools toward that end.

Entering the Schoolhouse Door

It is easy to criticize schools at a distance. Once you step inside, things become more complex. Even in the most successful schools, you quickly become aware of how busy everyone is. The label may be "public school," but except for special occasions like September open house and back-to-school nights, the public is seldom there. To really understand education, you need to visit classrooms. This sounds simple, but it isn't. The first challenge is to get inside. In some neighborhoods, you may feel that you are entering an armed camp. You search the ominously dilapidated building for the unlocked door, check with the hallway guard, make your way to the office, try to catch the secretary's attention as she deals with a gaggle of sullen "sent to the office" students, and ask for the principal (who is busy with an angry parent). It may be a while before you open a classroom door. Schools in nicer neighborhoods have more allure—attractive architecture and landscaping, windows splashed with the bright colors of children's paintings, an accommodating secretarial staff. Here, too, the principal may be meeting with a parent, but you will probably find your way to the classroom more quickly, easily, and safely.

Whatever the circumstances, the best way to understand and bolster today's schools is to take a firsthand look. Whether you volunteer as a tutor or serve as "Principal for the Day," you are likely to gain more empathy for the people who take care of our children—teachers, custodians, secretaries, and even principals. If you are a parent busy with many other matters, a visit may lead you to consider a greater investment in your children and the children of others. If you are a grandparent (especially a grandfather), you may discover the enormous value of your presence as a member of the outside world, an older person, a man.

Learning about schools is not easy. Merely having been a student or parent isn't enough. What do you look for? Whom do you talk with? What questions should you ask? How do you understand the answers? You have to become an ethnographer, a stranger in a strange land. You need to look beneath the surface routines of school life, find meaning in chaos, see creativity and individuality in conventional activities, and distinguish between experiences that are cognitive and constructive and those that are faddish and even foolish.

This section offers advice for the serious classroom tourist. It is organized around two situations: (a) you are welcomed into the classroom, with time to look around, observe activities, talk with the students, and maybe even grab a moment with the teacher; and (b) you are marched through the school by the principal, who takes you into a few classrooms, walks you around the playground or lunchroom, maybe has time for a brief chat in his or her office. How can you make the most of these opportunities to understand the school?

Three things to look for in the classroom. Once you are inside, how can you gauge the character and quality of the children's educational experience in this classroom? Our aim here is not to offer suggestions about how you can help—we'll discuss that matter a little later—but to help you make sense of what you see. You can visit after school or during recess, when classrooms are empty, when teachers and principal can talk with you, when you can study the environment. But the real insight comes from a room full of students. A surface view easily equates quiet with learning and noise with a lack of discipline. But quiet can also mean boredom, and noise can signify genuine learning. Here are a few guidelines for making informed judgments about the character and quality of classroom instruction from a relatively brief foray into this familiar but foreign territory:

First, *watch the walls*. Teacher and students share the same small space six hours a day, five days a week, so you can learn a lot by studying the physical environment. It's like visiting someone's home for the first time. You note room design and color scheme, artworks and artifacts, furniture and books. You form an impression.

What are you looking for here? Programs like Project READ offer an answer to this question. Visual graphics can tell the tale directly and obviously. Webs, weaves, story graphs, and other READ structures can instantly give you a handle on student thinking. Now, are you looking at immaculate teacher portraits or messy student efforts? Is the work organized or chaotic? Do you see only finished products or a succession of activities? Individual papers or collaborative efforts? Displays for students or grown-ups? It's amazing how often the ABC chart for kindergartners is tacked near the ceiling rather than down where the children live.

How is time spent? You may not be able to spend a lot of time in a classroom, but the daily schedule can be informative. If the subject matter changes on a regular basis—Reading, 8:30 to 9:15; Spelling, 9:15 to 9:30; Recess, 9:30 to 9:45; Writing, 9:45 to 10:15; Mathematics, 10:15

Figure 6.2
Storytelling in a kindergarten class.

to 11:00—you have stumbled on an artifact of the assembly-line era. Do the wall displays stress learning, or management? If the dominant chart is titled "Classroom Rules," this signals an emphasis on control. If instead you are overwhelmed by words and labels, then you are in the midst of a literate community. If you see lots of writing, if student compositions are strung from wires stretched across the room, if you feel overwhelmed by the outpouring of "stuff," then you are on the scent of critical literacy.

The physical environment is more than walls, of course. Public schools are public, so go ahead and explore desks, tables, boxes, folders, nooks and crannies. If you are impressed with neatness, then you are probably not in the presence of the "works in progress" that indicate active learning. Construction is a messy business. Teachers, brought up to value neatness, are understandably uneasy with this concept. Where can you look for clutter? It is sometimes in plain view on student desks, more often in folders. The teacher's table offers a source of information: loaded with papers read or to be read, scribbles showing the teacher's feedback. Do the red marks focus on spelling and grammar, or do they suggest structural revisions? Does the teacher assign a grade or offer opportunities for improvement? If you were the student, would you be inclined to put more effort into the project?

Look at the instructional materials. Do you find a plethora of worksheets asking students to do little more than mark the right answer or fill in the blank, or assignments requiring students to wrestle with a blank piece of lined paper? Do you see desks stacked with textbooks, or with a literary mélange—stories, anthologies, adventure tales, magazines, newspapers, how-to-do-it books? Is there a classroom library? What about pictures, which can be worth thousands of words?

Second, *listen to the voices.* Words—spoken words—are critically important. The students assemble, the teacher begins the lesson. It's easy to become distracted; you already know the answers. The key is to focus on the instructional process: Who is talking, who is listening? Research shows that teachers do most of the talking at all grade levels, but increasingly so at the later grades. Teacher talk certainly has a place, but students must also be encouraged to raise their voices and express their thoughts if they are to learn to use language to solve problems and to communicate. In the classroom, student silence is not golden.

Student talk is not necessarily golden, either. The teacher's job is to shape student conversation into significant discourse and to orient casual comments toward problem solving. If you think this is simple, try to recall your attempts to initiate conversations with your own children—"What did you do in school today?"

Listen to the questions. Assuming that most come from the teacher, what are reasonable answers? If "Yes/No" is the only choice, then the foundation for meaningful dialog is slim unless followed by "Why?" Multiple-choice questions—"Was Mary's hair dark or light?"—don't open up much territory either. Nor do leading questions like "Don't you think that. . . ?" Open-ended questions are much more stimulating.

Listen also for the big picture. How does the teacher organize the discourse? Is he or she a bottleneck, limiting discussion to one question at a time? Or does the teacher lay out a framework that invites students, individually and collectively, to absorb themselves in the topic? If this task seems simple, think about your experiences in formal meetings: Who sets the agenda? Is it reasonable? What is your role? What are your options? Do you have a voice? How do you assert your ideas? These questions, critical to effective participation in the adult world, have equal significance in classrooms, where children are learning to achieve as grown-ups.

Finally, listen for signs of enthusiasm and motivation. Do students seem sincerely interested in the work, or are they going through the motions? READ-like lessons are actually *fun,* often leaving students and teachers with a vague sense of guilt. But hard work need not be synonymous with pain.

You have looked and listened. Now *ask for explanations*. Feel free to take the initiative. Sometimes you find it impossible to talk with anyone, and that's a signal in itself. As a visitor you may feel invisible; you walk through the door, the teacher glances up briefly, students raise their eyebrows, and then everyone returns to the lesson as though you are not there. No opportunity to talk with anyone. In contrast stands the classroom where you are welcomed by teacher and students, where the flow of events opens to include you, where you are invited to join the activity.

Classrooms are busy places, and some activities (e.g., standardized testing) forbid interaction. Some times are better than others. The first and last two weeks of school are stressful. Mornings are better than late afternoons, Wednesdays better than Mondays or Fridays. But the essence of critical literacy is communication. Visitors—parents, other teachers and students, and even strangers—offer a chance to test the class's skills in a real-world way. The genuinely open classroom offers an environment in which students see visitors as an opportunity to display learning rather than as a distraction from it.

When you get a chance to talk with students about their work, a few simple questions go a long way:

- What are you doing?
- Why are you doing it?
- What are you learning from it?

Not exactly rocket science, but quite revealing. Students who are performing rote activities in a mindless manner will look at you as though you've just arrived from Mars. Those who are working on more purposeful projects and are more metacognitive about learning will demonstrate their strategic awareness of the lesson. In Orion School in Redwood City, California, students collect portfolios of schoolwork: writing samples, mathematics problems, book reports, science and social-studies projects. At conference time, when parents come to discuss their child's progress with the teacher, students actually run the conference. They use their portfolios to discuss plans during the past few months, review their accomplishments, and lay out goals for coming months. Orion students have no difficulty in handling questions like those posed above; they simply will show you their portfolios.

In listening to students and teachers discuss their schoolwork, you should attend to *content* ("We're doing a unit on Native Americans"), but also listen for *learning techniques*. Over the long haul, it's important for children to study the content featured in official textbooks and curriculum frameworks: the causes of the Civil War, the chemical formula for water, *The Red Badge of Courage*, and so on. But equally important is the acquisition of structures and strategies for approaching a task: how to weigh the various causes of the Civil War, how to visualize the meaning of H_2O, how to think through the themes of Stephen Crane's novel. It is one thing to memorize a problem-solving strategy; it is another to know how to frame a problem. It is important to know the steps in the scientific method; it is another to learn how to think as a scientist does.

If you can manage it, a few moments of conversation with the teacher can reveal a lot. In fact, you have learned a lot about the classroom if the teacher agrees to talk with you during class. It means that he or she has the confidence that the students can handle themselves. The noise level will probably rise; individual students may raise their hands or come up to the two of you. How does the teacher handle these matters?

Your questions for the teacher can be similar to those for students. What's happening in this lesson? What are your purposes? How is the class coming along? If you have already scanned the environment, you can inquire about specific instances. Ask for "war stories." Most teachers like to talk about children, and you can learn a lot about the teacher's educational philosophy by noting how he or she describes students and learning. Ask about the school. The goal here is not to provoke gossip, but to gain a sense of the teacher's collegiality with other faculty, and to understand development in other grades. As we noted in Chapter 5, teaching is an isolating experience in many U.S. schools—more so than, say, in Japan, where half a teacher's time is spent consulting with other teachers. If you find evidence of connections and common purpose, you have found a winner.

Listen for sounds of enthusiasm. When you "catch the spirit"—when virtually every teacher speaks with professional pride and personal fervor about their students, their colleagues, their school, and their community—then again you have found a winner. Teaching demands incredible energy. The chief rewards come from helping children achieve their learning potential.

Walking and talking with the principal. School principals in the United States have an impossible job. They are expected to be educational leaders, like the "head teachers" in Great Britain. They are expected to be efficient managers and effective businesspeople. They must deal with the problems of everyone in the school: students, teachers, and parents. They are accountable to external authorities—the superintendent and the board, but also the police and other child service agencies. Their doors are open and their phones accessible to virtually anyone at any time. When the school's intruder alarm goes off at 2:00 a.m. in the morning, guess whom the security service calls? The principal's daily agenda is driven by moment-to-moment demands beyond his or her control. Time for reflection and planning are virtually nonexistent.

And so, if you catch a few moments with the school principal, you will probably be walking. Not only will the exercise do you some good, but you will gain an interesting perspective. Is the tour purposeful or meandering? Does the principal tell you about the school or ask you about your motives for coming? Is most of the time spent in the office, in hallways, or in classrooms? Are you told what to look at or asked about what you see? Are you shown special programs or regular lessons, computers or people? If the tour includes classroom visits, how do teachers and students react to the principal's presence?

Ask the principal to explain the school. You can use the School Report Card design laid out earlier in this chapter as a framework: what about the program, the students, the outcomes, the plan? The book *In Search of Excellence,* by Tom Peters and Robert Waterman, describes successful businesses as focused and coherent, driven by a common vision stretching from the chairman's office to the workplace. As you move through the halls and classrooms, listen for a vision, a mission, a commitment.

During a recent visit to a Bay Area middle school, for example, the principal rhapsodized about the multimedia computer lab—top-of-the-line equipment and software! Unfortunately, we saw little evidence of how the lab was benefiting students. The work samples posted around the walls showed that the lab teacher was having a fantastic experience exploring the software, but we saw no student work. In an elementary school north of Stanford University, the principal told us about the success of her parents program. A "Family Room" provided coffee and goodies, the school sponsored weekly jazzercize classes, potluck dinners, and other social events. Special funding made it possible to hire a part-time parent coordinator. The program was clearly succeeding—the school office was alive with grown-ups! A great first step, but it appeared to be an end in itself and was not linked to educational outcomes. For instance, the program did not help second-language families with their children's English assignments; it did not connect with teachers' concerns (they thought about homework and tutoring more than potluck dinners).

Ask the principal about his or her job. Enthusiasm is a hallmark; you have to like this job to stay with it. But where is the enthusiasm directed? Toward the faculty and the students, toward programs, toward budgets and administrative tasks? Principals keep lots of balls in the air, but they differ widely in where they find their "joy" and in the extent of that joy. They also differ in how they use the power inherent in their position. You will find schools that are clearly top-down; indeed, in the past half-century, most schools have been managed like factories, with the principal as boss, teachers as workers, students as products. Recent years have seen a shift toward "shared power," collaborations in which faculty and principal are a professional community. You can find evidence for a sense of community by listening to how the principal describes the school's people and programs, and then comparing this account with what you see and hear from others. Some principals build their careers by filling the school with "cutting edge" activities like the computer lab and parent program described above. In the worst cases, the parts don't fit together and there are substantial human costs from juggling multiple agendas. In the best cases, principals help the school operate as a center of child and family services, a way to cut the Gordian knot of poverty, ethnicity, low educational attainment of parents and low academic expectations for children. This has some merit in communities where families and neighborhoods are failing their children. But achieving such a goal requires the involvement of the entire professional staff. The effective principal organizes the school as a developing institution, one in which teachers and parents play a role in the long-term planning and implementation of programs—where everyone's shoulder is put to the same wheel.

How the Home Can Help the School

An African proverb says that "it takes the whole village to raise a child." Our villages aren't what they used to be when the work of the school was undergirded by parents, extended family, and neighborhood. Many of today's neighborhoods have lost the sense of community. Except at work and in the home, we have few connections with others. And homes are certainly not what they used to be. In *America's Smallest School: The Family*, Educational Testing Service presents data on the positive effects of traditional family structure on student achievement, while also noting that the proportion of children living with single parents more than doubled over the past two decades, from 10 percent in 1969 to 22 percent in 1989. The figure for 1994 is 28 percent—more than one in four children! It's easy to show that single parenthood correlates with decreased school performance; the effects on two-parent children when both mother and father are working are more difficult to gauge. What's clear is that most families have less time to help children with school these days.

In addition, the kind of help that schools need from the home has changed. Report cards have become portfolios rather than grades, homework has become project plans and draft compositions rather than worksheets and spelling tests. That said, parents have many ways to support students. If you have young children, you can help at home by talking and reading to them; if you don't, you can work in the classroom as a volunteer, where you may be asked to tutor a student in need of help, monitor during recess to give teachers a break, accompany groups on field trips, tell stories in the school library, or act as a big brother or sister. Each of these activities is an opportunity to support children's language and literacy development.[3]

Throughout this book we have emphasized the acquisition of critical literacy—the literate use of language to think and communicate. Parents can take specific actions that support the child's development of literacy—not just the basic skills of reading and writing, but the attitudes that lead to a love of literature, an appreciation of good books, and a sense of competence and efficacy. At all levels of family structure and income, some homes are successful in promoting these outcomes. Research has focused on concrete artifacts: the number of books in the home (more is better), hours of television viewing (less is better, to a point), years of preschool (a worthwhile investment), and so on. The most important factor, however, is parent time invested in language development and literacy. Not every family can afford large book collections, blocks and magnetic letters, educational toys, computer games, special preschools, and so on. But all parents—even those with little money and limited literacy and for whom English is a second language—can talk with their children about the world around them. Those who can afford educational "goodies" still need to invest personal time, especially during the early years of childhood, in reading and telling stories and drawing out their children's ideas and interests. There is no substitute for lap time, for walking around the neighborhood, for committing yourself to your child's growth in language and thought.

Children's needs depend on a lot of factors, but age is especially critical. The rest of this section is accordingly organized around developmental levels. We begin with the years before school and move on toward adolescence.

The preschool years. Up through age four, our main advice is to immerse children in a language-rich environment. Talk a lot *with* children, not just *at* them. Ask questions. Explore answers. Expand and rephrase tentative thoughts. Encourage them to ask, "Why?"—even when you may not know the answer or feel pressed for time. Use the environment to stimulate conversation. Grocery stores offer numerous opportunities for discussion and wordplay. Think about the store as a gigantic "web": clusters of related items and activities. The meat counter operates quite differently from the produce section, and then come the frozen and canned goods. Fruits and vegetables vary marvelously in shape, size, and color—an enormous "weave." Talk about the process: How do you plan your shopping trip on different occasions—after work, before Thanksgiving, for a birthday party? The changing seasons open up other possibilities, no matter where you live. Night and day, heat and cold, rain and wind, sun and clouds—these variations affect us all and can be discussed by young and old. How do these changes feel? What causes them? How do you live with them?

Books are good—story books, ABC books, pop-up books. Quality is more important than quantity. A visit to the library lets a child try on different styles. Balance adult preferences with children's interests. "Educational books" may have less to offer than genuine literature. Skim resources like Jim Trelease's *Read-Aloud Handbook,* but don't let these limit explorations to the local library or bookstore, which can be valuable in their own right. The classics have much to offer, but the last decade has seen an outpouring of marvelous books by U.S., Canadian, British, and Australian writers.[4] Don't worry too much about age-level recommendations. Dahl's *James and the Giant Peach* may seem advanced for a 3- or 4-year old, but you may be surprised; read a chapter or two at bedtime and see what happens.

Young children are fascinated by "manipulatives:" blocks, letter tiles, and other concrete objects that they can handle. These can be fun to play with all by themselves, but they also promote engagement with language, with print, and with ideas. Parents are told to have their children memorize the ABCs, shapes, color names, and other basics; nothing wrong with this advice, but learning how to get along with others is equally important. Simple games can support social interactions with adults and other children.

What about television and computers? In this high-tech age, parents are often on tenterhooks about how to prepare their youngsters to travel on the information superhighway. Television is a particular concern. Some parents try to ban all viewing. Does watching television hinder the growth of literacy? The answer depends on how much children watch, what they watch, and what they do with the information. Viewing time matters. Children in the United States watch more television than anywhere else in world except Japan, but students in both countries have higher reading scores than their counterparts in other countries like Belgium and Switzerland, where children spend less than half as much tube-time.[5] Comparisons within nations reveal an "inverted-U" relation between viewing time and reading achievement; scores are highest for students who watch more than a little (an hour a day) but less than a lot (three hours a day). It appears that students are not harmed and may be helped by judicious exposure to the world of television. "Judicious" is partly a matter of quantity, but equally important is quality. The best programming in this country—*Sesame Street* and other offerings from Children's Television Workshop, for example—is truly outstanding. These programs introduce the child to the artifacts of literacy (letters, words, signs) while emphasizing ideas, social interaction, and communication.

Less is known about the influence of computers on children's development of language and literacy. Well-off families are more likely to have home computers, but libraries, museums, and preschools can fill the gap. What should you do with a computer if you have one? The preschool software market is packed with "educational games." Our advice here parallels our recommendations about books. Explore options with your preschooler, follow his or her interests, and don't insist on "drill-and-kill" exercises promising that your five-year-old will become a "reader." Reading is more than decoding, and the computer can be more than an automated worksheet. Explore opportunities for your child to create art, to make up his or her own stories, to play interactive games.

But whether the medium is book, toy, television, or computer, *what matters most is your investment of time and energy in your child and his or her friends.* READ strategies and structures can amplify the value of these investments. How do you read a story? How do you watch television? How do you walk through the park or the supermarket? How do you talk with a child? Thoughtfulness doesn't mean taking the fun out of parent-student interactions. Rather, by keeping a few key strategies in mind and by reflecting on what is happening, you can take advantage of natural situations to help your child become an inquiring person.

The CORE model from Chapter 3 (Connect, Organize, Reflect, Extend) offers a solid foundation for interaction. Preschoolers may seem difficult to *connect* with; the key is a genuine curiosity about what's happening in their head, what's going on in their mind's eye. Based on our own educational experiences, many of us feel compelled to tell children what to look at rather than ask them what they see; to tell them what they should listen to rather than ask them what they hear. They can use help, of course. *Cloudy with a Chance of Meatballs* is a crazy story about weird weather, which may entertain your child but not make much sense. Before opening the book, ask your child, "What would happen if food started raining from the sky?" You may have to wait for a moment, and it's better if you haven't already read the book so that the question is real for you as well as your child. Explore plausible possibilities, along with implausible ones. This brief activity connects with your child's emerging sense of plot and brings this capability to consciousness.

Connections can be stimulated by pointing out curiosities and commonplaces, to see what your child makes of them. Backyards and parks are great for this purpose; stop for a spider web or stoop for an anthill, a flower, or a footprint. Build a semantic web: What do you see, what is happening, how did it get started, how will it end up? Be flexible. If your child wants to do something else, don't turn it into an oral examination. Become a student of your child.

Can preschoolers really *organize* anything? Many parents may find this concept absurd. In fact, research shows that 3-year-olds are just beginning to form concepts that they can express, given a little help. To be sure, these concepts may not precisely mirror the way you have learned to organize the world. Let's go back to the supermarket. From your parental perspective, you may see things much as the store manager does: meat, dairy, frozen foods, bakery, produce, and so on. What a ridiculous conception! Before you had children, your categories were probably deli section, TV dinners, and snacks. What about a preschooler? The checkout counter is the highlight; that's where the candy is located! The point is that walks to the supermarket, the zoo, or the beach, and even around the neighborhood, offer opportunities to talk with young children about organizing principles, not as fixed categories but as ways of making sense of the world and communicating with others.

Finally, what about *reflection* and *extending* the child's world? Preschoolers are not naturally inclined to reflect. Jean Piaget first documented in the 1930s the four-year-old's tendency toward egocentrism. About the same time Lev Vygotsky described the progression from self-centeredness to social interaction and on to reflection. U.S. schools are only now learning about the work of these developmentalists.[6]

Children's literature opens the door for both reflection and extension. A well-written story can transport one person into the life of another, the essence of reflection. What did *Swimmy* think when all of his cousins disappeared into the tuna's giant maw! How did *Frederick the Mouse* feel when his cousins applauded his springtime speech? In Umberto Eco's *The Three Astronauts*, three Earthlings (from the United States, Russia, and China) suddenly confront an outrageous-looking Martian; what is it like to have green skin, six arms, and a six-inch nose? When the tiniest child in Who-ville yells out "Yopp" at a critical moment in Dr. Seuss's *Horton Hears a Who*, what would it be like to be Horton, the elephant-savior? To be the tiniest child? Questions such as these work not by forcing factual recall but by offering the child a chance to empathize. A daycare teacher may find it difficult to pursue a dozen different imaginations (although our experience suggests otherwise), but a parent's bedtime story offers opportunities to draw out the child's reflections and support children's efforts to build their own stories.

Aren't we just talking about what comes naturally? No! The attentiveness described above is anything but natural. Well-educated parents, like the teachers who taught them, know how to talk better than how to listen. The situation is no different for parents with less schooling. No one listens to children! It takes a special turn of mind to focus on the child's world. Our traditions are rooted in an image of children as "little people," small replicas of grown-ups, rather than in a developmental perspective.

Can parents learn to communicate effectively with their preschool children, and with what impact on later school achievement? Research suggests that parents can learn to communicate better with their children regardless of ethnicity, income level, or parenting style, and that the effect on school achievement is positive. One example comes from the HOPE preschool program developed and evaluated by the Appalachia Educational Laboratories in the 1970s. The basic premise was that preschoolers could benefit cognitively and attitudinally from television programs such as *Sesame Street*, *Mr. Rogers' Neighborhood*, and *Captain Kangaroo* when parents watched the programs along with their children and discussed what they were seeing. The program stretched from the hollows of West Virginia to tenant farms north of Huntsville, Alabama. All of the families were poor.

The researchers set up four groups: (a) *control* preschoolers were pre- and post-tested on a battery of cognitive and language tests, but were otherwise left alone; (b) the *packet* group was also tested, but each family received a monthly packet of materials linked to the television programs, the idea being that parents (actually mothers) would watch the programs, talk with their children, and work with them on the activities in each packet; (c) the *home visitor* group was tested and received packets, but in addition, each week during one of the television programs a "home visitor" stopped by to watch the program with the child and the mother, demonstrating how to use the packet and how to talk during the program (the home visitors were typically college students or unemployed teachers); and (d) the *Saturday school* group participated in all the above activities, but also provided preschoolers a Saturday session in a house-trailer staffed by a teacher or two.

The statistical results were clear-cut. The home visitor had a large positive effect on cognitive and language indicators. Sending a packet home made no difference, and the Saturday School did not in itself improve achievement. Low-income parents prepared their children for kindergarten better when a home visitor spent time with them modeling the simple task of watching educational television.

What happened here? The quantitative data tell part of the story; visits to participating families by a team of educators (including co-author Calfee) provided additional detail. The following snapshot from Huntsville demonstrates the possibilities. Our team piled out of a rented Cadillac into the dirt yard of a log cabin. Calfee walked across the yard toward two little girls, two and four years old, who huddled by the house in their Sunday best. He knelt down; "What's your name?" he asked the older child. Incredibly, given the circumstances, she answered. She introduced her sister and exchanged a few words. She said that her mother had told her that visitors were coming to talk with her sister and her. Inside the cabin, the young mother spoke with the visitors about her children. She would probably live out her life on this farm, but she was determined that her daughters have access to other opportunities. She described how the home visitor helped her to ensure that her daughters were ready for school. She expected her daughters to succeed in school and go to college. The home visitor had connected this mother with the (televised) world outside her log cabin and, more importantly, had modeled ways to help her daughters deal with the strangeness of school. The interaction with another person was important for this mother, far more than a packet of materials or a "Saturday school" disconnected from the family.

A family-support program must build on some level of family support. In another home that we visited, the mother was surprised by the group's arrival. Although the Laboratory had contacted her, she seemed uncertain about who we were, why we were there, and where her children might be. She said that she was happy to have the home visitor, but talked about it as child care. We suspect that the statistical effectiveness of the program resulted because more families fell into the first category than the second.

The first three years of school. What can you do once your child has entered kindergarten, and in the primary years through second grade? Kindergarten is relatively easy for the child who has been in preschool, but can be a shock for the child without any previous school experience. The passage from kindergarten to first grade is another shock, one that can challenge any child. When kindergarten emphasizes socialization and first grade demands that students be "ready to read," this mismatch can leave a child confused. The move to second grade is often equally abrupt. Fluent oral reading is expected by then, and students who, for whatever reason, are still struggling to decode printed words begin to attract attention. We draw the line at second grade because in many schools third grade is the boundary line for assigning poor readers to special-education programs.

What should the early years of schooling look like, and how can parents help their children during these formative stages of literacy acquisition? While American schools are organized by grade levels, the British ungraded primary school provides an alternative environment for supporting the development of language and literacy. In this model, a single teacher works with a cohort of students over a two- or three-year time span. Each year several new students join the class as kindergartners and several others "graduate." Most students stay with the same teacher for two or three years, allowing the teacher to adjust the program to accommodate developmental variations. The range of ages makes it possible to match early maturers with late bloomers. The aim is to help every child during these early years of schooling to optimize his or her potential, recognizing individual differences but downplaying competition.

While you should explore alternatives, you are most likely to find the primary grades in your neighborhood organized by grades. Ask about the program—not just kindergarten, but the years following. How do the teachers describe their approaches to language and social development, and to the acquisition of reading and writing? How do they handle individual differences among children? Don't wait until the fall; visit school during the spring to gain a sense of how "graduates" perform.

Far and away, the most important thing you can do during the primary years is to stay in touch with your child and with the school.

These are years when you are most likely to be welcomed as a parent volunteer, when class sizes are relatively small, when the teacher can offer personal attention to students and to families, when your child is likely to experience accelerated development in both language and literacy. Stay connected with your child's experience and with those adults who play a critical role in his or her development.

What about quick fixes like the commercial packages, computer programs, professional tutors? Statistics don't tell the tale for individuals, but the evidence provides some guidance nonetheless. Few commercial packages fulfill their claims. Computer programs for the early grades tend to rely on skill-and-drill, or to emphasize the entertainment value of the medium. Individual tutoring depends greatly on the tutor. Most of your child's educational progress depends on what happens during the regular school day—so focus your attention on this experience.

Spend time in the classroom and think about the curriculum and instruction that you see at work. Primary-grade classrooms, especially kindergartens, often provide caring environments for young children. Many tend to downplay academic skills and strategies—"It will come when the student is ready." It is not uncommon to find kindergartens where this philosophy is espoused in the same building where first-graders are expected to be "ready." Of course, you can find programs in which, from kindergarten on, curriculum is lockstep, instruction is teacher-centered, and learning is by rote. The challenge is to find a school that avoids these extremes, that offers children opportunities to explore while seeing to it that they also gain skills. A critical test is the degree to which the entire school offers a coordinated development program across the early grades, where teachers connect with one another to ensure that children are supported across the transitions. That is why you shouldn't just look for the "right" kindergarten teacher, but should also visit the first- and second-grade classes at the school. Look for linkages rather than for specialties. Look beneath the surface to the underlying structures. One kindergarten teacher may embody the 1960s style while another looks more traditional, but the two may have much in common when talking about students, learning, and literacy. If the kindergarten classes look casual while the first-grade classes appear regimented (a not uncommon state of affairs), you probably have reason for concern. If every class looks the same, something strange may be going on.

Ask yourself, "Do I feel welcome as a parent here?" The line between supportive parent and busybody can be rather fine. Anyone can overstay their welcome, and schools face the task of meeting the diverse and often conflicting needs of students and parents. Nonetheless, you have a right to know about your child's schooling, especially in the formative grades. Look for a school that reaches out to families, that takes the initiative in linking home and school, that invites you to participate as a partner in your child's growth, that offers opportunities to visit classrooms and serve as a volunteer. These connections are especially important for parents who work or have other responsibilities. When conferences are held only in the afternoon at the end of classes, then most fathers and many mothers will not be able to make it. You need to stay in touch, and the school should help you with this job.

The wonder years. The next important chunk of time in the elementary grades is the stretch that proceeds roughly from third through fifth grade. Often described as the shift from *learning to read* to *reading to learn*, this time span is one of rapid strides in independence and self-confidence. Textbooks grow rapidly in size, assignments become longer and more demanding. Children in this age range are still oriented toward parents and teachers, however, for guidance and support. They still act like children.

The primary educational question for parents during this period centers around their children's achievement level in reading and writing, and the school's response to individual differences in literacy. If a third-grader is not performing up to par, especially if the youngster is an overly active boy, the response may be to designate the student as learning-disabled and assign him to special education. Third grade is often a critical decision point, and fluent oral reading is the main criterion. In fact, the precursors of low reading achievement are rooted in early language experiences. The usual strategy for handling poor readers is extensive testing, diagnostic labeling, and remedial pullout programs. This policy remains commonplace although it has proved to be of limited effectiveness.

An alternative policy builds on a schoolwide approach that places virtually all students in the mainstream, while providing special support for language and literacy development within the regular classroom. The success of schoolwide programs for children with special needs depends on an attitude by teachers that asks, "What can we do to improve the program for all students?" Research on the effectiveness of pullout vs. mainstreaming policies is sketchy, but what studies of ability grouping do exist show consistently detrimental effects for children with academic problems when they are segregated from classmates. The results of low-tracking are well documented; these students are provided a less challenging curriculum, they are taught by rote, their motivation and self-efficacy suffers, and they show less growth in achievement and lower motivation than when they are included in the mainstream.[7] Moreover, mainstreaming has no deleterious effect on the performance of students in the middle and upper ranges. Gifted programs with an accelerated curriculum do offer benefits to more-able students—but the advantages of enrichment hold for other students as well.[8]

What can you do during these years? First, you should enjoy them, because adolescence is just around the corner! Second, you should take advantage of them, because this is a time when your child will still accept your presence in the classroom and on field trips. Follow your child's emerging interests and individuality. Through second grade, children are amazingly fickle—today an astronaut, tomorrow a nurse. By fifth grade, children have begun to develop more consistent allegiances and dispositions. They will continue to change and evolve, but you can begin to spot trends.

The emergence of adolescence. Beginning around fifth or sixth grade, you can expect to encounter the precursors of adolescence. The syndrome is well documented for our society: an increasing absorption with self and peers, a distancing from family and other established institutions, daily fluctuations in moods and interests. These symptoms are partly physical, partly social, and partly institutional. Physically, the onset of puberty has moved steadily down toward younger ages over the past century and is now commonplace by the fifth or sixth grade. The range of variation is enormous at these ages, however, with some youngsters attaining the size and shape of young adults and others looking like children. Socially, today's adolescents have a remarkable amount of freedom from home and opportunity for unsupervised time with their peers. Institutionally, the middle school has emerged to replace yesterday's junior high school. The middle school, typically grades six through eight, is designed to fit today's adolescents and to provide a smooth transition between elementary and high school. The idea is to provide a gradual transition from a sixth-grade experience much like elementary school—most of the day with a single teacher and an integrated curriculum—toward an eighth grade with multiple teachers and departmentalized classes.

What can you do to support your child's academic development during this tumultuous time? The advice ranges widely. One expert has recommended that reading instruction be delayed until adolescence; another suggests that adolescents be given a three-year sabbatical from school. School situations vary, but in general (a) the academic demands on your student are likely to increase substantially, with expectations of more independent work but with less instructional support, and (b) your student is likely to be less inclined to accept advice from adults, even when it is offered with the best of intentions.

Our counsel, as in previous sections, is that you stay in touch with the school and with your child and be ready to help out when the occasion arises, as the following anecdote illustrates. A teacher, the mother of a motivated, intelligent eighth-grader in a well-off community with an excellent school system, was attending a Project READ workshop where she had just learned about webbing and CORE. Later in the evening, her daughter, who had been assigned a five-paragraph essay for her English class, erupted with frustration: "This paper is impossible!" Not exactly a question, but you get the idea. The mother left her own work and sat down with her daughter, who had clearly *connected* with the topic—women's rights—and had spent her library period gathering notes on this issue from recent magazine articles. The trouble was that she didn't know how to *organize* the information.

The mother asked her daughter to go through the material with her. She asked for clarification about several items, listening more than talking. Finding herself becoming genuinely interested in the articles as well as her child's thinking, she finally suggested that it might help to cluster the material. She described for her daughter the webbing strategy she had learned about earlier in the day: "Write some key words from each of your notes on Post-Its, and put them together in piles on your desk until you begin to see some sense in each pile. Then you'll have the ideas for paragraphs. Try it out—I'll be in the kitchen if you need me." Half an hour later, the daughter came into the kitchen. "I think I'm close, mom, but I'd like you to look at what I've done. The problem is, I think I should write six paragraphs instead of five."

This story conveys several messages. One is to stay in touch, not to intrude but to be available. Another is to learn to listen as well as to tell—not exactly a new idea. Listening is not a passive act. Hearing how you sound to another is the essence of reflection, and it is during adolescence that individuals begin to appreciate the perspectives of others. Adolescent life can be messy and complex, and finding organization in the midst of chaos can seem almost magical. The READ structures that seem so simple in the early years of schooling may need to be modified for young sophisticates, but they are no less powerful.

Above all, adolescence in today's society calls for parents to attend to their children's social and emotional needs as well as to the academic

demands placed on them. Because critical literacy stresses the importance of problem solving and communication, its structures and strategies can be opportune during times that are troubling and confusing. Staying connected with the school is important, too, although it can be difficult. Your student may be embarrassed at the idea that you are planning to visit school: What will friends think? School may be difficult to deal with. Middle schools, which typically combine students from several elementary schools, are usually large institutions with complex configurations, almost like miniature universities. This is not kindergarten! Teachers emphasize content rather than student learning. Your child may have to deal with six different teacher personalities during the school day, not counting administrators, friends, or family. Volunteers are less welcome. Back-to-school nights resemble a carnival as you move in preset time blocks from one classroom to another. Parent-teacher conferences are hurried and hectic; each teacher may have responsibility for 120–150 students.

This book has focused on reading and writing, which may not be taught as subjects in the middle grades. The English teacher is occupied with grammar and literature, the social-studies teacher with ancient history, the math teacher with the binomial theorem, and the science teacher with the water cycle. Because they are specialized, teachers assign increasingly complex texts and demanding essays, on the assumption that your student can handle these assignments on his or her own and that the earlier grades have provided adequate foundations to support comprehension and composition.

As in the earlier years of schooling, you can help greatly by listening actively, by finding the time to go beyond "How are things at school?" to real dialogue and active interest. You can provide an audience for your adolescent's emerging capacity to reflect, to step back from a problem and think strategically. You may not understand some assignments; when was the last time you factored an equation or analyzed a DNA sequence? Your task is not to be an expert, however, but to ask questions; in fact, the less you know about the topic, the easier it is to ask good questions. READ graphics offer techniques for getting ideas out into the open, where you and your student can study the structure of a problem. Graphic organizers are far more common today in elementary education than in the middle- and high-school years; it is only when students graduate from college and enter business that they re-encounter the extensive use of graphic organizers, often supported by computer graphics and "smart charts" that can remember what is written on them.

Middle-school students confront enormous amounts of expository reading in their textbooks. Science and social-studies textbooks are dense with facts and skimpy with organizers. Passive reading of these materials is of little value. If the assignment is "Read Chapter 5 on energy," students need to internalize the strategy of scanning for introductions, summaries, and headings. Transferring this synoptic information to a large sheet of paper, moving the elements around until a comprehensible pattern comes into view—these are activities that you and your student can legitimately work on together. The idea is not to "do" your ward's homework, but to share information-handling techniques that are on the cutting edge, that will help you as well as your youngster.

Adolescents may also be assigned substantial amounts of expository writing even in literature classes. No longer is it enough to enjoy a story. Instead, "Compare the characters in Anne Frank's *The Diary of a Young Girl* and John Gunther's *Death Be Not Proud*"; "Discuss the relation between plot and theme in *The Monkey's Paw*." Narratives provide the starting point for these assignments, but both require the student to expound, to analyze, to organize. Whenever the task is to compare and contrast, sketching a weave or matrix offers a view of the relations and a foundation for writing. Drawing a story graph can reveal the flow of action and variations of character roles with surprising clarity. How do you divide a story into segments? What clues reveal an author's shift from one episode to the next? Both questions are reasonable enough, but language arts textbooks offer more advice about comma usage than about plot analysis. A lot happens along the way in the eight pages of *The Monkey's Paw*. How to carve up the events into digestible chunks? Reading along with your student, look for changes in time, place, feeling tone, characters. With a large sheet of paper and some Post-Its, it is easy to document the analysis: Father and mother, grieving the death of their son on a dark and stormy night in their miserable cottage, are interrupted by a knock on the door and the arrival of Sergeant-Major Morris—beginning of a new episode, as Morris describes his twenty-one years of combat in distant lands. The conversation then takes an abrupt shift when the sergeant-major hesitantly reaches into his pocket and withdraws the mummified paw of a monkey: "His three listeners leaned forward eagerly . . . " By the end of the reading, parent and student have constructed a plot graphic that reveals the flow of action and the role of the various characters, the rising suspense and the horrible irony as the story moves to its conclusion. The ground is now laid for writing a report about plot and theme. It can help to try these techniques first in nonschool settings like the

movies or television programs, situations that adolescents find more interesting and topics they find easier to talk about with grown-ups.

You Should Ask for the Complete Story

Decades ago families spent a lifetime connected with their local schools; it was not unknown for two or three generations to be taught by the same teachers. Standardized tests and national standards did not exist; local schools were where the action was. Today it's easy to lose touch with reality—"My kids have finished school, and I really don't know what's happening except for what I hear on TV and read in the paper." That's not a whole lot; today's television sound bites and *USA Today* "hot plots" leave little room for extended stories.

But stories—lengthy and searching treatments of topics—offer important insights. In this concluding section, we shall update a couple of the stories we began earlier. Some offer happy endings; others have turned out more sadly. Today's schools, teachers, and administrators are under siege from many quarters. It's easy to gain false hope from a successful short story or become discouraged by a snapshot. Virtually every innovation seems to work when first introduced; even the most effective programs are likely to seem like failures at times. We urge you to insist on the entire story, on descriptions of educational ideas and programs that offer lengthier, more detailed, and more analytic accounts. Some of them will offer little hope, but you can find expositions of brighter prospects, too: for example, John Bruer's *Schools for Thought*, George Wood's *Schools That Work*, and Sarah Lightfoot Lawrence's *The Good High School*.[9]

We now return to several schools described earlier, partly for a reality check and partly to reinforce parents' and citizens' drive to invest time and energy in our children's education, to become informed, to take action.

North Shoreview revisited. What is happening at North Shoreview in 1994, almost ten years after Evelyn Taylor contacted Stanford about Project READ? The spring of 1993 was rife with rumors, but everybody was busy finishing the school year and administering the new state-mandated CLAS tests. Then, just as school was drawing to a close for summer break, the school district abruptly announced that Taylor would be leaving North Shoreview to start a new school emphasizing community outreach and parent involvement. The district, preoccupied with budget cuts and other emergencies, provided little support for the transition. A new principal was assigned with little input from staff or parents. The impact on North Shoreview was substantial; for starters, Taylor was taking several teachers along with her.

As the new year began in September with a new principal and several new teachers, the North Shoreview faculty felt like strangers in a strange land. Individual teachers continued to employ READ techniques, but they no longer felt part of a professional community. The final blow came in early 1994, when the district announced that the school was to become a Montessori "magnet," a special districtwide program for preschool and primary-grade children. Once again, the decision was made with little consultation with either faculty or parents. Several teachers were reassigned to other schools. Some parents expressed fear that their children would also be moved, but raised little protest. By June 1994, the Inquiring School that Evelyn Taylor and her teachers built in 1985 literally from ashes was gone.

What lesson can be learned from this experience? One is that every strategy for school reform is vulnerable to the politics and frailties of today's public schools. Innovative programs for school change are flooding the nation; you can read about many of them in the daily newspapers and Sunday supplements. You should be cautious about accepting these claims at face value. What long-term evidence supports the program's effectiveness for students, for teachers, for parents? Standardized-test sound bites are quickly digested but of questionable trustworthiness. Stories, even those without happy endings, can be more informative. In fact, for almost ten years North Shoreview offered a productive experience for everyone involved and demonstrated the benefits of the Project READ/Inquiring School model for promoting high levels of achievement by students and teachers who previously had been written off. And it accomplished this task without large grants or "name brand" recognition.

The story does reveal the importance of leadership, community, and politics. Leadership in today's schools often falls on the principal's shoulders, and this was true at North Shoreview. When Evelyn Taylor moved to a new school—and such transfers happen for good reasons and are a part of life—what could have been done to help teachers sustain the best parts of the school program? Phrases such as "shared leadership" or "teacher empowerment" are found frequently in today's reform rhetoric, but the reality is that shared leadership is a difficult task under the best of circumstances. Teachers are ill prepared for leadership, either by inclination or by training. The teacher's workplace provides neither time nor occasion to act as leaders.

The Project READ/Inquiring School model can catalyze a transformation in these realities, but it requires a major shift in mindset by all involved, one that is explicitly supported by the district and the community. We are accustomed to top-down accountability. When there is a problem, we ask to see the boss. School boards, superintendents, and principals typically rely on a similar approach. But we are also familiar with examples of professional accountability. When you have a medical problem, the hospital board of directors and the department heads are seldom your point of reference: You may ask for different opinions, but you want to see a *doctor*. We propose a similar shift for schools and the teaching profession. Several efforts along these lines are now underway, including changes in the selection and preparation of teachers, certification of master teachers, and differentiated positions and salaries. These efforts are likely to bear fruit only as teachers find opportunities and encouragement for professional development at the level of the local district and school. As long as teachers are treated like clerical workers, the kind of educational program described in this book will be virtually impossible to sustain.

L.A. teachers take charge. If North Shoreview offers one lesson, Los Angeles provides another. Life is still tough in South Central schools. Resources are thin, pay cuts have become routine, schools are overcrowded, and innovations are centered on institutional and organizational changes: divide the district into smaller units, restructure the schools, involve business and industry, etc. The most pressing practical problem is an urgent need for additional teachers to fill the ranks of those who are retiring or leaving for plusher jobs in other districts. The District's intern program, mentioned in Chapter 5, has helped to take up the slack. Project READ has become a central element in the program. All teachers, no matter who they are or what they teach, need to work on reading, writing, and communication—this tenet is now a keystone of the intern program, largely through the efforts of Project READ teachers rather than external consultants or academic experts.

In 1992, at the conclusion of a three-year grant supporting Project READ in several South Central schools, several participating teachers created a professional network; they met regularly to compare notes and discuss expansion to other teachers and schools. When the district initiated the intern program, these teachers saw an opportunity and grabbed it, volunteering as instructors and mentors. The response of the interns has been very favorable; READ structures and strategies apply from kindergarten through high school, and across virtually all subjects. And for the mentors, "professional" and "empowerment" have become meaningful concepts.

Teach our children well. Sociologist Gunnar Myrdal noted several decades ago that "education has in America's whole history been the major hope for improving the individual and society."[10] These words are at least as true in our generation, maybe more so. The important decisions *seem* simple enough: what to teach, how to teach it, how to assess learning. In fact, these issues evoke profound feelings and reactions. They deal with aspirations and values. In a democracy, these matters are too important to be left up to authorities.

Who is responsible for our children's well-being: parents? schools? society? The proper answer is probably "all of the above." But the public school is the one institution that can offer a consolidated program of support, within reasonable limits, for all children. Given the enormous size of the American public-school system, the distressing conditions that confront today's children, and the frustration of policymakers in trying to reform schools, it is understandable that our leaders turn to panaceas like "higher standards."

The stories in this book have mostly been about the teachers who spend their lives with our children. But others are important as well. Certainly, if a family can support its children, it has the obligation to do so. All citizens, however, have an obligation to become more knowledgeable about schools and more understanding about the problems they face. You aren't off the hook just because you don't have young children. We are asked every day to support one globally significant cause or another, but our future eventually comes down to our children.

Can you make a difference? Absolutely! If you have school-aged children, you can make a difference for them, and for others as well. If you are a businessperson or a senior, you can also do a lot. In the small California town of San Juan Bautista, Granite Rock Construction (the largest local employer) gives employees flextime for parent-teacher conferences, allowing fathers as well as mothers to connect with their child's schooling. Bruce Wolpert, president of Granite Rock, initiated the flextime policy and went even further. He talked with employees and with teachers about conferences, and made an interesting discovery: Blue-collar workers were uneasy about meeting with teachers and unsure about how to talk about their children. So Wolpert and his wife, Rose Ann, arranged to personally host a Saturday brunch for local teachers and parents to talk about how to handle a parent-teacher conference. Participants found the session effective, showing what can be done for the price of a meal.

The world of 2001 offers possibilities for our children that we can only glimpse. If the past half-century is any indication, the one certainty is uncertainty. At their core, today's schools still resemble schools from the turn of the century. The rumblings of cognitive-social learning are only beginning to be felt. Translating what we know into practicalities for more than 40 million students and 3.5 million teachers and administrators will be a big job; schools will need all of the help they can get. But the returns to society of shifting from the factory model to one based on the principles of critical literacy are potentially enormous. Children walking into their first classrooms vary widely in experience and temperament; but for virtually each one of them, learning is as natural as walking.

Why teach them to march, when they can learn to fly?

Notes

Chapter 1

1. Berliner, D.A., and Calfee, R.C. (eds.), *Handbook of Educational Psychology* (New York: Macmillan, in press). The chapters in this handbook lay out the principles of cognitive teaching and learning.

2. These and similar terms will be explained in detail later on.

3. Coleman, J.S., *Equality of Educational Opportunity* (Washington, D.C.: U.S. Department of Education, 1966). This report described the conditions of schooling for African-Americans, laying the foundations for efforts to improve education. "Nationally, Negro pupils have fewer of some of the facilities that seem most related to academic achievement: They have less access to physics, chemistry, and language laboratories; there are fewer books per pupil in their libraries; their textbooks are less often in sufficient supply" (pp. 11–12). Jonathan Kozol describes similar disparities in today's schools in *Savage Inequalities* (New York: Crown, 1991).

4. National Commission on Excellence, *A Nation at Risk* (Washington, D.C.: U.S. Department of Education, 1983).

5. *Goals 2000: Educate America Act of 1994*, 103–227, *et seq.* 108 Stat. 125 (Washington, D.C.: U.S. Government Printing Office, 1994).

6. Keith Stanovich ("Matthew Effects in Reading" [*Reading Research Quarterly*, 1986, *21*, 360–406]) has shown that individual differences in early reading achievement are actually quite small, but are amplified during the course of schooling. Richard Allington, author of "The Schools We Have; The Schools We Need," in Graves, M., Taylor, B., and van den

Broek, P. (eds.), *The First R: A Right of All Children* (New York: Teachers College Press, in press), describes how teacher expectations and classroom instruction produce the Matthew effect.

7. We focus in this book on learning strategies in the elementary grades. Educators like E.D. Hirsch *(Cultural Literacy* [Boston: Houghton-Mifflin, 1987]), Alan Bloom *(The Closing of the American Mind* [New York: Simon & Schuster, 1987]), and William Bennett *(The Book of Virtues* [New York: Simon & Schuster, 1993]) emphasize the importance of content—e.g., familiarity with state names and Aesop's fables. We agree with this point, but simple "exposure" is pointless unless students can connect new material with their own experiences and see how it enlightens their lives as members of the larger culture.

8. Benjamin Bloom *(Developing Talent in Young People* [New York: Ballantine Books, 1985]) and Jerome Bruner *(The Process of Education* [Cambridge: Harvard University Press, 1960]), psychologists of very different backgrounds, have both argued that "everyone can learn." This position contrasts with the argument that intelligence is fixed by genetic endowment; see Herrnstein, R.J., and Murray, C., *The Bell Curve* (New York: Free Press, 1994).

9. Several other instructional programs incorporate principles similar to those described in this book. Two such programs, by Ann Brown and John Bransford, are described in Bruer, J.T., *Schools for Thought* (Cambridge: M.I.T. Press, 1993); two more are found in Michael Pressley's *Cognitive Strategy Research* (New York: Springer-Verlag, 1989) and Howard Gardner's *Creating Minds* (New York: Basic Books, 1993).

10. Whitehead, A.N., *The Aims of Education* (New York: Macmillan, 1929).

11. California State Department of Education, *It's Elementary* (Sacramento: California State Department of Education, 1992).

12. Testing is ingrained in American education. We take standardized tests for granted, relying on them to indicate how well we are doing, even though we know their limitations. The past decade has seen a call for more "authentic" assessments, requiring students to demonstrate that they can actually perform tasks rather than simply picking the right answer (Wiggins, G., *Assessing Student Performance* [San Francisco: Jossey-Bass, 1993]). National standards are now being established in all of the major disciplines, along with federal examinations. Genuine changes in testing practice pose substantial challenges, however (Calfee, R.C., and Perfumo, P., *Writing Portfolios* [Hillsdale, New Jersey: Lawrence Erlbaum, in press]).

Chapter 2

1. Stevenson, H., and Stigler, J., *The Learning Gap* (New York: Summit Books, 1992).

2. Elam, S., et al., "The 26th Annual Phi Delta Kappa/Gallup Poll of the Public's Attitudes toward the Public Schools," *Phi Delta Kappan*, 1994, *26*, 41–56.

3. Finn, C., *We Must Take Charge: Our Schools and Our Future* (New York: Free Press, 1991).

4. Ravitch, D., and Finn, C., *What Do Our 17-Year-Olds Know?* (New York: Harper & Row, 1987).

5. Whittington, D., "What Have 17-Year-Olds Known in the Past?" *American Educational Research Journal*, 1991, *28*, 759–780.

6. Cuban, L., "The Great School Scam: The Economy Is Turned Around but Where's the Praise?" *Education Week*, June 15, 1994.

7. Bracey, G., "Why Can't They Be Like We Were?" *Phi Delta Kappan*, 1991, *73*, 105–117. Also Bracey, G., "The Third Bracey Report on the Condition of Public Education," *Phi Delta Kappan*, 1993, *75*, 104–12, 114–118; Stedman, L., "The Sandia Report and U.S. Achievement: an Assessment," *Journal of Educational Research*, 1994, *87*, 133–147. Similar accounts can be found in Berliner, D.C., and Biddle, B.J., *The Manufactured Crisis* (Reading, Massachusetts: Addison-Wesley, in press); Schneider, J., "Beyond Politics and Symbolism: America's Schools in the Years Ahead," *Equity and Excellence*, 1992, *25*, 156–191; and Jaeger, R., "Evaluating Policy Inferences Drawn from International Comparisons," *Studies in Educational Evaluation*, 1994, *20*, 23–39.

8. Carson, C.C., Huelscamp, R.M., and Woodall, T.D., *Perspectives on Education in America*, third draft (Albuquerque: Sandia National Laboratories, 1991 [publication suppressed]). Also Stedman, L., op. cit., note 7.

9. This and immediately preceding quotes are from a series of colloquia held at the Education Writers Association Conference in 1991.

10. Cannell, J.J., "Nationally Normed Elementary Achievement Testing in America's Public Schools: How All 50 States Are above the National Average," *Educational Measurement*, 1988, *2*, 5–9.

11. "Writings Show Many Children Can't," *San Francisco Chronicle*, June 8, 1994, 12.

12. Government Accounting Office, *Educational Achievement Standards: NAEP's Approach Yields Misleading Interpretations* (Washington, D.C.: U.S. Government Printing Office, 1993), 34.

13. *Chicago Tribune,* February 16, 1981.

14. *Wall Street Journal,* April 13, 1993.

15. *Washington Post,* October 19, 1985.

16. Finn, C., op. cit., note 3, (page 88).

17. Berliner, D.C., and Biddle, B.J., op. cit., note 7.

18. Ibid.

19. Boylan, P.W., "A Letter from Japan," *Phi Delta Kappan,* 1993, 74 (7), 581–582.

20. Berliner, D.C., and Biddle, B.J., op. cit., note 7.

21. Elley, W., *How in the World Do Students Read? The IEA Study of Reading Literacy* (The Hague: International Association for Evaluation of Educational Achievement, 1992).

22. National Center for Educational Statistics, *The Condition of Education 1994 and Prior Years* (Washington D.C.: NCES, 1995), 68.

23. Education Testing Service, *High-School Course-Taking in the Core Subject Areas* (Princeton: ETS, 1994).

24. Center for Policy Research in Education, *The Progress of Reform: An Appraisal of State Education Initiatives,* (Rutgers, N.J.: Rutgers, the State University of New Jersey, 1989).

25. U.S. Department of Education, *Condition of Education* (Washington, D.C.: U.S. Department of Education, 1980–1994 inclusive).

26. Does money matter? Two recent samples of the debate appear in Hanushek, E., *Making Schools Work: Improving Performance and Controlling Costs* (Washington, D.C.: Brookings Institution, 1994), and Hedges, L., et al., "Does Money Matter? A Meta-analysis of Studies of the Effect of Differential School Inputs on Student Outcomes," *Educational Researcher,* 1994, 23, 5–14.

27. Organization for Economic Cooperation and Development, *Education at a Glance* (Paris: OECD, 1992).

28. E.g., the *Metropolitan Life Surveys of the American Teacher* (New York: Louis Harris and Associates, 1983–1994 inclusive).

29. O'Neill, B., "The History of a Hoax: The Media's Portrayal of Social Problems in Education," *New York Times Magazine*, March 6, 1994, 16.

30. Williams, S., "My Neighborhood," *Manierre Triumph*, (Chicago: Manierre Elementary School [printed informally], 1993).

31. Casserly, M., *National Urban Education Goals: Baseline Indicators* (Washington, D.C.: Council of the Great City Schools, 1992).

32. Rothberg, I.C., "*Surefire School Reform*," Washington Post, June 11, 1993, A21.

Chapter 3

1. Presidents Bush and Clinton both expressed commitment to the idea of "New American Schools," and a corporation was actually formed to pursue this goal; Kearns, D.T., "Toward a New Generation of American Schools," *Phi Delta Kappan*, 1993, 74 (10), 773–776. It remains to be seen what the final outcome will be.

2. Several researchers have studied basal textbooks; see Chambliss, M.J., and Calfee, R.C., *Today's Textbooks; Tomorrow's Minds* (London: Blackwell, in press); Fraatz, J.M.B., *The Politics of Reading* (New York: Teachers College Press, 1987); Tyson-Bernstein, H., *A Conspiracy of Good Intentions: America's Textbook Fiasco* (Washington, D.C.: Council for Basic Education, 1988).

3. A variety of authors and movements have emphasized "high-level thinking" and, occasionally, the importance of communication; Brown, R., *Schools of Thought* (San Francisco: Jossey-Bass, 1991); Resnick, L.B., *Education and Learning to Think* (Washington, D.C.: Academic Press, 1987); Anderson, R.C., Hiebert, E.H., Scott, J.A., and Wilkinson, I.A.G., *Becoming a Nation of Readers* (Washington, D.C.: National Institute of Education, 1985).

4. The potential impact of cognitive theory on education is discussed by many authors in Berliner, D.A., and Calfee, R.C., op. cit., Ch. 1, note 1; also see Gardner, H., *Multiple Intelligences: Theory into Practice* (New York: Basic Books, 1993); Bruer, J.T., op. cit., Ch. 1, note 9.

5. Estes, W.M., "Is Human Memory Obsolete?" *American Scientist*, 1980, 68, 62–69.

6. The impact of cognitive theory on reading and writing is covered by Calfee, R.C., and Drum, P.A., "Research on Teaching Reading," in Wittrock, M.C. (ed.), *Handbook of Research on Teaching*, 3rd Ed. (New York: Macmillan, 1986), 804–849; also Pearson, P.D., *Handbook of Reading Re-*

search, Vol. 1 (New York: Longman, 1984), and Barr, R., et al. *Handbook of Reading Research*, Vol. 2 (New York: Longman, 1991).

7. Nist, J., *A Structural History of English* (New York: St. Martin's Press, 1966).

8. Once the foundation of literacy instruction, the rhetoric fell by the way in the 1950s but is making a return. See Brooks, C., and Warren, R.P., *Modern Rhetoric*, 3rd Ed. (New York: Harcourt, Brace, Jovanovich, 1970); Welch, K.E., *The Contemporary Reception of Classical Rhetoric* (Hillsdale, N.J.: Lawrence Erlbaum, 1990).

9. The "great debate" in reading revolves around the importance of phonics versus comprehension in early reading instruction. The classic book is Chall, J.S., *Learning to Read: The Great Debate* (New York: McGraw-Hill, 1967). The history of the debate is discussed in Tuman, M.C., *A Preface to Literacy: An Inquiry into Pedagogy, Practice, and Progress* (Tuscaloosa, Alabama: The University of Alabama Press, 1987). Contemporary works include Symons, S., Woloshyn, V., and Pressley, M. (eds.), "The Scientific Evaluation of Whole Language," *Educational Psychologist* (special issue), 1994, *29* (4); Adams, M.J., *Beginning to Read: Thinking and Learning about Print* (Cambridge: M.I.T. Press, 1990); Chall, J.S., *Stages of Reading Development* (New York: McGraw-Hill, 1983).

10. The current fad is "literature-based literacy," which emphasizes stories as a foundation for helping children learn to read. The narrative form is clearly easier for children to understand (see previous references), and Moffett, J., and Wagner, B.J. *(Student-Centered Language Arts and Reading, K–12,* 4th Ed. [Boston: Houghton-Mifflin, 1992]) make a compelling case for this strategy. See also Lukens, R., *A Handbook of Children's Literature*, 5th Ed. (New York: HarperCollins, 1995).

11. Although today's teachers give less attention to exposition than was once the case, a substantial amount of research has been conducted on this topic; see Chambliss, M.J., and Calfee, R.C., op. cit., note 2; Britton, B.J., and Black, J.B., *Understanding Expository Text* (Hillsdale, New Jersey: Lawrence Erlbaum, 1985).

12. Brooks, C., and Warren, R.P., op. cit., note 8.

13. Julia Child, *The Way to Cook* (New York: Knopf, 1989), 123.

14. Vocabulary has been an important topic for reading research, and a great deal is known about how students acquire words; see Calfee and Drum, op. cit., note 6; also McKeown, M.G., and Curtis, M.E. (eds.), *The Nature of Vocabulary Acquisition* (Hillsdale, New Jersey: Lawrence Erlbaum, 1987).

15. Methods for teaching phonics go back to McGuffey's readers. Methods developed in the 1940s stressed phonics, the teaching of specific letter-sound relations. See Chall, J.S., *Learning to Read*, loc. cit., note 9; also Adams, M.J., op. cit., note 9.

16. These excerpts are from the early 1980s, the last time the phonics debate reached a climax: Flesch, R., *Why Johnny Still Can't Read* (New York: Harper & Row, 1981); Sharp, S.L., *The Real Reason Why Johnny Still Can't Read* (New York: Exposition Press, 1982); Bettelheim, B., and Zelan, K., *On Learning to Read: The Child's Fascination with Meaning* (New York: Knopf, 1982); Kohl, H., *Basic Skills: A Plan for Your Child, a Program for All Children* (Boston: Little Brown, 1982); Glushko, R.J., "Principles for Pronouncing Print," in Lesgold, A.M., and Perfetti, C.A. (eds.), *Interactive Processes in Reading* (Hillsdale, New Jersey: Lawrence Erlbaum, 1981).

17. Nist, J., op. cit., note 7.

Chapter 4

1. Sizer, T.R., *Horace's School* (Boston: Houghton-Mifflin, 1992); Lightfoot, S.L., *The Good High School* (New York: Basic Books, 1983).

2. *Silver Secrets* (Needham, Massachusetts: Silver Burdett & Ginn, 1989).

3. Flood, J., Jensen, J.M., Lapp, D., and Squire, J.R., *Handbook of Research on Teaching the English Language Arts* (New York: Macmillan, 1991).

4. Myers, M., "The National Writing Project: Literacy and Teaching," *Phi Delta Kappan*, 1985, *85*, 32–34.

5. Sharan, S. (ed.), *Handbook of Methods for Cooperative Learning* (Westport, Connecticut: Greenwood Press, 1994).

Chapter 5

1. Stories of teachers' lives seldom appear in the popular press, but an emerging research literature has now captured the essence of this occupation, which provides a livelihood for almost three million adults. We especially recommend Rosenholz, S.J., *Teachers' Workplace* (New York: Longman, 1989); and Little, J.W., and McLaughlin, M.W., *Teachers' Work: Individuals, Colleagues, and Contexts* (New York: Teachers College Press, 1993).

2. Kozol, J., op. cit., Ch. 1, note 3.

3. The Chicago "experiment" will take a long time to evaluate, and the political climate will make an impartial assessment difficult. But several institutions and foundations are making an earnest effort to document the results of this effort. The themed issue of *Education and Urban Society*, 1994, *26* (3), edited by G.A. Hess, Jr., cites several recent reports that provide an informative and balanced account.

4. Schaefer, R.J., *The School as a Center of Inquiry* (New York: Harper & Row, 1967).

5. Bean, R.M., *Assessing a Staff Development Program* (Pittsburgh, Pennsylvania: University of Pittsburgh School of Education, 1994); Creek, R.J., and Vollmer, M.L., *The Inquiring School at Falk Laboratory School* (Pittsburgh, Pennsylvania: University of Pittsburgh School of Education, 1994).

6. Judson, G., "Teachers in Connecticut Learning How to Teach Each Other," *New York Times*, April 3, 1994, 25.

7. *Julie of the Wolves, Roll of Thunder, Hear My Cry, And Now Miguel, Sounder,* and many other titles of good children's literature can be found in Trelease, J., *The New Read-Aloud Handbook* (New York: Viking Penquin, 1989), and Lukens, R., op.cit., Ch. 3, note 10.

8. Cuban., L., *How Teachers Taught* (New York: Teachers College Press, 1993); Tyack, D., *Public Schools in Hard Times* (Cambridge: Harvard University Press, 1984).

9. Wirt, F.M., and Kirst, M.W., *Schools in Conflict*, 2nd Ed. (Berkeley: McCutchan Publishing, 1989).

10. Glass, G.V., and Smith, M.L., *The Relationship of Class Size and Achievement* (San Francisco: Far West Laboratory for Educational Research and Development, 1979); also Hedges, L.V., Laine, R.D., and Greenwald, R., "Does Money Matter?" *Educational Researcher*, 1994, *23* (3), 5–14; Hanushek, E., op. cit., Ch. 2, note 26.

11. Smith, M.S., and O'Day, J., "Systemic School Reform" in Furman, S.H., and Malen, E. (eds.), *The Politics of Curriculum and Testing* (New York: Falmer Press, 1991), 233–267.

12. McLaughlin, M.W., "The Rand Change Agent Study Revisited," *Educational Researcher*, 1990, *19* (9), 11–16.

13. Op. cit., Ch. 1, note 5.

14. Kearns, D.T., op. cit., Ch. 3, note 1, 773–776.

Chapter 6

1. Coleman, J.S., op. cit., Ch. 1, note 3.

2. Reading instruction for children identified as low-achievers differs substantially from the earliest years, according to studies conducted over the last two decades by Richard Allington; see Allington, R., op. cit., Ch. 1, note 6.

3. The U.S. Department of Education, which initiated in the summer of 1995 a major effort—Read*Write*Now—to support family reading, provides at no cost a variety of booklets that offer solid advice. In its 1993 publication *Helping Your Child Learn to Read*, for instance, the "basics" include "Advertise the Joy of Reading," "Remember When You Were Very Young," and "Home Is Where the Heart Is." Parents (and other adults) are encouraged to immerse children in a wide range of interesting experiences, to talk about these, to read extensively, and to write as well as read.

4. Trelease, J., op. cit., Ch. 5, note 7.

5. Elley, W., op. cit., Ch. 2, note 21.

6. Ginsburg, H.S., and Opper, S., *Piaget's Theory of Intellectual Development,* 3rd Ed. (Englewood Cliffs, New Jersey: Prentice-Hall, 1988); and Vygotsky, L.S., *Mind in Society* (Cambridge: Harvard University Press, 1978).

7. Oakes, J., *Making the Best of Schools* (New Haven: Yale University Press, 1990).

8. Gallagher, J.J., "Ability Grouping: a Tool for Education Excellence," *College Board Reveiw*, 1993, *168*, 21–27.

9. See Bruer, J.T., op. cit., Ch. 1, note 9; Wood, G.H., *Schools that Work* (New York: Dutton, 1992); and Lawrence, S.L., op. cit., Ch. 4, note 1.

10. Myrdal, G., *An American Dilemma* (New York: Harper, 1944).

About the Authors

obert C. Calfee is a cognitive psychologist in Stanford University's School of Education. A professor in that School's Committee on Language, Literacy, and Culture as well as its Committee on Psychological Studies, he joined the Stanford faculty in 1969 after spending five years in the psychology department of the University of Wisconsin in Madison. Project READ, the subject of this book, commenced in spring 1980 when Calfee began working with teachers and administrators at Graystone Elementary School in California's Silicon Valley to develop an integrated language-arts program that was more challenging for the school's students.

Calfee's interests have evolved over the past two decades from a focus on assessment of early literacy skills to a concern with the broader reach of schools. He conducts practical research on the effect of schooling on the intellectual potential of individuals and groups, while his theoretical efforts are directed toward the nature of human thought processes and the influence of language and literacy in the development of problem solving and communication. He has authored and edited several books and written scores of peer-reviewed articles in the fields of education and psychology, including papers on the effects of testing and education indicators, ability grouping, teacher assessment, and the psychology of reading.

Calfee earned his doctorate at the University of California at Los Angeles and did postgraduate work at Stanford. His wife is a middle-school teacher working with students with special education needs. He is a devotee of river rafting.

ynthia L. Patrick has worked as a journalist for newspapers and magazines in Britain and the United States. Her education writing has received four distinguished-achievement awards from the Educational Press Association of America. She is also the recipient of Avery Hopwood, Broomfield, and other awards.

From 1988 to 1994 Patrick was news director of Stanford University's School of Education; from 1984 to 1988, she analyzed and synthesized findings for Stanford and the Schools, one of the nation's first school-university research collaborations.

Patrick received her bachelor's degree from the University of Michigan in Ann Arbor in 1977. She is the co-author of a previous book on education, *Inside Schools* (Falmer Press, 1989).

The Portable Stanford Book Series

This is a volume of the Portable Stanford Book Series, published by the Stanford Alumni Association. Subscribers receive each new Portable Stanford volume on approval. The following books may also be ordered, by number, on the adjoining card:

$14.95 titles
- *Teach Our Children Well: Bringing K–12 Education into the 21st Century* by Robert C. Calfee and Cynthia L. Patrick (#4064)
- *Love's Executioner* by Irvin D. Yalom (#4066)

$12.95 titles
- *(Nearly) Total Recall: A Guide to a Better Memory at Any Age* by Danielle C. Lapp (#4061)
- *The Disappearing Border: U.S.-Mexico Relations to the 1990s* by Clint E. Smith (#4058)
- *Race Relations on Campus: Stanford Students Speak* by John H. Bunzel (#4062)
- *Around California in 1891* by Terence Emmons (#4060)
- *Technology and Culture: A Historical Romance* by Barry M. Katz (#4057)
- *2020 Visions: Long View of a Changing World* by Richard Carlson and Bruce Goldman (#4055)
- *Brief Lessons in High Technology: A Primer on Seven Fields that Are Changing Our Lives* edited by James Meindl (#4045)
- *Terra Non Firma: Understanding and Preparing for Earthquakes* by James M. Gere and Haresh C. Shah (#4030)

$10.95 titles
- *Notable or Notorious? A Gallery of Parisians* by Gordon Wright (#4052)
- *This Boy's Life* by Tobias Wolff (#4050)
- *Ride the Tiger to the Mountain: T'ai Chi for Health* by Martin and Emily Lee and JoAn Johnstone (#4047)
- *Alpha and Omega: Ethics at the Frontiers of Life and Death* by Ernlé W.D. Young (#4046)
- *Conceptual Blockbusting* (third edition) by James L. Adams (#4007)
- *In My Father's House: Tales of an Unconformable Man* by Nancy Huddleston Packer (#4040)
- *The Imperfect Art: Reflections on Jazz and Modern Culture* by Ted Gioia (#4048)
- *Yangtze: Nature, History, and the River* by Lyman P. Van Slyke (#4043)
- *The Eagle and the Rising Sun: America and Japan in the Twentieth Century* by John K. Emmerson and Harrison M. Holland (#4044)
- *The American Way of Life Need Not Be Hazardous to Your Health* (revised edition) by John W. Farquhar, M.D. (#4018)

- *Cory Aquino and the People of the Philippines* by Claude A. Buss (#4041)
- *Under the Gun: Nuclear Weapons and the Superpowers* by Coit D. Blacker (#4039)
- *50: Midlife in Perspective* by Herant Katchadourian, M.D. (#4038)
- *Wide Awake at 3:00 A.M.: By Choice or By Chance?* by Richard M. Coleman (#4036)
- *Hormones: The Messengers of Life* by Lawrence Crapo, M.D. (#4035)
- *Panic: Facing Fears, Phobias, and Anxiety* by Stewart Agras, M.D. (#4034)
- *Matters of Life and Death: Risks vs. Benefits of Medical Care* by Eugene D. Robin, M.D. (#4032)
- *On Nineteen Eighty-Four* edited by Peter Stansky (#4031)
- *The Musical Experience: Sound, Movement, and Arrival* by Leonard G. Ratner (#4029)
- *Challenges to Communism* by John G. Gurley (#4028)
- *Cosmic Horizons: Understanding the Universe* by Robert V. Wagoner and Donald W. Goldsmith (#4027)
- *Beyond the Turning Point: The U.S. Economy in the 1980s* by Ezra Solomon (#4026)
- *The Age of Television* by Martin Esslin (#4025)
- *Insiders and Outliers: A Procession of Frenchmen* by Gordon Wright (#4024)
- *Mirror and Mirage: Fiction by Nineteen* by Albert J. Guerard (#4023)
- *The Touch of Time: Myth, Memory, and the Self* by Albert J. Guerard (#4022)
- *The Politics of Contraception* by Carl Djerassi (#4020)
- *Economic Policy Beyond the Headlines* by George P. Shultz and Kenneth W. Dam (#4017)
- *Law Without Lawyers: A Comparative View of Law in China and the United States* by Victor H. Li (#4015)
- *The World That Could Be* by Robert C. North (#4014)
- *America: The View from Europe* by J. Martin Evans (#4013)
- *An Incomplete Guide to the Future* by Willis W. Harman (#4012)
- *Murder and Madness* by Donald T. Lunde, M.D. (#4010)
- *The Anxious Economy* by Ezra Solomon (#4009)
- *The Galactic Club: Intelligent Life in Outer Space* by Ronald Bracewell (#4008)
- *Is Man Incomprehensible to Man?* by Philip H. Rhinelander (#4005)
- *Some Must Watch While Some Must Sleep* by William E. Dement, M.D. (#4003)
- *Human Sexuality: Sense and Nonsense* by Herant Katchadourian, M.D. (#4002)